ELECTRIC VOICES, HUMAN HEARTS

Memories, Mayhem and Music

PAUL. E. SMITH

Published by Paul Smith 2016

Cataloguing-in-Publication data available
from the National Library of Australia

ISBN: 978-0-9946421-0-3 (pbk)

Design and layout
by Publicious P/L
www.publicious.com.au

Cover design by Paul Smith & Laura La Roche (Publicious)

Published with the assistance of
Publicious P/L
www.publicious.com.au

ACKNOWLEDGEMENTS

Dedicated to those who listen without prejudice and speak without criticism.

But especially to my son Alexander, whose passion for and knowledge of music exceeds even my own.

To my daughter Natalee who appreciates where I am coming from even though at times I may not.

To my mother Sylvia Beryl Smith and my late father George William Smith.

To Rob Stormont the only person I know who is an even bigger Beatles fanatic than myself, enough said.........

To Leo the Beagle who was my best friend and staunchest companion. Rest in peace old boy, you were truly one in a million.

Last but by no means least, to my dearest wife Jutta, who without any pressure or coercion on my part, acted as proof reader, analyst, literary agent and coffee maker, all at the same time. A truly remarkable juggling act. Her enlightenment, understanding, careful guidance and words of wisdom have made this book possible.

LEGEND

Individual songs or Albums with Artist name listed and referenced throughout this book are *underlined* and asterisked* accordingly.

Shown in parentheses ( ) a number from 1 – 10 indicates my *personal assessment rating*. 10 being the highest level and worthy of a long and intimate association. As would be expected very few achieve this ranking. Conversely those nominated at the other end of the scale provide curiosity value only or better still, should be reserved strictly for those who gain total satisfaction by punishing themselves. To be fair even the most cringe worthy, banal or ordinary songs are given a value higher than (0). Further, to minimise any damage to artist pride or ego, no songs have been included that rate less than a near passable (4).

I make no apology for the fact that the comments and ratings contained herein are totally *subjective.* What pleases one ear may not necessarily please another.

Wherever possible the Year of release is also provided.

I felt a little strange, a little awkward and that was all. Once it was established it didn't move any more, it lay low and I was able to persuade myself that there was nothing wrong with me....

Jean-Paul Sartre NAUSEA

Yesterday morning was good.

Today was even better.

A crisp wind blew in across the open waters and the great god of the universe came out of the sky in a silver dragon ship that breathed no fire.

At least the rain had stopped. A few leftover clouds partially obscured the last crescent moon as it dipped behind the snow capped sawtooth mountains. Beech trees sang and whispered, while woodferns, musk root and bluebead crackled as we passed. Below, a thin veil of mist settled on the forest floor. In the clearing, near a bend in the river, a pack of hungry wolves set upon their prey.

You took my hand and squeezed gently to make sure you would not lose your way again. We stepped out of the line of shadows and into the machine and were no longer afraid. Now a light hung all about us, brighter than a thousand yellow suns burning in a thousand giant chandeliers.

With a whirring sound the heavy door slid into place, blocking out the stars and everything else around. I fumbled with the T-shaped lever for a moment, moving it slowly downwards centimetre by centimetre, until the time dial clicked over to the month of February in the year nineteen hundred and fifty three. The needle on the temperature gauge came to rest at a comfortable seventy two degrees Fahrenheit. The console began to hum and the grey metal floor pulsated beneath our bare feet like the beating wings of a dying moth. Through the small plexiglass porthole, the colourless landscape outside shifted and changed, becoming almost transparent in appearance. Transformed until our eyes could distinguish nothing, except the pitch black void of space.

Then in a gentle rush of air, we were gone.

INTRODUCTION

There are those who dare to dream and those who have no dreams at all.

Robert Leroy Johnson most likely will be remembered as perhaps the greatest exponent of Delta blues the world has ever seen. Shrouded in mystery and rumour, the truth behind his story and the exact details surrounding *that* ill-fated excursion down to the crossroads[1] remain open to conjecture and debate. As little is known about the man himself it is difficult to untangle the myths from the facts. Legend has it that in a secret contract made with the devil, Johnson in fair exchange for his soul, was endowed with remarkable playing skills unmatched by any of his peers. According to those performers who knew him best, Edward James 'Son' House Jr and Willie Brown, Johnson's transformation from ordinary musician to the ranks of genius was astonishing. To most, the devil's pact theory seemed the only credible explanation that could account for such a rapid change. However, despite the popular so called Faustian myth that now surrounded

---

1. *Those with expertise in this matter seem to locate the crossroads at the intersection of highways 49 and 61 in Clarksdale, Mississippi. Although subsequent investigation has thrown up increased speculation and conjecture as to the true location. Other reports place Rosedale (highway 8 and highway 1) as the most likely site of the actual pact. Whether Johnson did or did not sell his soul, the plain truth of the matter remains, that after his death the blues emerged as an unstoppable, supernatural force.*

him, fame and fortune did not come in his own lifetime. Unable to achieve the success and recognition he no doubt deserved, Robert Johnson died on August 16, 1938 at the age of twenty seven[2]. Some three days after performing in a popular jook joint[3], he was found in his room in the "Baptist Town" section of Greenwood, Mississippi, apparently the victim of poisoning, most likely the act of a jealous husband of one of his many female companions. Varying reports and eye witness accounts exist about the tragic circumstances surrounding his final hours, including a note which indicated complications from syphilis to be the cause of death.

In a brief, turbulent career, Johnson left behind a remarkable legacy of recordings that proved to be a critical catalyst in the formative years of rock and roll. His songs were not uplifting. They plumbed the dark depths of intense loneliness, tortured existence and hungry desire. Yet Johnson's aura never waned. Thanks mainly to the iconic King of the Delta Blues Singers*(8) compilation release in 1961, his music somehow became increasingly more popular for an entire generation borne out of the post war gloom. His nimble and unique, clipped acoustic playing style profoundly influenced the development of many first wave British acts seeking to put their mark on the world. These so called *new age white disciples* included the Rolling Stones (Love In Vain, Stop Breaking Down Blues) Eric Clapton (Crossroad Blues, From Four Till

2. *Members of the 27 Club (those who died at the ripe old age of twenty seven) include such artists as Jimi Hendrix, Jim Morrison and Brian Jones.*

3. *A commonly used term for an often ramshackle establishment of ill repute found in the south eastern parts of the USA. They featured music, dancing, gambling and drinking and were operated mainly by African Americans. Also known as Barrelhouses. Sources indicate the place to have been Shaples General Store in Three Forks.*

Late) Led Zeppelin (Traveling Riverside Blues - which they turned into The Lemon Song), Fleetwood Mac (Hellhound On My Trail) and others.

Some twenty two years or so after his tragic demise, I stumbled quite by accident, headfirst into the wonderful and often chaotic world of music. A place of bewilderment and imagination clearly unbounded by the clichéd parameters of normal, everyday life. Indoctrinated initially into the realm of the big bands and swinging jazz combos such as Glenn Miller, Tommy Dorsey, Duke Ellington and Dave Brubeck, it wasn't long before the inevitable shift to primal rock and roll occurred. With unreserved appreciation to those pioneering American heroes, Bill Haley, Little Richard, Chuck Berry, Buddy Holly, Jerry Lee Lewis, Elvis Presley and others, the transition was smooth and totally painless.

The wheels had been set in motion. The avalanche express rumbled down those high and mighty tracks. Tearing down barriers. Taking restless hearts and childhood dreams with it. And like the first kiss shared by innocent sweethearts, nothing would ever be the same again.

1

NO ONE SAID IT WOULD BE EASY

It is not where we have been and where we are now that matters, it is where we end up and what we become that counts. Do not waste the precious moment, it will not return this way again.

What follows in these pages is not a long story. Neither is it a sad story. This is not War and Peace in magnitude, nor is it by any means Anna Karenina in narrative and scope. Not in the least bit Animal Farm or Brave New World. Light years away from the enigmatic, mind picture creations of Philip K. Dick[1] and much closer I think, to Rod McKuen or that revered poet turned singer/songwriter Leonard Cohen.

It would of course be nice if it were all these things. Then I certainly would depart this world a happy man. The simple truth is, it perhaps lies in another comfortable space somewhere between. Maybe not quite on the same astral plane as those gone before me, but snuggled in that special place reserved for marshmallow childhood memories and adult whimsy.

---

1. *Renowned American Science Fiction author. Why not try a tempting morsel of Do Androids Dream of Electric Sheep? The story was later successfully adapted into the classic motion picture Blade Runner starring Harrison Ford.*

Still, god willing and with a fair share of luck, at the end of the road wherever that may be, I shall rest at peace with a smile on my face.

Like good old Hazel in that cosy burrow, deep beneath Watership Down[2].

---

2. *That most popular English pastoral themed novel by Richard Adams describing country life and death from a rabbit's unique ground level perspective.*

2

A STATE OF MIND

Please, someone feed the hungry beast. Press the number and it shall be released. Relax, take a deep breath and step through time. Behold the machine shivers and shakes. Awakens from deep sleep and casts out its offerings piece by precious piece. Spins and crackles, each to each as the needle descends into the black. The music plays and with one fell swoop takes me like a flaming rocket back into the years of my youth. I am dissolved and am nothing and yet I am everywhere.

For those out there with any modicum of interest, there is one irrefutable fact not to be skimmed over lightly. *I am a tragic Beatlesphiliac. Simple though it may be. That is the reality.* This frank admission might seem rather sad. Especially when the hot topic is raised around those less fortunate among us who through no fault of their own, casually surf through the bubbling cosmos of life on an entirely different wavelength. Although said with clear disclaimer attached, many of them choose to ignore the glorious past as though it never existed. They observe the world through an inferior pair of rose tinted glasses. I am not surprised therefore that any attempt to convert the unconverted with verbal lunacy is doubtless condemned to fall upon deaf ears.

My daughter for example cannot see what the fuss is about. The Beatles were just another pop group (albeit in her words, *a very good one*) from another time and place she has no connection to. No more no less. It so happens she would much prefer the formidable renditions of those from her own generation. The familiar sounds she grew up with. Be they good or bad. Sounds that strike a chord or ignite a special moment hitherto held in temporal suspension. Sounds of sadness, sounds of joy, even sounds of anger and confusion. Not that I have a problem with this lopsided opinion for I too share that faculty of feeling. Where events and sensations fall into place. That particular nanosecond when the neurons, transmitters and impulses within our bodies are provided the perfect opportunity to court and spark. Biased the process may be, but when analysed on a deeper, more emotional level, this of course makes total sense. This reaction, common to us all, is an integral part of the life process: a stimulus response operation. Being able to express pleasurable or painful conditions of the mind and absorb and understand the sensibilities and perceptiveness of others. All through the medium of word and song. It is the capacity to relate to the music of the times and be blinded by its overwhelming power to move. There is nothing new or earth shattering in this point of view. Like our parents before us, we looked at music in much the same way (blinkered in our thoughts and attitudes) and did exactly the same sort of unexpected things in our rebellious, flippant manner. However, most of us are too stubborn or far too fixated with our shallow lives, to ever care to admit it.

I confess I am guilty of giving short shrift to the talents of those from the distant and not too distant past. Artists and musical pioneers whose works I never gave a second thought to, nor had any remote appreciation of. Fortunately, the passage of time and the inevitable realisation of growing old, certainly has a way of righting these wrongs, thereby opening up a whole new perspective on the origins of popular music. The landmark studio recordings of such luminaries as Francis Albert Sinatra, Ella Fitzgerald, Sarah Vaughan, Billie Holiday, Big Bill Broonzy, The Kingston Trio and The Weavers to mention but a few, have been (largely) consigned to the mists of another less complicated era. But that does not dilute the substance of their contribution nor make it any less valuable than say that of the Beatles, the Beach Boys, Paul Simon or even the Rolling Stones. Without the genuine frustrations depicted in the powerful, heart wrenching folk songs of Woody Guthrie and Pete Seeger, perhaps Robert Zimmerman[1] would not have found his rightful place in the music pantheon he now clearly occupies. Without the smouldering Delta Blues magic of Charlie Patton, Son House, Lead Belly, Robert Johnson, Sonny Boy Williamson, Willie Dixon, Elmore James, Blind Lemon Jefferson, Howlin' Wolf, John Lee Hooker and others, it is doubtful popular music as we have come to know and love, would exist at all.

It never ceases to take me by surprise, how the mind can conjure up dormant images that spring once again into full and vibrant blossom almost instantaneously out of the depths of a complex cognitive map. One that contains a catalyst, able to suddenly transport an individual to an exact place and an exact time whenever a specific song is played on the radio or even mentioned in casual

---

1. *The one and only Bob Dylan who took his surname from the famous Welsh poet and writer Dylan Thomas.*

conversation. I am sure that most people have at some point experienced that unique hair raising moment, when they are able to recall without fault, precisely where they were and what they were doing when they first heard a song or a particular line from it. What the scientific term for this phenomenon is called I do not know, but rest assured we all seem to share the same intricate trigger mechanisms and chemical bonds. It is what makes growing ragged round the edges far less daunting. Being able to rekindle in a mere snap of the fingers, visions, landscapes and cherished moments from our fleeting past. Pangs of yearning. A desire to be returned to the source of our delirious happiness or the depths of our despair. Flashes of that youthful existence we so vigorously nurtured and today still proudly share with others via the medium of music.

For as long as I care to remember (and much to my parent's disappointment), my innate passion for the Beatles has been the steady state of affairs. Indeed, for a considerable part of my formative years, their influence both on a musical and cultural level held dominion. Comparable I suppose, to a stubborn narcotic predilection, or something in the blood capable of igniting the senses like a fire coursing through one's veins. Once taken hold, it never let me go. Upon painstaking reflection, this may or may not have been a good thing.

The picture I am trying to arrange, becomes much clearer by degrees. Slowly and inexorably. Resisting any urge for radical change, with my hairline not in the exact same place it was when last I looked and with my character turning more J. Alfred Prufrock[2] with each passing

---

2. *The Love Song of J. Alfred Prufrock by T.S. Eliot. A most remarkable description of one's journey through the twilight years of life.*

day, I am regardless of this similarity, now confident and far more at ease in my midlife hiatus. Content and comfortable in where I am and where I have been and where I may or may not fit in. Yet, still blessed to have that same adrenalin rush of spirit and amazement whenever the Beatles music is played. That special *joie de vivre* moment when a dense, impenetrable fog is lifted from the eyes and electricity jumps and crackles from every conceivable pore. When I am a king and suddenly sixteen, doesn't seem all that very long ago. Not that my early years in any way could not be described as happy, but they were a completely *different sort of happy.* Special years experienced from a slightly skewed angle of appreciation. You know the kind I'm talking about. Carefree, child wild and full of silly questions. Now my life has gone full circle.[3] Today things are far more cautious, less serious, not nearly so wild, measured (perhaps to the point of tedium) and crammed to overflowing with answers. Even if those answers might be wrong. Or worse still, biased in their content. And you know the strangest thing I've found: age is a state of mind, not a mind of state and father time forgives many sins.

In short, I cringe to think what sort of a world it would be without the music of the Beatles.

---

3. *Reflecting on the words of Harry Chapin, something about life and death and circles. From the song* Circle* (6)

3

THE TRAVELLER

Living on cheese cake, watching those white waves hit the west coast 'til dawn. Well here I stand easy, happy and breezy, taking care of the old folks, back in the old home. Where rust is a business booming like never before. That's why I'm dandy, all soft hearts and candy, tripping the sun light to keep myself warm. So if you should find me, in gold chains that bind me, lost in your footsteps tattered and torn. Just think of it easy, happy and breezy, living on cheesecake, never thinking of corn.

It is stating the obvious: despite overwhelming mechanisms of socio economic inequality and circumstance, music has the unique ability to cross great divides. From the scattered tribal villages of darkest Africa, the swamps, everglades and delta country of the American deep south, across the wide muddy reaches of the Ganges, the sweeping plains of Russia and Mongolia, to the arid lands of outback Australia, music is the universal panacea. Mankind can relate to and interact with it in one form or another. This *world* music as we might choose to call it, has a heart and soul worth nurturing. It is spiritual and yet non spiritual at the very same moment. It is the heavy stuff of dreams, culture, ethos and entity. It both unites and separates. It celebrates great occasions and it transcends boundaries and prejudices with ease. Music is the substance of life as much as life is music. The two are intertwined and virtually inseparable.

You, the laid back casual observer, will have a different outlook and visual and auditory perspective to that of myself. What one may seek to embrace with a strength and passion, another is sure to contravene and ridicule. What affects you in a distinct way and stays with you forever, may be but a fleeting, passing shadow for someone else. Yet they also, somewhere along their great life journey, will be driven and moulded by a simple, defining event. An instant of pleasure or of pain, exuberance or melancholy, over which they have absolutely no control. Nor should it be any other way. The world would be a very boring place indeed if we were all so much alike and so predictable. Beings moulded without character, devoid of any ability to feel. In the final analysis, individuals will be measured by the lives they have led and the choices they have made along that rugged path traversed. Music to a certain extent determines and shapes these life choices.

I am glad therefore, that I like music. And by all accounts, music agrees with me. There is something obsessive and magical within its timeless framework, which both bleeds and feeds the restless spirit. A sort of ambrosia of the gods. An omnipotent elixir I find totally addictive. And funnily enough, satisfying. It enables me to focus on the world around and keeps me sane through even the most crazy, uninspired moments (which of late there seems to be an awful lot). I do not feel uncomfortable in my shrinking sexagenarian skin, for music fills me with great joy and likewise great sadness. It projects images that may forever haunt, it can make or break relationships and torment the soul. It can build bridges and tear down walls. Yet music can produce mind altering landscapes and take me on wondrous journeys, over immense distances, without the need to ever leave the confines of my warm, cosy room. In this way, I am a simple man with simple desires. But a traveller no less.

I have visited the majestic snow-capped peaks of Annapurna, trembled in awe at the foot of ancient ruins, walked the dense jungles of Amazonia and seen starships on fire above the icy rings of Saturn. I have traversed an adrenalin charged super highway, lost and found love and been turned upside down in the process. These facts are not in doubt. Like the unforgettable words of _Across The Universe_* (7)[1] intimate, one only has to close their eyes and listen to realise that nothing is what it seems and nothing lies beyond the imagination and the realms of human possibility.

I appreciate the absolute power of melody and lyric and the interconnected elements of instrumentation, whether they be sparse or symphonic in quality. Songs for the most part, can be considered unique entities[2], structurally and word different from each other and are an art form in themselves. Some art I would proudly display on my living room wall for all to see and admire. Be it a Renoir, Van Gogh, Turner, Da Vinci, Titian or similar

---

1. *This was originally recorded by The Beatles in February 1968. At the behest of Spike Milligan it was released for inclusion on the World Wildlife Fund Charity LP (with bird sound effects added to the beginning and end of the song) in Dec 1969. A slightly different stereo form appears on the album _Let It Be_ 1969*

2. *Stop and analyse this basic premise, then consider how George Harrison must have felt after losing a protracted legal battle over copyright breaches with his worldwide mega hit _My Sweet Lord._ The court adjudged the similarities to the Chiffons' _He's So Fine_ to be more than simple coincidence.*

great master of their trade. Others though, especially in this modern, fast moving commercial and throw away electronic age, I am afraid I am yet to be totally convinced about. In the eloquent musings of Graham Gouldman and Eric Stewart[3] perhaps there is more than a little truth echoed in the obtuse lines of *Art For Art's Sake** (6).

I hope that on this brief sojourn I can share my thoughts and experiences with others of similar passion and persuasion, who appreciate the great rewards that lie out there in the vast, music ether. A realm keen to reveal its innermost secrets, whether these be rare, beautiful diamonds or buckets of gravel and stone. It is your choice, whatever your mood or disposition, simply pick whichever pie takes your fancy. There is no right or wrong way where matters of the heart are concerned. Endless riches are there to be discovered with a spin of turntable and the warm crackle of stylus surfing the silky concentric waves of black vinyl. Or for the strict modernists and technophobes amongst us, audio information neatly sorted and packaged in the pristine and some would say clinical, non-hiss and pop of the super silver compact disc and the ubiquitous, insincere download world of mp3[4]. Trite as it may seem, one man's earthly pleasure is the absolute treasure of no other man.

To finish therefore, let me say that this is not a book about music per se, nor is it a music book. I would not be so daring as to attempt such a bold endeavour. I leave such

---

3. *Two of the original members of eccentric nineteen seventies British band 10 C.C. Graham Gouldman in particular proved to be a talented songwriter. His early work had been covered by artists such as The Hollies, Herman's Hermits and The Yardbirds.*

4. *This format is highly popular with Generation Y who seem more than happy to ignore its all too obvious audio shortcomings – specifically the deliberate removal of a large percentage of the music information. However MP3 encoding software has over the years improved and is now able to extract greater audio quality from fewer bits.*

meanderings to the so called experts, those professionals, scholars and musicians alike who know far more about the technicalities and sublime qualities of music, rhyme and meter than I surely ever will.[5] It is, by deliberate design, a loose selection of handed down phrases, anecdotes and narratives. Most are real, while the remainder, less based on fact but more on fiction are snippets of concepts and ideas that for far too long have gathered dust in the corner of my mind. What I have accumulated here is a montage of events and recollections from childhood and adolescence through to later years. Stories, graceful or otherwise, of growing up and growing old, of people both ordinary and extraordinary whom I have been fortunate to have met along the way. There are places visited or relayed to me by friends and acquaintances, whose influence has been nothing short of extraordinary. Pictures and pieces extracted from dreams. Together with the simple indulgences life has to offer. Oh, and of course the entire bundle would not be complete without some obvious music references and casual asides. Just to keep the ledger on an even keel.

I rest content in the fact that the road travelled upon in the quest for knowledge and understanding, is full of twists and turns, but is a journey surely worth the effort.

I wish nothing but good will and enjoyment to all who dare to enter here. No need for a special introductory offer, key code or a ticket. Get on board, buckle up, take a deep breath and keep your fingers crossed. Who knows, it might just be the best ride you ever take.

---

5. *For those wishing to burn the midnight oil, try David Byrne's superb account of the history of music 'How Music Works'*

4

GOING BACK TO THE START

At last the heaviness of space left me. I opened my eyes slowly. The machine had come to rest in a large field full of wild flowers: wood cranesbill, buttercup and pignut. A soft light danced and flickered. The hairs on the back of my neck stood upright. Overhead a yellow sun shone in a deep blue sky. It was three forty five on the first day.

In the small, uncertain hours when the wind blows through the branches of the trees, I often scratch my chin and wonder at what might have been. *If only.* If only I had taken the left turn in the road instead of the right. Or better still, put my foot down and gone straight ahead.

Now from the inside looking out, I am an entity comfortably enriched around the waist and with more than a little time to spare, able to brood and contemplate upon the fast approaching years of old age. It would be nice to sit back in my favourite chair, admire the changing scenery of the seasons or the transit of the stars and planets high above, smile and without any further hesitation utter the words: *This is my slice of the cake. This little piece of heaven. Here is my humble story, do with it what you will. Remember of it only what you wish. It is just me gathered up along the stone filled way. But you know, when it comes right down to it, if I could have my time over again. I wouldn't change a thing.*

Shall I dare tempt fate and begin here with something banal and trivial? Or indeed slightly odd. In so many ways I can set the ball in motion. How about *'once upon a time in a strange yet wondrous land'* or perhaps *'somewhere in a cloud at the very, very, beginning'* may be more appropriate. Either way, I am afraid that would be far too simplistic or even presumptuous on my part. So suffice it to say, *'there were no pyrotechnics nor trumpets blown and no special prizes handed out when I was born in that small insignificant room on a cold, dark grey winter's morn'.* Sounds Simon and Garfunkle good. Precise and to the point.

However, to be brutally honest I have no idea who came and went or what the weather was really like on that auspicious occasion on the eighteenth of February nineteen hundred and fifty three. The day may or may not have been average and I suppose that with a gentle stretch of the imagination it might even have been full of delights and unexpected events. I too may have been unexpected, though given the circumstances that is highly unlikely. One thing however would be fairly safe to surmise, not many paid too much attention to what transpired around them. Least of all, one Sylvia Beryl Moss.

My birth father was nowhere to be seen. He didn't have the decency to stick around and smell the roses or see the fruits of his philandering. Without so much as a rosary bead and mea culpa, he vanished into thin air as quick as the melting snow in some now forgotten spring. Never more to be seen or heard from again. Gone on a steel breeze. Extricated from our lives.

It was not the best of starts, but mother however, despite the dire predicament, never once raised her voice in bitterness or complaint. I am sure she saw the future in a different light and with a little help from her friends in unusual places, soldiered on bravely with the hand god had dealt her.

After all, as described in the concept of *samsara* or *wheel of life*[1] ours is a cyclical and meaningful existence that is limitless and knows no bounds.

Life is what you make of it. It is what it is.

Around the same time, other events unfolded. Some minor, some major. Joseph Stalin died. The Korean War ended. Watson and Crick discovered the intricate structure of DNA. United States Air Force pilot Chuck Yeager set a new speed record in the experimental test machine X-1. Edmund Hillary and his faithful companion Tensing Norgay scaled the heights of Mount Everest. The Soviet Union in its quest for dominant super power status, exploded the Hydrogen bomb thereby ensuring the continuation of the Cold War.

It was that kind of year.

---

1. *The teachings of Buddhism prescribe that human beings travel a continuous cyclical pathway: birth, death and rebirth.*

5

ROAST BEEF AND YORKSHIRE PUDDING

In My Life* (10) 1965 The Beatles, Rubber Soul
It did not take me long to figure out that God
indeed works in mysterious ways.

Having been thrust into the world from the dark confines of a fairly unremarkable hospital ward somewhere in a quaint, but fairly unremarkable town should not in any way be held against me.

My subjective shortcomings aside, Doncaster and the surrounding region must have had a lot going for it. So much in fact the diligent Romans in their insatiable drive to conquer Britain, saw fit to establish a small wooden fortress on the banks of the babbling River Don sometime around the year A.D.71. A defensive stronghold built to keep the local heathen clans at bay. It is worth noting that the Coritani and the Brigantes, the fiercest of these tribes, had proven themselves on more than one occasion to be a formidable giant thorn in the side of Imperial Rome. The Antonine Itinerary[1] (which had recorded pertinent details of the occupation of Britain), referred to this place as *Danum*. In Anglo Saxon times it was known

---

1. *The Itinerarium of Emperor Antoninus. This is a complete register of the Roman stations and the distances along interconnecting roads.*

as Doneceastre (derived from the words *Danu*[2] meaning rapidly flowing river and *castra* meaning fort). From these harsh and simple beginnings sprang up a fine, prosperous market town in the very heart of the Yorkshire coalfields.

The largest and perhaps most diverse County in all of England, Yorkshire is a virtual cornucopia of sights and sounds. Visually stunning from border to border. Ancient abbeys, majestic manors, old stone walls criss crossing over green rolling fields, rugged seascapes and mist covered moors greet the inquisitive eye. And of course from a culinary point of view there is always the much renowned, traditional fare of Roast Beef and Yorkshire pudding. The kind mother and her mother before her used to make. If that tickles your particular fancy.

Many a famous person has been the product of this wondrous place. Michael Parkinson having emerged from the veritable wilderness of Barnsley, got his start in newspaper journalism, before successfully making the transition to television host. Jeremy Clarkson of BBC Top Gear notoriety came from Tick Hill and soon took the high road out of there. Kevin Keegan one of the finest footballers ever to grace England's famous team, was born in Armthorpe and played for Liverpool because good old *Donny Rovers* didn't think he could make the grade. Dianna Rigg (who played the part of Emma Peel in the iconic television series The Avengers) was born in Doncaster and of course went on to bigger and better things.

Stoic Geoffrey Boycott from the village of Fitzwilliam, took his cricket whites and trusty willow and like a good,

---

2. *This was the name the original Iron Age inhabitants of this area gave the river. To the Celts, Danu was a river goddess.*

Yorkshire fellow, did his utmost not to let anyone else have a bat.

The most notable export of them all, a certain Captain James Cook[3] sailed a converted coal barge out of Plymouth harbour and the rest is as they say *'history'*.

3. *Cook was born in the village of Marton, near Middlesborough in 1728.*

6

LET'S SIT HERE AWHILE AND DREAM OF TRAINS

All The Nasties* *(7) 1971 Elton John from Madman Across The Water.*
Colorado bound. Here we sit on the back seat of the Greyhound bus, watching the landscape of our lives drift by.

The cold air was surely the root of my problems. Well, that's what everyone with a mouth and an expert opinion told me. Those who knew best. Those with no sense of fair play or common streak of humour whatsoever. From Constable Hutchinson to the neighbour from number 295 who couldn't help herself, I was a lost cause and they told me so. The fickle finger of *"See, look what happens if you don't take the necessary precautions",* pointed fair and squarely at the abominable weather. Their boredom and my belligerence had nothing to do with it. It boiled down to hydrogen and oxygen atoms and the effect they had on some people more than others. It came as no great surprise. It was also not unexpected that a young boy growing up in such an inhospitable environment had to find something to keep himself amused. Something to hold the dour winters at bay. Although come to think of it, even the far too short summer days were not that much better. Seemingly dogged by those on and off again showers that for some unknown reason hung around just long enough to be a damn nuisance. You could bet London to a brick that the sun would only make an appearance late, when it was time for all good children to go to bed. It was indeed fact that the sun in these high latitudes would set as late as nine thirty. By stark contrast, in January it was almost dark by four.

The vagaries of clouds and water droplets, referred to so succinctly in the obtuse meanderings of *I Am The Walrus** (9) 1967[1] did not deter me one bit. I was happy as a pig in mud and content with my simple lot.

Never was a sharp mind dulled and never was an idle moment spent. Not with friends like mine anyway. For the most part, we found ourselves preoccupied. Kept far too busy with football and cricket in the wide open spaces of Elmfield Park or kite flying in the town fields to be considered for the scholar of the month award. Marbles, hopscotch and other rowdy games were often played on the local pavement, which pleased grey follicled Mrs Coughlin and grumpy Mr Gardner no end. Not the type to mind their own business they could only watch and salivate about their once childhood years spent in harmonious bliss. "*Can't you rotters find better things to do*" became the popular neighbourhood catch cry. We could of course, but we never let on. That would be far too easy.

Thoughts turned to endless summer hikes and strolls in Hexthorpe Flats along the banks of the muddy river Don. Tossing dried cow pats at each other or chasing after

---

1. *As a child I was inclined to spend far too much time lazing about in pretty English gardens waiting for the sun to shine. On reflection, it is indeed one of life's great pleasures.*

elusive peacock and cabbage butterflies with a bent willow stick and a net full of holes. For the most part with little success.

Hours at rest on freshly, rolled haystacks and even longer hours fishing for sticklebacks, newts and tadpoles in the local stream then storing the day's meagre catch in a jam jar so mother could show off her be kind to slimy creatures side and say "*What were you thinking? That's cruel to keep them in such a small container*". That and more. And after all the great hardships we had gone through to bring back our prized possessions in one piece. Still we didn't mind the embarrassment her words brought or the extreme discomfort we felt from the grass stalks and prickly burrs hiding in our jumpers, or our soaked breeches and shoes caked in mud. Not to mention not getting home until dinner was cold or the fact Michael got a headache from too much positive thinking. It was a price worth paying.

There were even daring escapades deep behind enemy lines where the ominous threat of those *Strictly Private Property, Keep Out If You Know What's Good For You* signs, could not deter the Baxter Gate brothers. Our famous clandestine sorties took us far and wide, over field and brook and under barbed wire fences. Zig zagging our way through a minefield of security personnel at the World War Two tank graveyard to forage for ball bearings and other notable keepsakes became the highlight of our Saturdays. The steel *"bollies"* made a great addition to any worthwhile marble collection.

We knocked together primitive billy carts (constructed from only the finest wooden orange boxes and discarded pram wheels) then raced them helter skelter down steep cemetery hill with its avenue of giant elms and birch. Past the broken headstones and weathered crosses. Leaving treacle trails and thumbtacks on the road behind us. Raced the damn contraptions until they fell apart before holiday's end, then drained of all energy we lost interest in resurrecting them.

If such digressions were not quite enough to whet the appetite, there was always the peculiar pastime of *train spotting* to fall back upon. An odd turn of phrase, but delightful occupation requiring maximum physical effort and minimum brain capacity, that conjured up a bountiful manmade landscape of rugged English dysfunctionality. A balancing act between body and soul. A leisure pursuit etched in granite and venerable to an entire culture that had no idea whatsoever, on who to blame for inventing such a mind numbing activity. To become a member of this gender exclusive club was indeed a boy's greatest privilege. The girls for their part however, were not interested in huge, coal fired engines that ran around on tracks and made rude noises from their pistons and their funnels. To them it was strictly dolls and dress ups or nothing at all. Such was the accepted order of things. We didn't want it any other way.

Complete with pen and illustrated compendium of useless information (bought at great expense from Mr Cuttriss's *we have far more than you can possibly imagine* Hobby Shop), all of us would scramble up the steep nettle lined embankment to catch the twelve o'clock Flying Scotsman[2]

---

2. *We didn't know so at the time but we were witnessing the very* Last of the Steam Powered Trains. *Take a listen to the Anglo-centric paint pictures in your head album* The Kinks Are the Village Green Preservation Society* (8) 1968

thunder its way under Balby Bridge. Lost in the bliss of thorns, thistles and soothing whistles we were on board that train bound for destinations unknown. Our happiness was bliss and it came in a circular motion.

Ah, the joys of the age of steam.

7

TAKE ME WHERE THE
MERSEY RIVER RUNS

*The smell of the restless sea is strong as it drifts like
smoke across the bay. It makes me think of the places
seen and the faces we once played. And though the
time we shared has gone, the waves that break upon
the shore, reminds me that memories like songs can
mend the heart and soothe the saddest day.*

It was a period of uncertainty that hit us where it
hurts. Creeping out of the ruins like storm clouds on
a mission, bringing great upheaval as well as new found
hope and inspiration. It was the age of the *Baby Boomer*
and I happened to be right in the thick of it.

The conflagration of the Second World War had left
its brutal scars and indelible marks for all to see. An entire
nation, exhausted and almost at the point of bankruptcy,
stoically carried on and looked towards a better future.
The intervening twenty years or so after war were the
realm of wishes and fantasies. A time to reflect in an era
of rapid and yet subtle change. Bold explorations and
conquests. The climbing of Mt. Everest[1]. Technological

---

1. *One of the proposed working titles for the Beatles' Abbey Road album was 'Everest'*
(after Sound Engineer Geoff Emerick's favourite brand of cigarette).

advancements hitherto only dreamed about took place: Saturn V rockets and communication satellites to orbit the earth. The production of nuclear energy. The jet engine. The hovercraft. The heart transplant and other miracle developments in medicine. Pretty soon man would conquer the moon. There appeared to be no bounds to the capabilities of humankind. In a few short years the world was no longer the world our parents had grown up in. To most, the change came as a complete shock to the system.

The nineteen sixties exploded out of the fragile progress made during the previous decade. Almost overnight, a strange thing occurred in a rather grimy port city in the north west of England. Popular music would be turned on its head as one seemingly innocuous foursome calling themselves the Beatles, emerged out of the Jacaranda Club in Liverpool[2], morphed offshore in Hamburg, Germany[3] before returning to perform sold out gigs at the Cavern and eventually sealing a recording deal with EMI Records Parlophone division. Under the watchful guidance of manager Brian Epstein and maestro producer George Martin (often referred to as the *Fifth Beatle*) they soon became the greatest pop phenomenon of all time. As an aside, it is worth noting that for some inexplicable reason Decca Records were less than impressed with the (rather poor quality) demo tapes the Beatles presented them with in an early audition. In a masterstroke of human foresight the company declined to sign them to even a modest contract[4]. The commonly

---

2. *At this early stage they were called The Silver Beetles*

3. *The Beatles secured a German club contract with the aid of local Liverpool promoter Allan Williams*

4. *The famous faux pas is directly attributed to the legendary Dick Rowe.*

accepted management spiel issued at the time, was that the experts of the industry, the recording executives, were of the unanimous opinion that guitar groups were on the *"way out"*.

The decision proved to be perhaps the most celebrated error of judgement in pop music history.

And thus it occurred in modern music: a radical transformation unlike anything seen before or since.

What might have been referred to, rightly or wrongly as inferior British music, (now) digested and moulded the American R & B and Jazz sound. It successfully converted the form into something unique and totally different. These enterprising groups made it their very own style, delivered with a raw, unencumbered energy and mannerism and to top it off, a quirky, pop dress fashion unfamiliar to their American counterparts. Minor hits (albeit with some notable exceptions) and curious B sides by mostly African-American artists became the source of inspiration to the up and coming groups soon to form the nucleus of the *British Beat*[5] juggernaut. The Beatles, the driving force behind this transformation, recorded a number of slick, catchy cover versions of a host of artists. Chuck Berry, Wilbert Harrison, Smokey Robinson and the Miracles and Carl Perkins readily spring to mind. Not bound by American constraints, their working class background and cultural ideals proved to be a winner. They playfully dabbled with the lyrics, song structures and arrangements and added distinct Beatlesque harmonies unashamedly based around those put together by the Everly Brothers. Compare the clever call and response

---

5. *Highly recommended for further reading, the vivid and compelling account of* <u>The British Invasion</u> *(Barry Miles)*

passages evident in *Please Mr Postman* with the Marvelette's rather innocuous 1961 original effort and be enthralled by the whirlwind power and dynamics of Lennon's crisp rendition of *Twist and Shout*[6] (a 1962 minor chart hit for Cincinnati family act the Isley Brothers). The staple music sets and exhaustive song lists performed during their famous stints at the Cavern, Kaiserkellar and Top Ten Club (these latter two were renowned Hamburg drinking and live performance venues), included a vast smorgasbord of fifties and early sixties American music. Even the Animals (though not a Mersey group) with the rasping, charged vocals of Eric Burdon up front and Alan Price on organ, reworked a traditional deep south song piece, *House Of The Rising Sun** (10) (also a hit for Joan Baez at the start of the new decade) and promptly scored a massive number one on both sides of the Atlantic.

Not to be outdone, The Rolling Stones and the Yardbirds put down strong music roots by manufacturing into their own unique brand[7], the mostly overlooked, but never the less formidable works of Willie Dixon, Bo Diddley, Muddy Waters, Howlin' Wolf and others. The original incarnation of Fleetwood Mac with guitar supremo Peter Green at the helm could not resist the temptation to get on board the blues / jazz infused band wagon. Continuing the latest trend, The Hollies, John Mayall, Manfred Mann, Them and so many other contemporaneous artists, produced memorable recordings of almost overlooked music gems. At the height of the so called *invasion*, Eric Clapton sporting his Cream persona

---

6. *Many analysts believe this to be perhaps the most famous single take in rock history*

7. *The Rolling Stones raw, pull no punches rendition of Willie Dixon's* Red Rooster, *gave dirty blues a whole new meaning. It was released as* Little Red Rooster. *Covers of this seminal number have been recorded by various artists including Howlin' Wolf.*

still preferred to expand upon and experiment with the unmatched refrains of _Crossroad Blues*_ (8)[8] recorded some thirty years earlier by Robert Johnson. Suddenly those previously insignificant British acts were the hot flavour of the month.

It was but the beginning, for what had started out as a ripple soon became a tidal wave. Full of light, magic, youthful exuberance and rebellion, it swept out of the bleak cities of the industrial north. American R & B, jazz and even folk music, perhaps not by choice but by sheer accident (and with a little luck along the way) became a virtual treasure trove of new sounds and endless possibilities for the _stark and rough edged_ British groups. Far removed from their transatlantic neighbours, they adapted and annealed this music into a mouth-watering stockpot with a distinctly English flavour. This _sound_ evolution, combined with a surge of public optimism not seen for years, brought about a rethinking of what at the time was considered to be acceptable music.

The Yardbirds' versions of Bo Diddley's (Ellas Bates McDaniel) I'm A Man and Pretty Girl can be found on Five Live Yardbirds* (8) 1964

Jazz and blues though popular with predominantly poor, black audiences, for so long had struggled to gain recognition, garnering no more than moderate mainstream radio airplay in the land of their birth. However, from a different cultural perspective half a world away and driven by a mostly disengaged post war youth eager to shake off the shackles of conservatism and all remaining signs of stiff upper lip convention, it was an entirely different ball game.

---

8. _Cream's classic electrified interpretation of this piece became Crossroads_

At the same time, still struggling to come to terms with the brutal after shock of the death of John. F Kennedy, America sought some form of tangible comfort and new social direction to replace what had become stale and stagnant. They found this and much more within the radical, framework of the Beat invasion. It was like a breath of fresh air blown in through once closed windows.

The great music, now re-energised and revived, had been right under their noses all along. All it needed was a push and a shove and a tweak from just the right source. The irony of course, was that America had rediscovered its own unique brand of music. And they couldn't get enough of it.

The revolution, germinated and grown from humble beginnings would alter our lives and the way we viewed the world forever. The road ahead was paved with free love, incense, sequins and gold. We could adopt and follow the idealist philosophy echoed by The Beatles in _Tomorrow Never Knows_*(10)[9] or find solace in the clichéd, turned on tuned out words of chemical minded Timothy Leary. Although I think I would much prefer the safer option: to sleep, to dream, to grow a beard then put some flowers in my hair. Just like good old Scott McKenzie[10].

---

9. _This song's original working title was Mark I. (Takes 1-3 put down in April 1966). A highly experimental mind altering piece from the ground breaking Revolver* (10) 1966. Source: The Complete Beatles Recording Sessions Mark Lewisohn._

10. _Those out there from the Hippy era are best likely to remember this timeless classic San Francisco (Be Sure To Wear Flowers In Your Hair)* (8) 1967_

A LITTLE SOMETHING TO PASS THE TIME AWAY 1

IS THAT A SITAR RINGING IN MY EARS?

Within You Without You (9)	The Beatles	Sgt.Pepper's Lonely Hearts Club Band
Blues For My Baby And Me (9)	Elton John	Don't Shoot Me I'm Only The Piano Player
Paint It Black (9)	Rolling Stones	Aftermath (U.S Version)
Do It Again (9)	Steely Dan	Can't Buy A Thrill
Paper Sun (7)	Traffic	Mr Fantasy (U.S Version)

WHAT ABOUT THE SAXAPHONE?

Candle In The Window (8)	Creedence Clearwater Rev.	Cosmo's Factory
The Year Of The Cat (8)	Al Stewart	The Year Of The Cat
Baker Street (7)	Gerry Rafferty	City To City
Urgent (7)	Foreigner	4
Don't Bang The Drum (6)	The Waterboys	This Is The Sea

COUNTING BY NUMBERS DOESN'T HELP

One After 909 (8)	The Beatles	Let It Be
25 Or 6 To 4 (7)	Chicago	Chicago II
1,2,3 Red Light (5)	1910 Fruitgum Company	1,2,3 Red Light
Rainy Day Women #12 & 35 (8)	Bob Dylan	Blonde On Blonde
Happenings Ten Years Time Ago (8)	Yardbirds	Roger The Engineer

WHAT'S THE WEATHER LIKE TODAY?

Here Comes The Sun (10)	The Beatles	Abbey Road
She's A Rainbow (8)	Rolling Stones	Their Satanic Majesties Request
Rain (9)	The Beatles	Past Masters
Shelter From The Storm (7)	Bob Dylan	Blood On The Tracks
Flowers In The Rain (8)	The Move	The Move

NAUGHTY BY NAME, NAUGHTY BY NATURE

Desdemona (6)	John's Children	Single Release only
Mrs Robinson (7)	Simon and Garfunkle	Bookends
Gloria (7)	Them	The Angry Young Them
Mustang Sally (5)	Andrew Strong	The Commitments (Soundtrack)
	Wilson Pickett	
Maggie May (8)	Rod Stewart	Every Picture Tells A Story

DON'T GO DOWN TO THE WOODS TODAY

Lodi (7)	Creedence Clearwater Rev.	Green River
High Sheriff Of Calhoun Parish (7)	Tony Joe White	Tony Joe
Hotel California (9)	Eagles	Hotel California
Tower Of Song (8)	Leonard Cohen	I'm Your Man
Lake Marie (5)	John Prine	Lost Dogs And Mixed Blessings

8

ERNEST EDWARD

Brave were they who lived and died, working for the corporation on the darker side. Out of mind, deep underground, where the sun's light never shines. Brothers in arms on a human tide, working that endless black seam together.

The sad truth of the matter should not surprise anyone. I hardly knew my grandfather. Which on reflection was no fault of his. Children for some reason, have a bad habit of being concerned more about tomorrow and far less with yesterday. Of course, they don't look at it in such a simplistic way. Now as a grown up, wrestling with the harsh realism of mortality, it doesn't seem quite so strange to think about the past and the people in it. Yet try as I may after so many years, my recollections of that proud, grey haired man with the strong, calloused hands and piercing gaze, I am afraid are rather obscure. Like the worn and faded surface of an old photograph, they remain but snippets of memories accounted to me by my mother. Pictures painted in my head over and over, from a time far removed from the here and now, where only the ghosts of Christmas past remain.

Ernest Edward Moss, the youngest of two children was born in the village of Stavely, Derbyshire in the year of our lord 1889. Salt of the earth. Hardworking, proud husband of fair Georgina and father to eight. Six boys and two girls. One child did not live to see his first birthday.

Ernest was a coal hewer or seamer as they were more commonly known. Like his father before him and his grandfather before that. The dark belly of the pit was the only world they ever knew.

If you want to better find out what a miner's lot was like, look no further than that so brilliantly evoked and captured on celluloid in *How Green Was My Valley*.

Ernest Edward was 68 when the black coal eventually consumed him. The company he broke his back for never shed a tear.

From that day onward, Georgina carried his lonely shadow to her grave.

9

DAFFODILS AND PRETTY MAIDS
ALL IN A ROW

Onward, Christian Soldiers marching as to war,
with the cross of Jesus going on before...
Forward into battle see his banners go.
Onward, Christian Soldiers. Traditional
English Hymn

Five years might seem a mere drop in the ocean of numbers and hard knocks to most, but to these confused brain cells it felt more like a hundred. It also didn't help make matters any easier that a great deal had been crammed into such a short twinkling of time. I can remember. We packed up the canary and the tortoiseshell cat and relocated from my grandmother's cottage in nearby Bentley to our (new) domicile on dire sounding St. Sepulchre Gate. Now strictly speaking the home was not new, far from it, but sadly rather tired and run down from lack of care and attention. It was one of a dozen or so modest terrace houses together with a few convenience shops that had been built in the mid nineteenth century to accommodate the surge in demand for itinerant workers employed in the booming railway industry. Indeed, the main rail link from London to Edinburgh passed almost within spitting distance of our front door. Although I wasn't game to test out that theory. Fact was, we couldn't actually see or hear much, as the line ran at a level much lower than the road and a large red brick wall at the top of a vertical embankment conveniently blocked out any noise that came our way. However, the wall no matter how high, did not stop the smoke. We could smell it. That thick odious substance was everywhere. It crept about the buildings. It stained the clothes that dangled on the washing line. It fogged our minds. It even blackened our faces, but never once our hearts.

What should have been a normal lie in and think of muffins Sunday turned out to be nothing of the kind. This particular day I fell out of bed earlier than usual, perplexed by the sound of music drifting down the street. It was deep winter, the cold Yorkshire concoction one had become accustomed to. The threat of snow hung heavy, but somehow the air was filled with the scent of daffodils and hyacinth and a sweet cinnamon wind that wound its way through the long grass of a sun kissed meadow. It was the Salvation Army Brass Band and for the first time ever, I had the privilege to witness such a decorative and rowdy procession. You can imagine how that felt. For a young boy, barely half awake, with a head full of stars and the leftovers of last night's dreams still whizzing around the room, it was difficult not to be impressed.

The atmosphere must have been contagious for everyone except Tom Turner the boilermaker had the same idea. Out onto the narrow pavement they came. Tall and short people of working class persuasion, anxious to see what all the fuss was about. Extricated from their cosy nests by those most mellifluous, melodic pied pipers. Each onlooker jostled and groaned in unified anticipation, until excitement reached a fever pitch. Charlie Pecks the rebellious Staffordshire terrier from three houses down, showed his complete indifference to proceedings and cocked his leg at the first available car tyre he could find. Always the last to get in on the action, Mr Whittaker taking a well-earned break from his mundane corner shop duties, stumbled into the fray. In an effort to catch his breath he propped his bulky frame against the only lamp post that didn't have a no loitering sign affixed to it. Lifting his striped apron to wipe the sweat from his brow, he almost dislodged the spectacles that sat precariously atop his large crooked nose. There was a distracting hum of voices that hung about. So much so, he hardly noticed skinny Florence Thistlethwaite as she rushed by, rubber band arms flailing in every which direction, her body all lit up in *that* multi coloured macintosh she wore no matter the hour or the season. Always in a hurry, with no place special to go. She never had the time for ceremony or useless chit chat and frowned her disapproval at the idle gathering. Not that it had any effect. The noise just got louder and louder. Soon she was a ghostly face lost in a shifting tide of bodies.

A pretty lass with flame red hair tied back in a bun barely visible beneath a broad peaked cap, marched at the head of an ensemble of men carrying all description of wonderful, sparkling instruments. Such a vast array I had never seen before. There were tubas and trombones, flugelhorn, flutes and lutes, timpani and triangles. And other various items, but no guitars. It seemed that the good lord in his wisdom frowned upon such misplaced hedonism. At the rear, looking remarkably distinguished in his full military attire and bearing two small silver stars on his epaulets, came a handsome captain of the guard.

Another associate with long, curling beard, pounded relentlessly on a bass drum almost too large to carry. To compliment his valiant efforts, cymbals crashed like waves breaking on a beach. Each wave a little louder than the one before. Until at the crescendo there was a long pause before a short drum roll, followed by a sigh and a clap of hands. The men were singing about brave soldiers from some long ago sacred war. The very same hymn we often sang in our school assembly. It sent shivers down my spine and made most of the inquisitive onlookers want to march along with them. Stirring stuff indeed for martyrs of the Pentecost.

A girl barely out of her teen years, held an emblazoned banner. Though with her slight physique, she struggled to keep it upright in the strong, blustery wind. Occasionally the pole would slip from her grasp to be rebalanced at the very last moment in a precarious juggling act that would have made a circus performer proud. Directly adjacent, another woman rattled a metal canister with boundless joy and enthusiasm. It was expected of the model citizens of the town, that they be most charitable and donate to the worthy cause. Otherwise god in his anger would perhaps strike them down. Then it suddenly occurred to me in that awkward spiritual moment that refused to let me go, that god was indeed someone to be feared. Not wanting to tempt fate at this hour of the morning, I put some pennies in the tin as did Mrs Broadbent, Mr O'Leary and a few other repentant souls. The very thought of blood and fire was enough to make even the most rebellious stick to the straight and narrow. Redemption was a cause worthwhile and a far better choice than the alternative of burning in hell. Mr Whittaker, who must have known a thing or two about the mysterious workings of the Christian faith, winked and went back to the safety of his shop.

As if she could read my thoughts, the woman holding the receptacle smiled. She had travelled this road before.

For what seemed an eternity, I stood in hypnotic state, listening to the magic sounds and watching the parade slowly disappear from view. Before running headlong and almost breathless to tell my mother that I wanted so much to join the formidable brothers and sisters of the travelling Celebration Marmy and see the big, wide world. Before it was too late. Before I grew out of my shoes. Wouldn't that be a wonderful way to spend the rest of your life.

"My word of course it would" she chirped *"now come and have your breakfast."*

10

MYSTICAL VISIONS OF RHUBARB

*Music was at its very best when I was young and
mostly foolish.*

Before too long, we found ourselves somewhere near
the hump back iron bridge and old stone ruins,
between the water filled quarry and the brick houses
teetering on the edge of the dark at the narrow lanes. It
was late morning when the sun's rays struck upon the duck
ponds. Now almost at the halfway mark of our journey,
you were relieved that the sweat and hard work was not in
vain. The prize at the end of the rainbow would surely be
worth a few cuts and bruises.

After a mad scramble down the slippery, clay
embankment and through the bramble bushes that
bordered the market gardens, we fell exhausted into a vast
carpet drift of dog daisies and towering red sorrel. A wild
bloom of colour that mixed with the starburst of your
cheeks.

The heavy canvas knapsacks rubbed hard against
our shoulders and all the running had made us thirsty
and tired. So we drank like gods from the bottle of
freshly squeezed orange juice your mother had prepared.
Rested a short while in the dappled shade of elm and

elder. Laughed aloud and spoke about dragonflies and Wuthering Heights, then took a deep breath to plot our next strategic move: the assault on farmer Riley's giant patch of irresistible rhubarb.

11

SUSANNAH'S GREAT FEATHER
BED BY THE SEA

*The air was full of crystal drops and vapour trails.
Eclipsed by a pale moon, I came out of the burning
sky, close behind you. The restless heart of a comet
forever homeward bound, I quivered in my new
transparent skin. Then your eyes caught mine and
would not let go. Until like rivers of blue ice we
became entwined.*

Anyone who knew the slightest bit about rest,
relaxation and ergonomics had one. Be it a
grandmother or other family member of any importance,
they would have a feather bed. It was the answer to
their nocturnal problems. Simple and most effective.
A panacea for tired, aching bodies, far better than hot
milk and Horlicks. And for kids growing up the world
over it was a symbol of security and good old fashioned
values. Something to be revered, especially by those most
unfortunate not to have one. They didn't know what they
were missing.

Now, as it so happened we fell into the latter category.
We didn't have one but wished for all money we did. My
mother always made excuses, said we had no place for such
a great wooden artefact, particularly the solid four poster

variety. They were heavy and too awkward to manipulate up those tricky narrow stairs that defied even the most flexible furniture movers and shakers in the land. To accommodate such a monstrosity would certainly mean wholesale changes. In other words something had to give or something had to go. However, in both departments, George was adamant it wouldn't be him, pointing to the fact that in the Smith castle, nothing ever got removed or relocated unless it was absolutely necessary. Not even the cat. Therefore, we were more than happy to go along with the next best alternative. So whenever the opportunity arose, Mum gladly accepted Aunties kind invitation for a weekend stay over on the coast.

Susannah, a widow with no formal education proved to be a better business woman than she looked. A lady of the manor, of highest scruples, who ran a large, comfortable bed and breakfast in that most unlikely town of Blackpool, Lancashire, just a stone's throw away from the rippling shores of the bleak and inhospitable Irish Sea[1]. Fortunately for her and the many dedicated clientele who returned year after year, refreshed and invigorated, in search of that elusive strip of sand, wholesome sunshine and double dose of vitamin D, the house was not located on the main neon infested promenade, famous for its inedible striped rock candy, glitz and carnival atmosphere[2].

This was a blessing in more ways than one.

---

1. *Referred to quite simply as the Northern Sea on* <u>Military Madness.</u> *From Songs For Beginners* (8) by Graham Nash 1971*

2. *The seaside resort situated between the Ribble and the Wyre estuaries. It attracts many thousands of visitors annually to its golden mile of buildings, amusement parlours, piers and of course the highlight attraction, Blackpool Tower itself.*

The road from Doncaster to Blackpool was long and winding and full of pot holes of every possible shape and size. I did not have the time nor the slightest inclination to count them however[3], so I amused myself by turning my attention to sheep instead. My father, at the blunt end of his good natured tether and suffering from a severe bout of hunger and motorist back spasm, suggested we should have gone to sleepy Llandudno instead, far from the bustling crowds and burning lights.

By some miracle of Fatima, we arrived at our destination still in one piece, thirsty and much wearied after our bumpy ride. Holding a large bunch of freshly picked geraniums, Susan greeted us at the front gate. After surviving the hazardous barbs from our back seat driver, it was a comfort to see someone with a smiling face and a thick skin. George was on tenterhooks, keen to get a move on, least of all because he could already see himself stretched out on the pier somewhere between a deck chair and a hard pebble. Waiting for the tide to roll in.

For a brief moment, as we exchanged pleasantries and gifts, it felt warm in the afternoon sun. I think it was summer. Or at least the abridged version of that most anticipated of the seasons. Yet Great Aunt Susan did not have any remote interest in temperature or humidity, for no matter the time or the occasion she always wore her favourite knee length fur coat with matching stole and leopard skin cylinder hat that perched on top of her head like a drunken sailor's cap. First impressions she said, made the loudest noise. Particularly in these here parts.

---

3. *John Lennon made reference to this fact: According to a news article published in a local paper, someone for lack of anything more productive to do, had meticulously counted four thousand holes in Blackburn, Lancashire. As succinctly described in the Beatles' epic* A Day In The Life* (10) 1967

Sour faced Howard, whose middle aged appearance and crop of wispy thin hair disguised the fact that he was a fit and sprightly Lancastrian, did not shirk one bit when it came to carrying luggage. He thrived on hard work and insults. Howard with an unflappable bent and a nose for excellence, never batted an eyelid and always seemed to be one step ahead of everyone else. Susan said he had been the porter and chef de mission for as long as she cared to remember. Even when she first purchased the property, large as life Howard had been there taking care of business. Not wanting to throw a screwdriver in the works she agreed it for the best that Howard should continue on in his accustomed position. And in any case, most of the patrons thought of him as something of a northern English oddity and a charmer of high standing. A true Bolton boy made good.

He placed our bags inside the room, nodded and then doffed his hat before disappearing into the baroque themed music parlour. Moments later we could hear the gentle piano refrains of Chopin's *Nocturnes* as they drifted through the house. Howard just couldn't stop himself when it came to impressing visitors. Especially those from over the green hills and faraway in Yorkshire.

The star chamber as we called it, was a wonder to behold. Situated on the first floor it was full of light and smelled of peony and sweetest lavender. Decorated with vases of moon beams and damask roses on every table, even if it was dull and overcast outside, the room never failed to impress. Next to it, a small but comfortable annexe contained a library of rare leather bound books, a single curved chaise lounge and the obligatory tough as teak aspidistra in a traditional Grecian pot. From the arched window, if you held your breath and balanced on your toes long enough, it was possible to catch a glimpse of the steel grey sea over the roof tops of the houses lining the promenade.

Subtlety was not George's strong point. Particularly when sore and perplexed. And here he was at a complete loss to explain why anyone in their right mind would bother to stop by here to scale the lofty heights of a metal tower that looked disarmingly a lot like that famous one in Paris or to dangle their legs in the foamy brine. For the water at best, was ice cold and coal dark. Certainly not for the faint hearted. For the most part it proved to be downright uninviting, something to be avoided at all costs. Somewhere George did not want to venture even when in a good mood. And of course being Blackpool, as much as you could count on the carousel and constant flashing lights to make the head spin, you could count on the rain. Day in day out there was always the rain to dampen a good holiday. That was a fait accompli.

The most important room in the entire guesthouse however, was the Grande bedroom, crammed with priceless memorabilia and keepsakes from an almost forgotten era. Taking pride of place therein, was a much admired oaken post ensemble with the largest quilted eiderdown imaginable, hidden under a draped fabric canopy and cascades of satin curtains. Susan always insisted Queen Victoria had once slept in that very same bed. Howard cultivated serious doubts. But however pointed his polite grumblings and misgivings might have been, we liked the very thought of royalty and regalia and as mother with a touch of humour remarked, *'If it was good enough for the dowager queen herself then it was most certainly good enough for us.'* Anyway, regardless of the truth it was a rollicking story to tell the family, especially on a winter's night huddled around a roaring fire with nothing else to do.

Three weeks later we too joined the exclusive brotherhood of the illustrious feather bed. Trouble was, we just didn't have anywhere to put it.

12

AT STORM BAY
(EIGHT YEARS ON AND COUNTING)

I like it when she talks underwater.

We arrived in Whitby in time to catch the dying rays of a melting sun fall out of a broken sky. Robin wrapped the thick Shetland wool scarf his mother had knitted for the occasion of his fifteenth birthday around his neck and rubbed his hands together in a comical but vain effort to keep warm. Alexandria with the enormous pigtails, insisting we get to our rooms before dark, tugged at his trouser legs to make sure he would listen. It was so cold she couldn't feel her nose and anywhere other than here, was a better place to be.

A biting wind blew out of the north east, bringing ice arrows down upon the clustered row of houses. Across the black slate rooftops and through the narrow half lit streets and alleys it bucked and thundered like a wounded beast. Getting louder by the minute. Bellowing at door and threshold *'Come with me, it is time to go.'*

In the harbour the last of the speckled trawlers headed to safety, dragging to rest its heavy kelp filled nets. Then shifted sideways into the flotsam currents of the bay, taking shelter near the old stone breakwater.

Waiting for another chance to ply its trade. Waiting for another day.

'Now it is the time to go.'

We stood and watched the grey enclose around us, piece by piece until there was nothing left to take and nowhere left to hide.

Overhead, a band of sooty terns and anxious herons swooped and churned the heavy air, each one in its fashion screeching at the fast approaching storm. Giant shadows shifted into strange shapes and patterns and the birds thinking better of it, took flight and headed south for winter.

'Soon it will be here. Soon it will be time to go.'

The rain fell in short bursts, at first softly tapping on our skin, then quickly turned as sharp as thorns upon the bramble. While from afar, sultry siren voices rising from the open waters, once more called *'Take my hand, follow me. It is time to go.....'*

13

DAYS OF BLACK VINYL, NOT PEARLY SPENCER[1]

Reflections of Charles Brown* (8) 1967 Rupert's People.

One day full of Rowntree Good News and peppermint drops, my father arrived home from work earlier than was his custom, with a broad grin on his face which at first suggested he had been given a promotion or had struck the mother of all mother lodes on the football pools. Unfortunately it was neither. Nor was it a birthday celebration or any other such event out of the plain old ordinary. Except this particular day, George was in an especially good frame of mind and wanted to share the mood with everyone. He had, tucked under his arm a 78 rpm shellac recording by new English heart throb sensation Craig Douglas. The song was a version of Sam Cooke's *Only Sixteen** (7)[2], later to be revived and turned into a huge worldwide hit by Dr. Hook[3].

---

1. *David McWilliams scored a minor chart hit in Britain late 1967 with* The Days Of Pearly Spencer* *(7)*

2. *Released in 1959*

3. *Released December 1975*

Sylvia was nervous. She paced up and down the floor over the exact same spot the carpet had already worn thin from previous amblings. What had gotten in to him? It was not an unreasonable question as it was most un-George like to suddenly become an expert on things he had absolutely no idea about. I too thought it rather odd at the time, as regardless of his musical leanings and generous intentions we had no means of playing the damn thing. For that matter neither did anyone else we knew. For in the entire neighbourhood of lower Balby by the bridge, there was not a single record player to be seen or heard. And only popular Mrs Winterbottom with the endless supply of fruit juice and custard tarts she kept aside for the well behaved children in the street and whose husband was a roaming shoe salesman (with a chronic case of gout), had a new-fangled, state of the art television set. One to die for. You know the sort. Plush cabinet made from timber sourced all the way from Borneo, with special louvre doors behind which hid the largest cathode ray tube ever made by human hands. And as a nice touch, the cabinet was finished off with mirrored cocktail drinks bar. The whole unit was about six feet long and as heavy as a pregnant pachyderm.

Not long thereafter, we scraped enough money together to buy a rather cumbersome Dansette record player. A wonderful device of great pedigree, a conversation piece that took pride of place in our humble household for many a glorious year. We were astounded by what it could do. Via a long chrome spindle, it somehow balanced the large black discs on top of each other. With bated breath we couldn't wait to hear the glorious clunk of the record as it fell onto the rotating rubber platter. Followed by the crackle and hiss of the heavy needle in its special groove. There was an aural pleasure in the entire process, not unlike the sensation experienced in the muffled roar of waves beating from a seashell pressed against the ear.

The machine could even play the latest 45 rpm[4] single discs which in those early days came with a push out centre piece. These could quite easily be removed and reinserted if one chose to, but for what earthly reason you would do so I never really knew. Monaural (mono) sound recordings mostly were available. Stereophonic was in its infancy. Quadrophonic was still nearly a decade away and a fad destined to quickly disappear. But that's another story altogether.

No one took much notice but our parents listened mostly to the symphony classics or the sounds of the big bands along with such notable crooners as Frank Sinatra, Bing Crosby, Nat King Cole, Dean Martin and Perry Como. My mother, bless her cotton socks, was a fan of Mario Lanza, Andy Williams, Johnny Mathis, Doris Day and Brenda Lee. While my father enjoyed the tremolo tonsils of Joseph Locke, The Bachelors, Hank Williams, Johnny Ray and Johnny Cash. His greatest love without doubt however, was any recording that featured the bagpipes. The infernal noise made us fear for our sanity. But not George. For some unfathomable reason they brought tears to his eyes. I am sure he would have been right at home ensconced in the ranks of the Royal Scots Dragoon Guards. How he adored those banshee moments and ear piercing reverberations. Sitting there as pleased as Punch with his plate of pickled cabbage and Stilton cheese, watching on television, the stirring performance of the

---

4. *If my memory serves me correct the first 45 recording available in Britain was Bill Haley's anthem to rebellious youth, Rock Around The Clock* (9).*

Edinburgh Military Tattoo, especially during Christmas holidays when family goodwill and merriment forgave his indiscretions. Much later, in his mellow years when the waters had calmed and Sylvia had better things to do and didn't bother him quite so much, he often listened to the Highwaymen and Merle Haggard.

I do know that the very first record that really made me sit up and take notice, was the up tempo remake of the classic *Rock Island Line** (8), by Lonnie Donegan and his skiffle group.

Where the song originated remains unclear. Clouded in history, it was a traditional piece that had its roots in the American deep south and was often sung by prison gangs working in the fields or on the railroad. It appears to have been first recorded by pioneering field musicologist John Avery Lomax in 1934 during his frequent travels and visits to the Louisiana State Penitentiary, Angola. The song was originally performed acapella by the inmates. The great Lead Belly who was incarcerated during this time[5], later released his seminal version in 1937. However, it was Donegan's unique cover rendition put out on the Decca Label in 1956 that created all the fuss, garnering the attention of the up and coming beat movement. The single went on to sell more than a million copies worldwide. I think I peeled the paint from the walls belting out the lyrics to that infectious song. Sang it over and over until my voice went hoarse. Sang until my mother threatened me with a nasty fate. Sang it until we got another record to replace the old worn out one. Then started all over again.

---

5. *American blues musician Huddie William Ledbetter (born 1888 died 1949). Convicted for murder (1917) and attempted murder (1930) and pardoned both times. His singing literally earned him his freedom. Source: Rock and Roll Hall of Fame Museum rockhall.com*

Perhaps skiffle can best be described as *do-it-yourself music for not much cost*, in essence a user friendly concoction easily produced at minimal expenditure and by just about anyone who had the time and inclination to do so and mainly by those whose talent in the first instance often took a back seat to ambition. Originally it was a generic term applied to poor non-white musicians who by virtue of that very fact, incorporated into their act only the simplest of improvised instruments such as washboards, broom handle base and kazoo. Skiffle's beginnings can be traced to the turbulent, backwaters of New Orleans circa 1900.

Some sixty years down the track, emerged a daring collective of British acts, keen to sample, replicate and reinvent the jazz, blues and folk flavoured American music wave that now washed away what had gone before. Influenced in no small part by Donegan and his revival of the almost obsolete art of skiffle, groups fervently sought out the lesser known, obscure recordings by African-American blues based performers and moulded this unsophisticated, traditional form into their own.

It was easy to see the profound effect this had on the younger population, an entire generation still shackled and bound by the giant economic sinkhole that had resulted from the disastrous consequences of the Second World War. Money was not readily available, especially to the struggling majority and certainly not an item to be squandered on short lived fads and expensive instruments. Improvisation out of necessity, proved to be the key to unlocking the inner secrets of Pandora's box. Almost overnight, across the entire length and breadth of England, skiffle acts sprang up from a hitherto music wasteland. They generated a raw, basic sound which in a strange way was also rich and vibrant and filled with an infectious energy difficult to resist. It did not take long for the rough edges to be smoothed and streamlined. Thereby providing a springboard for modern rock and roll.

And so the winds of change blew throughout the land. The _Magical Mystery Tour_* (6) had begun.

We couldn't wait to see where it would take us.

A LITTLE SOMETHING TO PASS THE TIME AWAY 2

LET US PRAY

Hallelujah (10)	Leonard Cohen	Various Positions
	Jeff Buckley	Grace
Let It Be (10)	The Beatles	Let It Be
Son Of A Preacher Man (5)	Dusty Springfield	Dusty In Memphis
My Sweet Lord (8)	George Harrison	All Things Must Pass
God (8)	John Lennon	John Lennon/Plastic Ono Band

COSMIC PSYCHEDELIA

I Had Too Much To Dream (Last Night) (7)	Electric Prunes	I Had Too Much To Dream Last Night
White Rabbit (7)	Jefferson Airplane	Surrealistic Pillow
It's All Too Much (7)	The Beatles	Yellow Submarine (Soundtrack)
In A Gadda Da Vida (6)	Iron Butterfly	In A Gadda Da Vida
Set The Controls For The Heart Of The Sun (8)	Pink Floyd	Saucerful of Secrets

SOMEONE SPECIAL TO MEET MOTHER

Brown Eyed Girl (8)	Van Morrison	Blowin' Your Mind
Caroline (5)	Status Quo	Hello
Josie (8)	Steely Dan	Aja
Sister Golden Hair (7)	America	Hearts
Rosanna (7)	Toto	Toto IV

A NICE PLACE TO VISIT

Come To Milton Keynes (6)	The Style Council	Our Favourite Shop
Itchycoo Park (9)	Small Faces	There Are But Four Small Faces
Blackberry Way (7)	The Move	Single Release only
Monterey (8)	Eric Burdon and the Animals	Single Release only
The Village Green Preservation Society (6)	The Kinks	The Village Green Preservation Society

INVITE AT YOUR OWN PERIL

Werewolves Of London (7)	Warren Zevon	Excitable Boy
Roxanne (5)	The Police	Outlandos D'Amour
Sexy Sadie (8)	The Beatles	The Beatles (White Album)
Stainsby Girls (6)	Chris Rea	Shamrock Diaries
Wild Thing (6)	The Troggs	From Nowhere... The Troggs

DEAD TO RIGHTS

Lady D'Arbanville (8)	Cat Stevens	Mona Bone Jakon
Ballad Of Sir Frankie Crisp(Let It Roll) (6)	George Harrison	All Things Must Pass
Matty Groves (5)	Fairport Convention	Liege And Lief
Eleanor Rigby (10)	The Beatles	Revolver
Sky Pilot (7)	Eric Burdon & The Animals	The Twain Shall Meet

14

THE HOUSE ON ARBITRATION STREET

*Have you gone, or are you somehow disconnected
from this place.
I chase the shadows on the wall. Faces form,
strange voices call and patterns dance through
time.
Outside, the cold wind blows. It cuts like a knife
through the endless molecules of the night. And
across the open fields something stirs and then calls
my name. I wonder, have you gone and turned to
dust. Or are you just disconnected.*

The red and blue painted building with the crooked
chimney in state of collapse, was a mere shadow of
its former self. Forlorn and long neglected it appeared to
be not unlike all the other houses that stood side by side
in the dingy, narrow street. On first glance there was
nothing special about it to grab the attention or get the
imagination running wild. But once inside, well that was a
different story altogether.

It was more than odd. One might even be as bold to
say peculiar, but each time we went there to quench our
overwhelming curiosity for things that go bump in the
black of night, something unusual happened. Now what
to an inquisitive ten year old might be considered unusual,

may to an adult be quite normal and even plausible under the circumstances. The truth of the matter was the vacant Victorian terrace we had become accustomed to in our weekly quest for adventure, had some devious tricks up its sleeve or in its cloistered closets. Or wherever else you might care to look. That is, if you dared to look at all.

The tiled parlour had seen better days. It was plain uninviting. Musty and damp, thanks to the rainwater that for years had seeped between the broken bricks and rotting woodwork. We sneezed the moment we set foot inside. The masonry was festooned with a complex network of spider webs that hung between pillar and porch. The delicate strands and fibres sparkled in the half light, each one of them lined with a thousand silver sequins. A staircase swept upward to a number of rooms on the first floor. The treads were badly worn and twisted and the central section had given way altogether, making it difficult and dangerous to climb. At the top a wedge shaped area containing a small cabinet and a torn leather arm chair, opened into a wide corridor and an additional three rooms, two of which were nurseries. The third it seemed, had served as a utility or sewing annexe, as numerous cotton spools, spindles and pieces of cloth lay scattered about. The middle floorboard creaked when you walked on it. In places, some of the wall panels were missing or splintered and you could see the sky through a large hole in the ceiling above. Amongst a row of empty picture frames a sepia photograph (torn at the edges) hung from a wire fixed to a dado rail. It was a portrait of a sad young girl sitting astride a speckled rocking horse. In her left hand she held a small object.

The front room was the largest and boasted a fine, high, decorated ceiling of pink plaster rosettes and a central chandelier. Other delicate features completed the cornice which was covered with mould and unsightly stains. Water trickled down a rusted gas pipe and into the kitchen below. The basement, a simple, rectangular cellar that had been carefully cut into the stone foundations contained a pantry with a thick wooden bench and a large copper tub for washing clothes. Behind this, a small, separate enclosure stored coke and coal. More than enough to see through a cold harsh winter.

It was something Angela said. A cursory remark that drew an inquisitive response and a shrug of the shoulders. But nothing more was made of it. That is until the raggedy puppet with the sharp as needle eyes caught our attention. Those black marble beads that cut right through us. Set wheels in motion. Got the adrenalin rushing through nervous veins.

At our last rendezvous, we had noticed the doll sitting upright on the bedroom floor. Before that we had found it in the sewing room near the floorboard that creaked and moaned like an old man's bones. Yet earlier still, in the cellar and on our very first formal introduction there she was perched bold as brass in the chair at the top of the stairs. Of course, we did what any normal kid in our situation would do. We grumbled and cursed and pointed at each other, reluctant to accept the distinct possibility that poltergeist or other powerful forces were to blame. We could not hide from the most obvious fact that not one amongst us had touched that dreadful object. But the devil it seems was surely in the detail. There for all to see.

And even far more unnerving. The child in the photograph was holding that very same toy. The one first discovered weeks ago. Then again. And again. The doll that refused to go away. Caught in some pagan ritual of the senses or hit by a bolt of lightning in a storm, the hairs on our arms stood upright. A faint figure of white light moved slowly across the room. Then dimmed. A kaleidoscope of shapes and patterns danced on the ceilings where hollow faces called. Whispers hung in the air like mist above a meadow. Questions ran around inside our heads. Who was that pretty little stranger and why had the previous occupants not taken the picture with them? What had become of her? Had she suffered with illness and tragically died and what was that stain that seeped through the very fabric of the wall itself? Pieces of puzzles yet to fall into place. The truth no doubt lay somewhere between perception and logic.

Expecting to hear whistles and voices from the other side, Eunice put a finger in her ears. She just wanted to get out of there, quick smart. Colin was convinced he could smell burnt bacon on the stove and threw daggers at whoever had come up with the great idea to explore the world of the supernatural in the first place. Not quite sure what to do, Jacob twitched. He had heard this story before.

The wind rattled the doors and the window frames. Metal rubbed on metal. A piano played in the back of my head. Darkness fell and something scuttled through the roof space. Disturbing thoughts of the Jabberwocky and the raven rose from the ashes to haunt us.

Our tails between our legs, we departed that forbidden house in haste. Never more to return.

15

APPLE STRUDEL HEART

Seems to me we could have used some <u>*Savoy Truffle*</u>* (9) 1968 The Beatles*

Now, looking back through the years it should have been a simple freeze frame Woody Allen moment to remember. One taken straight from The Purple Rose of Cairo. The unforgettable scene where the gallant hero steps from the glowing picture screen and slap bang into the arms of the beautiful girl. There they would kiss and from that moment on live together happily ever after. A fairy tale come true. End of story, full stop. Perhaps, but in this instance, not quite. Here, it was just part of the intricate plot, where things would become inextricably entwined.

So it played out, with roles reversed, that prim and slim Miss Buttercup came to save us. As if heaven sent, she jumped right out of that movie theatre and into our mundane lives. Drawn from a heavy fog that at once clouded the senses and made the head swirl. The angel with a heart of gold, she came all the way from Birmingham via Billingsgate with nothing but a suitcase full of exotic food recipes and John Donne poetry to protect her. Our very own Miss Buttercup who spoke fluent Spanish and had a distinct penchant for continental cooking. Especially in the patisserie department. Apple strudel was her particular favourite and it quickly became admired the district over. Across the local parish, the children were unable to resist its light and fluffy pastry, stuffed with nothing but the finest diced and blended Somerset apples and baked for just the right length of time at just the right temperature. Next to manners and cleanliness, temperature and timing was everything, she said. The resulting product then finished to sublime perfection with a generous serving of thick, whipped Devon cream. Oh, how our mouths watered at the sight.

Miss Buttercup was a tall and imposing figure. And for the most part looked just as one would imagine a noble countess should look. Or at least like those pictures I had skimmed over in *The Everything You Wanted To Know About Deutschland (But Were Too Afraid To Ask)* tourism book, strictly for those who never travel. Dressed in long pleated skirt, season matching bright floral blouse and finest of alpaca jumpers that hugged that perfect torso as if they had been specially made for her. Light brown hair gathered tightly in a bun and adorned with black cloche hat tilted modestly to one side. Her hands were small and delicate, white as finest alabaster.

To our great delight, she also happened to be the most popular and glamorous teacher St James Public School ever employed. Mrs Petty the bespectacled headmistress, growled and scowled at the very thought, but deep down, recognised our Miss Buttercup to be a rare talent indeed. The school's excellent grade results and standing in the community, were testimony to that impressive fact.

Those in the right circle, said she reminded them of someone grand and famous. Not from these barren parts. In that regard, I am sure they had a classic silver screen starlet in mind. One thing was certain, Miss Buttercup would give Ingrid Bergman a good run for her money.

Yes, our favourite erudite teacher was definitely not your slash and burn, now you see me now you don't school madam type.

She wasn't married (though for what possible reason, remained a complete mystery) and so as a consequence, enjoyed a quiet, semi reclusive lifestyle taking care of her frail invalid mother and doing all the things a woman in such a position could possibly do. Even taking into account her single status, Miss Buttercup was a happy soul indeed.

She lived not beyond her means in a neat, middle class suburban setting, on the other side of town, along a tree lined avenue full of dancing elms and golden birch and opposite a Presbyterian boarding house once a refuge for wayward girls. Her home was typical Edwardian. From the foundations to the rafters. A well preserved, grand architectural example, solid and finely built, employing generous use of oak and other exotic timbers and decorations to adorn the large, light filled rooms inside. Most featured, as a focal point, a granite fireplace complete with hand carved mantelpiece. It seemed that none of them had burnt a fire in years.

Outside, a grey stone wall not much more than knee height, enclosed a bright green lawn surrounded by scented English roses, towering foxgloves and a lilac bush that blossomed fervently in early spring. On the southern side, a fragrant honeysuckle twined its way around a hawthorn tree.

Far removed from the nervous strains and pains of the school week ritual, Miss Buttercup always found time on weekends to dabble in her favourite music recitals, ad hoc pencil sketchings in the glass roofed conservatory or to apply herself the best she could on the potter's wheel. Then of course, there was Woodbine and Player (apparently so named after her late father's favourite habit of vice), an indomitable pair of cute Cavalier King Charles Spaniels to keep her company. Especially on dim and grey rainy days. In these parts, there were always a lot of those to go around.

Roly poly Mr Brampton, the widowed next door neighbour, the man with a passion for nouveau French fashion and dark chocolate, secretly fumed and protested that the rogue duo took great delight in digging up his vegetable patch. They fancied above everything else, his meticulously manicured row of giant beans. The same beans that had won him first prize three years running at the annual horticultural fair. He swore those dogs had a secret way of getting through the fence. Though he never quite could figure out where. With a puzzled look, what good he contemplated, was a garden without a secure barrier to keep out unwelcome intruders? Especially catastrophic canines hell bent on a mission to sniff, eat and destroy. However, deep down, Mr Brampton had a marshmallow soft spot for Miss Buttercup, so he never ever complained about naughty dogs and their dirty deeds. And every second week, just to make a suitable impression and show there were no hard feelings, he brought around a large bag of his famous legumes, especially for her. She had melted his heart. For sure and certain.

Each time we came to visit (which happened to be on a most regular basis), we would pick the very best blossoms from her well-kept bed of nasturtiums and pansies. Arrange them carefully in colourful wrapping paper and with an innocent smile and shaking hand that almost certainly revealed our guilt, give them to her when she answered the door bell. Funny how she blushed and thanked us for the impressive bouquet. Played the perfect diplomat by not once mentioning where they had come from. Then without so much a a blink and with a bright sparkle in those deep blue eyes, said how busy her day had been and that she could never understand how the gift horse worked in mysterious ways. No matter, it was nice to take a break and shake out those Saturday morning cobwebs. But I think she enjoyed the company more than anything else. Even if it meant sharing the product of her fastidious baking with her marauding students.

Miss Buttercup had a definite way with words. *"You know, it really is about time I got someone in to take care of those nasty aphids and pesky caterpillars"*. As if speaking underwater, she burbled in a murmur that brought a gentle hint of sarcasm and almost no conviction. *"Ah, the roses never seem to last, especially the prettiest ones"*. That was the Miss Buttercup we all knew and admired. We laughed out loud until our tummies ached. Couldn't help ourselves. We thought all the flowers in the garden were pretty.

In the delicate afternoon shadows she brushed her way past the privet bush and the border of blushing hollyhocks. *"Mmm, I don't suppose Mr Brampton would have the slightest inclination to help out in my hour of need, not with his mind set on vegetables and cow manure? That dear man and his beans, he really must find himself another hobby!"* Anxious heads nodded in agreement and a cloud of white butterflies swarmed into the warm, moist air. It was hard to believe she couldn't find a knight in shining armour.

"Now let's go and eat. Before we lose our appetites".

It was like listening to the wind scurrying through a broad, grassy meadow.

16

WHEN THE CARNIVAL CAME TO TOWN

It wasn't often the trucks and brightly lit wagons lurched into town, but when they did, the pungent smell of sawdust, toffee apples and a wild rush of electricity came with them. For miles around there were huge smiles and the greatest of expectations, none more so than in our home where I was always the first to roll out the red carpet and show any sign of genuine enthusiasm. Then again, I suppose being young and easily impressed by frilly clowns, baggy pants and painted faces had its own rewards. An added benefit of course, was I never got bored of seeing or doing the same things over and over again and as I was soon to discover, that very fact alone would stand me in good stead. It also helped, if somewhere along the way one possessed a vivid imagination and had a degree of difficulty in getting one's tongue around certain words and phrases. To complete the picture, a sense of humour only George at his most cynical could possess, made such delicate matters far more tolerable than they otherwise might have been.

In general, I was hard headed but easily pleased. My favourite fairground attractions were the big d(r)ipper (which mother always insisted required a special drip to get on board such a hair raising ride), the house of mirrors, ghost train and last but by no means least, the irresistible but hard to spell *doghumms*. In my case pronounced with a soft 'g'.

Over hill and dale, cleft and swale, from Cleethorpes to Brighton and points in between, the wretched unresponsive blighters proved to be as popular as cheese and cucumber sandwiches. Everyone liked them but weren't quite sure what to do with them. But that didn't stop those long heated discussions about personal safety and how they seemed to possess a devious mind of their own. Those most ridiculous Noddy cars only someone as twisted as Enid Blyton could dream up, that attracted the wrong people for all the wrong reasons. That was no deterrent though, for at their very sight I quivered, my eyes grew wide as saucers and my mind ran off in every which direction. At this rate my future looked secure. I would soon be joining the ranks of Formula 1.

They were machines of Machiavellian substance, that thanks to some principle of physics I never completely understood, produced sparks from nothing more than a carefully placed hook on an overhead track. The sort of giant sparks George emitted each time he risked life and limb by climbing into one. The purpose of the exercise, which on careful analysis seemed rather futile, was to weave around a congested circuit with other people of dubious intelligence. Once behind the wheel, strangers and friends with limited powers of concentration who may or may not have been close to the edge of insanity, tried their very best to be the last man standing. Or should I say sitting. To have any chance, pre-emptive strike was the name of the game. The choice was easy. No rules is good rules. Bump or be bumped. Which was fine provided one had not consumed a hearty meal of fish and chips beforehand.

We spent painful hours moving in ever decreasing circles and notwithstanding George's prodigious talent for avoiding those drivers determined to destroy us, not once did we complain that somehow regardless of our sterling efforts and honourable intentions, we never crossed the finish line.

Still, it was agreed, a carnival wasn't a carnival without the mayhem and mirth of such frustrating jalopies.

Come rain, hail or high water we persisted in subjecting our bodies to bone rattling ruination for the sheer thrill of the chase. In order to keep up with our neighbours the Browns who I swear must have been going for some Guinness Book world record in absolute stupidity. And each time the outcome never faltered from its course: when those words I loved so much trickled out of my mouth no one had the slightest clue what I was on about. Was it a member of the flower family related to the dog rose? Or was the connotation more sinister? It was as though speaking in riddles was the accepted norm, that is until suddenly lining up at the Ace of Diamonds shooting gallery, in a eureka moment, the consonants fell into place. A veil had been lifted. To celebrate, hawk eye George with itchy finger on the trigger finally gave the elusive duck on the top row what it deserved. The man in the jacquard jacket shrugged his shoulders and put it down to pure beginner's luck. George put it down to his nervous disposition and the years spent on the army rifle range.

When the smoke finally cleared we were awarded a pair of fat goldfish in a small plastic bag and a not so funny, furry monkey with a crooked tail and flat nose.

The irate stall owner twisting the ends of his Jimmy Edwards' moustache said we should find another way to vent our frustrations. Perhaps the dodgems would do the trick.

17

TIME OF THE SEASON
(WAITING FOR THE MELTING SNOW)

Put some Sand In Your Shoes* (8) 1975 Al Stewart from Year Of The Cat.

The unforgettable winter of 1962–1963 was one of the worst on record. For want of a better name, they called it The Big Freeze. And for good reason. People complained and grumbled and no one wanted to see another like it again. Starting on the 22nd December 1962 it lasted an interminable sixty eight days. Burst out of the wild north east and swept across mainland Europe. Hit England and Scotland with a vengeance. The River Thames froze over in many parts for the first time in almost a hundred and fifty years. Ice blizzards cut off vital transport and halted most essential services. Almost dark by three pm it seemed as though an eternal blackness had descended on the country.

The snow fell without a break. It piled up so high against the kitchen door, we had to dig a narrow trench between it and the back gate. Icicles of all sizes hung from the eaves of the house, like glistening daggers ready to fall whenever the wind blew. They were a decoration to behold.

At the rear of the yard, an old brick water closet adjoined the laneway that ran between the rows of houses. The heavy wooden door with a missing hinge, had a hole at the bottom large enough for a rabbit to crawl through. Like Scott of the Antarctic dressed for the task at hand, my father strategically placed kerosene lanterns on the walls inside to keep the water pipes from freezing. For the most part it was an exercise in total futility. The pipes had a mind of their own and froze and burst anyway.

Only the most fool hardy souls would dare venture out in such atrocious conditions.

I suppose that's why some clever person caught up in one too many bad winters, came up with the idea of the under bed pot or jerry[1] as we fondly called it. At times like these it was a godsend. Along with the crackling coals that burned in the stone hearth. We spent many a long night roasting chestnuts or marshmallows on the open fire.

Waiting for the spring to melt the snow away. Wishing for the bluebells and wild primrose to bloom like never before.

---

1. *Most probably derived from the word 'jeroboam'*

18

WILLIAM, THE WILD HORSE CHESTNUT

The Boxer *(10) 1970 Simon and Garfunkel from Bridge Over Troubled Water*

Roll with the punches and listen to the crowd roar

Ten sixty six was a very good year for brave knights in shining armour. Not so for damsels in distress. Boggle eyed William of Normandy with the one track mind (this description may or may not be entirely accurate) was in no mood for benevolence or sightseeing tours. Battles, dark dungeons and fire breathing dragons more befitted his unquenchable thirst for fame and fortune. With substantial forces he sailed across the narrow sea and smack bang into the middle of a family disagreement. Though when he did this horrid act, that shallow body of water no doubt may have been known as something altogether different. Perhaps *Norman Waters* or *Le Petit Canal* would have been far more appropriate a name, for at this particular point in history the keepers of this fair isle were not yet considered important in the great world order. Unlike the French.

Fast forward a few thousand more wars and a couple of centuries. So it happened that in the rather ordinary spring of 1963 (with little thought for what had transpired nine hundred and three years earlier) and under much less duress than poor Harold and his ill prepared brethren, I assembled a formidable band of rag tag friends and set off on a wondrous crusade to parts barely known. Complete with favourite picnic lunch and sharpened cutting shears we traversed over fields and streams to pillage and plunder the wild woodlands on the outskirts of town. In search of the perfect horse chestnut seed. If such a beast did indeed exist. We no doubt would find it. After a day's strenuous work which left us with tattered pants, skinned knees and a variety of bruises, we managed to procure a large bagful of those reddish brown and almost perfectly symmetrical weapons of mass destruction. We were pleased with our endeavours.

Colloquially referred to as the *conker,* the innocuous looking nut had a reputation far larger than its own circumference. Now, how this name came to be derived I have absolutely no idea. I am convinced however, that this terminology was perhaps a simple misnomer and the more applicable description should have been *bonker(s).* Which after all, is what one clearly needs to be to indulge in such a frivolous, non-productive pastime.

To succeed in the (delicate) and refined art of *conkery*, quality control is paramount, as only the biggest and brightest seeds are selected for battle. Each nut scrutinised and examined by magnifying glass to check for imperfections, then carefully drilled through from top to base with a hole just large enough to thread a piece of twine. During the delicate procedure, it is essential not to crack the conker. A cracked conker is a useless commodity. Once completed, the seed is placed into an oven for a prescribed period of time in order to harden the lethal product. Everyone knows that the secret to a strong, reliable conker is of course in the baking.

The rules of the game allow each player in turn to strike the opponent's nut. This is done in a smooth, precise swinging motion aimed specifically to inflict the most damage and continues ad nauseum (though most times usually for a short duration) until only one remains intact.

I named mine in honour of that brave man from nearby foreign shores. And a very logical name for a nut. Considering the trouble and turmoil he had caused, it seemed the least I could do.

William accounted for many a would be champion before finally succumbing to the inevitable fate destined to befall all beloved horse chestnuts. Split asunder by a strategic blow from your worst enemy.

But at least for a short time I had my special place in the English sun.

19

A ROSE BY ANY OTHER NAME

Names, Tags, Numbers and Labels * (7) 1972
*Albert Hammond from It Never Rains In
Southern California*

Big Louigi was a fourth generation Italian market
gardener and proud of his heritage, which could be
traced back to large landowners from Catania on the island
of Sicily. Long before the Great War, the last of his family
had uprooted and with a pocket full of seeds and precious
few other possessions, left behind their native land in
search of a better life in Britain.

With his beautiful wife and two young girls he ran a
small, but profitable free hold property on the outskirts of
town. They grew all kinds of vegetables along with rhubarb
and apples and also farmed free range pigs, ducks, chickens
and some fine feathered grouse given to him by his good
friend Angus McCloud. In those days there was no such
thing as battery hens and restrictive cages, so the eggs
were always large and tasty and the meat from the plump
poultry made even the driest mouth water. Especially
the way Pepina cooked the meals. The Italians sure had
a knack when it came to good food and wine. Not to
mention, conversation.

Louigi owned an old and rather pedestrian sow called Henrietta Turnpike and a trusty, go anywhere male companion Peter Piper, a loveable black and patchy white hog with large trotters, huge snout and lots of spiky bristles, who thought himself to be more of a quaint, inquisitive canine than a cumbersome Berkshire pig. Every Saturday morning bright and early without fail, Louigi would despatch his fine produce to the local market in a weather beaten truck almost bursting at the seams with tightly packed wooden crates and cardboard boxes. Henrietta and Peter would amble to the gate before the goods departed and then return again at midday, anxious and ready to catch Louigi offload the leftovers and other food scraps for all the animals. Being very intelligent and the best of time keepers where food was concerned, Henrietta and Peter were always first to the trough and last to leave and for that they were well rewarded.

One grey, storm filled weekend after a long dry spell, Louigi casually remarked, he knew from his younger travelling days, a mild mannered railway man, a thin sprig of a fellow with biblical ambitions, who for some inexplicable reason took great satisfaction in naming his children after Scottish towns. Large towns or small it didn't much matter, the man just couldn't resist. It might have been the fault of the weather in such latitudes, his skewed political outlook or simply because he came from Fife. Perhaps deep down he even held a morbid fascination for Andy Stewart, haggis and heather and other such things of the tartan ilk. That would explain it.

After eight offspring however (and another on the way), it was becoming increasingly more difficult to find a suitable sounding town. One that would live up to his high expectations. The man proposed therefore, that for the ninth child, he should look elsewhere for inspiration. His wife trembled at the thought, closed her eyes and wished that his awful affliction was just a passing phase.

This revelation soon became a heated topic of discussion for Louigi and his closest companions. Whenever guests arrived for dinner and drinks, out would come the Monopoly board together with the illicit jugs of homemade red wine and the towering cheese platter that looked more Mont Blanc than Trentino Asiago. With a gentle hint of sarcasm, everyone chided Louigi as to why he had not followed in his friend's footsteps when it came to the fate of his own children. Was he afflicted with a serious ailment? Did he have a strong aversion to towns and cities? We all concurred that towns for the most part anyway, had nice, pleasant names. Otherwise people would not live in them.

It was suggested that if logic and parochial inclinations faltered, perhaps he could fall back on famous streets or thoroughfares. Even rivers sprang to mind. That way he would never run short of ideas.

Louigi who could not see the funny side of the argument for all the letters in *consternation*, shook his head and scowled at such a ridiculous notion. He possessed more sense than they gave him credit for. Quips and shenanigans aside, could you imagine being so cruel as to call your sons and daughters Trafalgar, Angel Islington, Marlborough or heaven forbid, Picadilly? That would be the end of him for sure and certain. It was a dangerous road he would not take. He kept reminding everyone however, as he filled up their glasses to drink a toast to Enrico Caruso, the last of the great tenors, that this would not be practicable for any good Sicilian worth his weight in pasta. In Louigi's case that was an awful lot of pasta.

Ambrosia and Vincenzina crossed their hearts in a fitting gesture, forever grateful that when it came to *praenomens*, sanity and Italian common sense had prevailed.

Louigi never did work out what the fuss was about.

As for the infamous railway man, he's still out there somewhere riding that north-south line, in search of divine guidance and a little love and understanding.

20

SONG FOR OBEDIAH JOHNSON

Got some rainbows in our pockets, sunshine in our hands. Reminding us of the good times we spent hatching our precious little plans.

At first light we rushed. In such a fluster we fell over our own feet in our secret quest for ugly amphibians and giant mushrooms of the edible kind. Myself, good old Roy and faithful Shepherd with the black spots and large floppy ears.

Lily said *"Best to be home before dark, otherwise there would be trouble brewing"*. So with nothing between us but the blue stone road and the disused quarry, we ran and ran until our sides ached and our faces turned the brightest rhubarb red. Past the broken street lamps that never shone and the higgledy piggledy houses near the common. Past the cricket pavilion on the village green and the YMCA community hall, with its huge brass bell and weathered panel door that was always in need of a coat of paint. Ran until our feet hurt and almost out of breath, we found ourselves down by the water's edge. The sun burning hard upon our backs. The wind blowing a symphony through the trees. Looking up to see the cloud people close behind us.

There we were, snaking like streamers through the long grass and the twisted reeds that stuck fast to our trouser legs and shirt sleeves. With not a care in the world. It was easy to imagine we were the last of the intrepid explorers lost somewhere in dark Africa. Compass in hand. Our calico bags stuffed in pockets full of holes, ready to bring back the great bounty of our special day together.

Hearts on fire and Shepherd by our side, chasing those elusive shadows for bespectacled Obediah.

21

OH STARRY NIGHT!

Something waits for us beneath The Dark and the Rolling Sea* (8) 1975 Al Stewart from Modern Times

After a most forgettable long night's journey that took us all the way from Doncaster to Harwich, where no one got any sleep except Rover the driver's faithful Labrador, we caught the early ferry to the Hoek Van Holland. Then a brief stopover before a slow but comfortable train ride to Rotterdam and on to Utrecht. Past farms and fields, filled to overflowing with towering tulips of every possible colour. Finally ending up in the pleasant market town of Enschede nestled near the German border and where we subsequently stayed with our good friends and hosts Minnie and Jaan.

On our novice travels, we encountered a great number of windmills. Large and small. Each one in appearance identical to the others we had seen. However, the Dutch being a proud and industrious people, built their windmills very well. That is the reason I suppose that so many can still be found and most of them in tip top working condition. We also discovered endless miles of stone walled dykes along the Zuider Zee with fair haired little boys at the ready should the need arise, to put their fingers in any part likely to spring a sudden, embarrassing leak. Needless to say, just like those carefully constructed sail machines, the dykes were very strong and constructed to last.

And no matter where you looked, lots and lots of people riding bicycles. Which meant hard work. Indeed one could perhaps surmise that the Dutch despised cars and were either very fit or very foolish.

Amsterdam, world famous for its canals, was our final destination. Armed with only a well worn guide map and Swiss army pocket knife my father had procured from a persuasive odds and sods vendor, we set off to inflict ourselves upon the best sights the city had to offer. First and foremost a visit to the Grachtengordel district was high on the itinerary, complete with comprehensive water tour aboard one of the many sleek, glass roofed boats. Sipping peppermint tea we cruised beneath a procession of curved iron bridges and past bobbing wooden barges. Lost in the moment. Thinking about chocolate and clogs.

Now and then we felt the urge to stop awhile in an inviting small café or curio shop we found along the narrow cobbled ways. The bright window lights shimmering in the pools of water that had collected between the stones. Every street corner alive with fruit sellers, shoe sellers and sellers of good faith. Where colourful buskers, Marcel Marceau impersonators and other strange acts performed in a whirlwind cabaret as though this day would be their last on earth.

The worlds of Rembrandt Van Rijn, Vincent Van Gogh and Johannes Vermeer opened up before us, a wondrous tapestry to behold.

In need of a pick me up, we found ourselves tongue tied and not so pretty, standing in the great hall of the

Rijksmuseum in the illustrious company of The Night Watch.

Amsterdam was all of this and much, much more.

22

SAG MIR WO DIE BLUMEN SIND

Before The Deluge* *(8) 1974 Jackson Browne from*
Late For The Sky

Cologne (Köln) had 4711 and much pilsener. Though definitely not to be confused with each other. To make things especially interesting, it also boasted a large, outdoor music and entertainment venue, a nice international zoo for all the family to enjoy and six grand bridges that spanned the broad river Rhine. Or at least that was the count when we last visited there in the summer of 1963. Which is one generous splash of aqua mirabilis, a very good beer, a whole lot of wild animals and quite a few bridges more than can be said for most other towns.

To further enhance its enviable status, there was also the magnificent gothic cathedral (*dom*) located in the city centre, a hop step and jump away from the newly refurbished and restored *Haupt Bahnhof.*[1] The giant cathedral stood proud and defiant, overlooking a vast wasteland of rubble that still remained as stark reminder of the atrocities and stupidity of war.

It was obvious, even to the most parochial observer, that German cities like their English and European

---

1. *Translsates in English as main railway station.*

counterparts, had not escaped the rain of deadly bombs dropped from the enemy planes. Seemingly overnight, whole blocks had been virtually wiped off the map. The wonder with Cologne, is that anything was left at all. With Dresden nothing was.

Poor Billy Pilgrim[2] would never see things the same way again.

We had German friends whom my mother and father had met on a previous holiday. Their home was a compact two bedroom basement apartment in the Ursulaplatz district that somehow survived the incessant air raids. For the nineteen years since the end of the war, they continued to live in the dangerous, crumbling ruins, without so much as a murmur of discontent.

Franz and Carla always said they hoped the future would forgive the sins of the past.

Their daughter Gertrude with the pretty smile and elf like ears just wanted to watch old black and white re runs of Laurel and Hardy.

Far better she thought, to laugh at where we were going than cry for where we had come from.

---

2. *The time travelling soldier from Kurt Vonnegut's bleak, satiric novel <u>Slaughterhouse 5.</u>*

23

THE DOGS ARE SILENT NOW

(Old Dogs, Children And) Watermelon Wine * (7)
1972 Tom T. Hall

Evening fell. Soft and almost velvet to the touch, drawn out of the grape dark sky until there was just a simple folded shadow left upon the farmhouse. That's when the cold, harsh winter came and took the dogs away.

No more scuffling or shuffling of padded feet across the stone yards. No welcoming tails to wag. No wet noses. There is only a numbing mist that hugs the land and rushes hard along the valley floor. Scurrying for a phantom bone. Nothing more. Nothing left to breathe or spark the senses. No noise.

After all these years, the dogs are silent now. It is hard to believe they're gone.

He loved those dogs. Deep down inside, you knew. They were as much a part of him as anything could ever be. He loved their smell, their touch, their company.

Of course you knew. How could you not.

The endless hours spent out upon the open fields, with carpet drifts of purple heather in their fur. Nostrils flared and hearts on fire. Running like sparks along a wire, chasing the elusive hare and cunning fox. Chasing until the world itself would stop.

Let me stay here for a while. In this place where they shall roam, forever young and carefree. As things were meant to be. I am afraid to ask for more. Those dogs will be the death of me.

Morning breaks the eggshell silence. Shakes itself upon the grey slate roof, settling into all the cracks and moss filled crevices. A seamless, ghostly white. A spectral hue.

Between a corridor of leafless birch and elm, the narrow, red stone road twists and turns towards the town. One solitary, bright light shines above the ridge, casting its strange glow upon the soft drifts of freshly fallen snow.

I think the dogs are somewhere in that other meadow. Wild and free. They shall be until we meet once more.

Underfoot a thin layer of ice crackles. Like it has never hissed and crackled before.

He sheds a tear and walks alone without them. Carrying his lamp in the dappled, sooty darkness. Searching for the answer. But there is nothing. No words can take away the pain.

A haunting shallow breath of wind remains, that lingers for a brief moment on the ground, like methane to a fen. Then shifts and crawls beneath the barren hedgerow and the thorn and once more around the old brick wall. For the last time. Just for old time's sake.

The dogs are silent now.

Gone to rest where voices sing, in that endless sea of grass.

24

MARCH 1915: A LETTER TO A WIFE

Everywhere we look there are small spaces that surround us. Some remain grey and shapeless and pass on by without warning, never seeming to notice what we have done with our lives. Others are full of fire and light and remind us of our place in the great ever changing cosmos.

Out of the choking dust clouds the black cars came. Carrying tall men wearing tired crinkled suits with artificial roses and bibles in their pockets. They brought with them letters that tumbled out of the steel grey sky and shook the very ground on which she stood. They were only words on a small piece of paper. But how those words cut hard and deep.

Dear Madam: It is with great sadness and regret I write to inform you....

Her knees trembled and a heaviness fell upon her like a dark immovable shadow. A lump formed in her throat that could not be swallowed.

He will not be dimmed nor broken by the passing of the years, though a mother's salty tears may haunt us still, until they shake us to our very bones.

And I recalled the first time I came across that awful news.

Shall these monsters crouched upon young shoulders weigh us down and turn our thoughts from other fancy.

The crunch of autumn leaves beneath our feet. Soft green fields lit up in the morning sun. A child's caress. The pale white skin of tangled lovers lost and now forever gone.

Though the beast of fire and brimstone beats its scaly wings, shall the stench of death that hangs like smoke above the mud filled trenches, numb our youthful spirits. Even dim our bright and restless souls? Shall it melt us with fetid breath into the sodden earth? No more to rise and touch the stars above.

Yet these souls held so dear, are not ours to give.

With tattered golden banner held forever high, the crown of heaven beckons with all its promised riches, while the thorns that stab the flesh and pierce this aching heart, now streak unnoticed across a blood red turning sky.

25

BETTER LATE THAN TREVOR

The straight faced man from the bureau of statistics and convoluted stories, had all the answers. Even if they were the wrong answers. In the long run and when the dust had settled, he said it really didn't matter which way was up or which way was down. Things somehow always work out. Whether you want them to or not. For better or for worse.

Early January and so far no sign of any snow. The moon in its phase was bright and waning gibbous, Jupiter was in the first house and the stars in the heavens had mysteriously aligned. Not that we could see much through the heavy cloud cover that had crept in overnight.

The news of the day gave us goose bumps and palpitations but the weather forecast at least was fair to mildly optimistic. The fat man in the striped grey suit who looked like he wanted to be somewhere else in a big hurry, said in a trembling voice and with no great confidence, '*Very cold with just a slight chance of sleet and intermittent flurries. Farmers would be well advised to keep a close watch on their sheep*'. He also made a brief remark about wind chill factor, isobars and atmospheric pressure and the expected arrival of a weak occluded front shown on the map by black squiggly lines that looked for all the world like children's scrawl. He wasn't much of an artist when it came to painting winter landscapes and his eyes gave him away. A hot chocolate to settle the nerves was what he needed. He looked befuddled and bewildered. But nowhere near as much as us, who when it came to meteorological events were none the wiser and merely passed them over with a shrug of the shoulders. In other words no one had the faintest idea what he was talking about.

The big morning came, bringing a sudden drop in temperature. With some degree of difficulty, Mr Ley dressed in full length gabardine coat and billowing huge pillows of steam from his mouth each time he spoke, got all the equipment on the bus. Barely raising a sweat, the rest of the St James football team promptly boarded. One by one in single file as if tethered at the waist with strands of invisible twine. Our red faced driver who wore an appropriate St. Nicholas beard for the occasion, shifted awkwardly in his padded seat as he cursed and muttered something about golden sands, swaying palm trees and staying home in his cosy little bed. The thermos flask of vegetable soup perched precariously at his side, would not last long in this weather.

Out of odd necessity we were created. The product of small minds and great matter. The district powers that be wanted a team for all occasions, and they got one. Some bright spark on the student board called us the Hornets. I suppose thanks mainly to the influence of our surly headmistress, who happened to be a dab hand tipster when it came to the weekly football pools and who had an annoying fetish or two for flying insects of the stinging variety. She also had a soft spot for cats and dogs (preferably those of the miniature kind) and was very fond of knitting to pass the time of day. We breathed a collective sigh of relief when the sports committee, thirteen against and two for, vehemently rejected the name the Pearl Stitch Poodles. Thankfully they saved that one for the attractive girl's hockey team, who as a matter of public record, never complained and never won a single match. Most of us thought we knew the reason why.

Picture this if you can. Something to put in the *Memories are made of this* scrapbook of human enterprise. Eleven hardy souls kitted out in the very latest fashion accessories: knee length baggy shorts with plenty of space to accommodate three years worth of growth spurts, orange and black hooped shirts and matching socks, with customary protective pads. Though why on earth they called them shin guards, was anyone's guess as they didn't really seem to protect much at all. We were a sight for sore eyes, a proverbial bunch of pests not to be trifled with and ready at short notice to fight for the noble cause. Although huddled together like penguins on an ice floe and with our teeth chattering in three four time to the sound of our knocking knees, we looked anything but dangerous. So we were very impressed when bushy haired David with ears that always aligned to magnetic north, said how we looked didn't really count, as appearances can be deceiving. He was a classic case in point.

We alighted the bus, to be met with an arctic blast of air that had waited for this very moment before springing to life. In a mere crack of the whip, the conditions deteriorated and a heavy flindrikin[1] set in. At that instant, barely able to see our hands let alone anything remotely resembling a football field, we began to brew serious

---

1. *Of Scottish derivation, a seldom used but rather delightful term for snow shower.*

doubts. Somewhere out in the middle, trekker John put in a request for a compass to get his bearings right. Eric began to turn every shade of blue imaginable and Tony who never ever raised his voice in anger, complained he couldn't feel his toes. For that matter none of us could, so to help things along, Trevor who kept a rabbit's foot in his trouser pocket for just such occasions, called it right and won the toss. The Hornets would kick off and run with a stiff breeze that now blew strength 5 on the Beaufort Scale.

Unable to move in any direction without tripping over, Mr Ley chipped in at the last moment to give a subtle discourse on the gentleman's finer principals of football. Eager to tell us the whys, the wherefores and the whatnots of the game he loved with a passion. Adamant the vital key to success under such conditions, was to keep possession no matter the cost. *"Flick it down the flanks and surprise them. Take no prisoners. Never forget lads, the do's and the don'ts. Especially the don'ts."* Mr Ley shuffled crabwise to the sideline proud of his Churchillian speech. Now all he had to do was turn the other cheek, find a comfortable spot, sit back and hope the strategy would work.

The whistle blew and not thinking about the consequences, we launched forward on our first attacking foray. It was then I had a certain fuzzy feeling inside that today might just turn out to be something special. Call it what you will-finding a four leaf clover in a meadow full of mud and rocks, falling into the lap of the gods or Irish luck. Between the sign of the cross and a prayer to the patron saint of circular objects, we struck gold. Although looking back now I am sure that whatever it was, that mysterious occluded front played the biggest part in our success.

The snow was thick and driving hard upon our backs. Visibility was down to about twenty feet give or take a few studded boots. So depending on where the opposition stood, our mission was akin to chasing shadows or playing hide and seek with a blind man. It didn't take long for our nervous adversary to get the wobbles. Their *we'd much rather be beside the seaside in Bognor Regis than stuck out here* attitude soon kicked into full swing. So alas, while Mr Ley sipped his mug of luke warm Nescafe, contemplating his next holiday on the Costa Del Sol, the other team never knew what hit them. Especially the poor goalkeeper who by the time he could react to the dark shapes that emerged like deadly doodlebugs out of the white mist, it was too late. The damage had been done. The only sound he heard was the ominous ping of the ball as it hurtled into the back of the net.

By game's end the poor blighter was sick and tired of picking up that heavy leather Mitre[2] that seemed to follow him around everywhere. No one would have blamed him if he had retired forthwith from that perilous and prickly predicament.

Four nil our way after twelve minutes. Not too bad. Considering. But still we pinched ourselves for affirmation.

With those stern words still echoing throughout the shire, we obeyed our coach's instructions with formidable resolve. "*Remember John Wayne and the Alamo.*" We sure did. Graham even said he'd seen the movie twice. "*Always cross your legs before you think, dot your i's before you wink and most importantly never give a sucker an even break.*" Tick that box too. In fact we ticked every square box he brought with him. And then a few extra to calm his nerves.

---

2. *The famous English make of football.*

Half time. Ten nil. Chance to stop for a breather and some homemade cupcakes and hot tea. Score line slightly lopsided and plenty of sour looks all around, but not from our boys and even though most of us were now sympathetic towards our bedraggled visitors, we continued on our mission with great gusto. *"Would they react the same way if the sock was on the other foot?"* Tommy Toledo chimed with a wide grin that stretched from one half of his face to the other. However profound the sentiment, we thought the pun was rather harsh and quite intentional.

The match referees shivering in unison, put their collective heads together with some haste and ordered that to be fair to both parties and because of the foul and inclement conditions, the second stanza would be reduced to fifteen minutes duration. Plenty of time for our opposition to salvage something out of the mess they found themselves in. Or for the Hornets to show sympathy and generously declare their innings. Then we could all go home, have a nice warm bath and a steaming brew of Bovril to blow away the cobwebs. Just to put us in the right frame of mind for the approaching spring.

The end couldn't come soon enough to stop the maelstrom. The final scoreboard read: Hornets twenty nine, Mudlarks no score. Check that and confirm. Big round zero. Nada. Nix. Zilch.

That must have set some sort of world record we thought. Impressive that, keeping up with the clock. Nineteen goals in less than a half of near faultless football. A triple hat trick, two double hat tricks, three French hens, two turtle doves and a partridge in a pear tree and every player on our team scoring except for the keeper. Whom it might be said, for most of the game was in a catatonic state from lack of attention. He left the field suffering from hallucinations of the grandest kind.

And they somehow have the nerve to call this sport.

The New Year had started off with a resounding bang. The dynamic Hornets proving they were far from being a one kick wonder, went on to win the local schools championship in fine style and strange as it may seem, packed up their duffle bags, boots and laces and were never heard from again. They took their fearful name and achievements with them and disappeared like gentle ghosts into the football hall of fame.

That didn't seem to bother Mr Ley any. He subsequently retired to the sunnier south of England, a very happy and respected coach, more than thankful the weather man got it wrong on that memorable day.

26

NUMBER ONE WITH A BULLET / SOMETIMES A HIT IS AS GOOD AS A MYTH

*Two Of Us** (9) 1969 The Beatles from Let It Be

Hank B. Marvin didn't know a Jack Russell about it, but he really was the cause of our woes. At least we thought so. In a nutshell that's what we put it down to. Him and his merry band of restless strummers we had never seen or heard of until one day out of the ocean blue, they came. Drain pipe trousers and foot tappers anonymous. Sending cryptic messages over the airwaves. Giving *Flingle Bunt*[1] a torrid workout on the wireless. Whoever that odd, mysterious character was, he made his mark and got our creative juices flowing.

The exact details remain dim and sketchy, but I guess proceedings started with rambunctious Tony Mace, George Alfred Leyland and one other whom I have now completely consigned to the forgotten names basket. We were the neighbourhood kings of moderate thinking. A couple of primary school rowdy romantics and football team friends, who as fortune would have

---

1. *The Rise and Fall of Flingle Bunt** (9) *released in May 1964. A UK Number 5 hit.*

it, amalgamated our talents into a rather accidental pop group. For better or for worse. In sickness and in health.

It was summer and like most summers we had known, it was raining. This time heavier than usual. So confined to the indoors for days on end, devoid of useful ideas, it suddenly came upon us. Somewhere between the exploits of Bill and Ben the Flowerpot Men and the Daleks Invade London, in a moment of brilliance that blazed a trail of fire through the night sky, we agreed to call ourselves *Cool Hands EleKtriK*. Though what the dickens K had to do with anything I am not quite sure. Still, standing there in the cold north haze searching for answers, it seemed the perfect name choice. Though in hindsight, perhaps it was far from the perfect time.

Tony who had been scratching a musical itch for months, said he'd had a vision splendid and of course the rest of us believed him. The words rang out like honey in the morning dew.

A man riding a chariot drawn by six winged stallions, fell to earth. In the centre of a satin quilted baldachin stood a red and silver Wurlitzer jukebox wrapped in strands of frosted seaweed and sprigs of holly. A noisy crowd soon jostled at the sight. They placed their coins into the slot and sirens danced to the tune of a thousand Rickenbackers. Out came the blues just as they were meant to do.

The morning headlines read: People prefer happy news and a simple Yorkshire diet. One that lingers long upon the palate. A fine mixture of herbs and tonics gathered from lush green, rolling fields.

Take a sip from this special cup and you will become number one with a bullet. In the days that follow so it shall be written on the wind.

It had the makings of a Homer epic, although what it meant at this time was not quite clear. Harbouring great ambitions to conquer the world, we put aside our inhibitions and stepped out into a whole new landscape of cardinal delights.

As a collective, we were under-priced and over rated. For the princely sum of a penny a peep, our rough and tumble live act became the talk of the town. We performed after school and on weekends if the weather was favourable. Did it out of some form of perverted kindness. Strictly for those we knew who somehow convinced their mums and dads that the act of listening was the greatest gift of all. Therefore it was not unreasonable to hand over an entire piece of vacant concrete garden (an area no larger than 3 or 4 square metres) to a bunch of cherub faced kids who couldn't even play their instruments properly. Still, we looked the real deal and anyway, it was the thought that mattered.

I had been a particularly good boy that year and mother must have been overwhelmed with all the hints and clues I had scattered around the living room. So impressed, that on the occasion of my eleventh birthday I became the beneficiary of a sturdy second hand acoustic guitar made from finest Canadian maple. To complement appearances there was a red curved infill strip on the main body near the breathe hole. For most of its productive life however, one stubborn string flatly refused to follow instructions. Like that great rocker Chuck Berry, when it came to playing, it had a mind of its own. Tony with his slicked back hair (that would make Gerry Marsden or Billy Fury raise a sweat in envy) was from a different mould completely. Without fuss or fanfare he dabbled and he jangled until he got the hang of those elusive chords.

In the end his persistence proved the perfect foil to our contrition. He turned out to be a pretty fine guitarist and could even pluck a mean riff when in the right frame of mind. Which fortunately for us was every time Mrs Sullivan threatened to take back our fresh out of the oven slice of cherry pie for any wilful damages caused to the audience. We appreciated her noble sentiments were for the greater good, as Tony's sunburst stratocaster with the spring tensioned tremolo fitted the bill nicely, thank you very much.

Bit by bit the train was gathering momentum and our mojo was working overtime. Along for the ride came ambidextrous Georgie Porgie wearing a pork pie hat that sat on top of his large head like a skewed pavlova. He was the youngest member of the quartet and although he had a strong urge to play glockenspiel, drums and washboard was the best deal we could offer. Using sticks carved from mighty oak he happily beat out jungle rhythms on a dented oil can salvaged from a local wrecker's yard. On rare occasions he also covered on tea chest bass. Georgie would have a go at just about anything. His reckless enthusiasm knew no bounds. Being a multi-instrumentalist he claimed, was another arrow in his impressive quiver. The rest of us however were just grateful he never tried his hand at pianoforte.

The sound we made was a bit off key and perhaps somewhat disturbing. But we could sing or at least the girls we tried to impress thought we could. Oblivious to the cotton wool in the ear syndicate who stood in defiance furthest from the action, Angela T, Shirley Bell and Sarah Jane Parkin always took the best seats in the house. From where we stood it was impossible not to notice their pretty hair held back with ribbons and delicate bows. Hands clapping and feet shuffling to the music. Long, slim legs hidden by their modest sense of dress. We knew they had attractive limbs from the countless times we somehow got to catch them perform their special gymnastics routine every Wednesday at school. It was easy to tell when the girls had PE lessons by the line of anxious boys clamouring to get prime position next to the podium.

No one objected about our shortcomings or the fact that compared to others in our neighbourhood, we operated on a strictly limited seven song Beatle repertoire. Counting on two hands kept things nice and simple. We didn't let that get us down one little bit and we somehow managed to cover without too much trouble _She Loves You_*(8), _I Wanna Hold Your_ Hand*(9) and a few others. _Twist and Shout_*(9) was a particular favourite as it was such a fantastic number to give the tonsils an exercise in futility. Tony was a shoe in new wave Bob Dylan. But without the nasal drawl and trimmings. Even went so far as to attach a battered old mouth organ to his shoulders via stiff wire cable. The sad part was he ended up looking more like a mannequin in a shop window than a pop singer.

John Winston Lennon was the cool Beatle everyone aspired to emulate, so to look authentic I strutted around wearing my black leather Marks and Spencer's cap as well as a hand me down pair of dark sunglasses. Strictly for star appeal. That's as close as I ever got to matching it with Moondog Johnny[2]. Then somewhere down the line things changed. In a twinkling, Johnny had a change of heart, soon forgot there ever was a "Y" on the end of his name

---

2. _Johnny and the Moondogs was the name briefly adopted by John Lennon, Paul McCartney and George Harrison in 1959 when they competed in the ABC TV's talent show Star Search hosted by Carroll Levis._

and fell out of favour leaving cuddy wifter[3] Paul to become everyone's national hero. From that point on, Mick Jagger's swagger and swivelling hips got our undivided attention. In the background, poor Ringo and George could only pick up the pieces.

Smooth waters quickly turned to giant waves and Tony's fair weather friend departed not long after, blaming irreconcilable differences for his rash decision. Having had enough of all the quibbling and considerable lack of attention from the female crowd, he marched off into a winter haze, taking his amplifier, Fender bass and supply of Quality Street toffees with him. For a while we tried short fused Nicholas C. to plug the leak, but his conservative Greek background made him more suitable for bouzouki than guitar. He was just a square peg trying to squeeze into a round hole. Out of desperate measures and because we had a crush on his sister, we elected Robert into the fraternity, hoping for a phoenix to rise from the gathering ashes. But the wings had well and truly fallen from that chariot of great hope. When the snow had gone, we pulled up stumps and by unanimous vote flew off in different directions. By my account, we stuck together approximately two hundred and fifty seven days and sixteen glorious hours. What started out with a bang ended in a fizzle and our dreams sadly, never came to fruition. In the harsh light of day we realised we were never ever going to be like the Beatles.

Damn Mr Marvin and his Shadows. What we needed now was another hero.

---

3. *A seldom heard old English term describing a left handed person. Another favourite is Sinistral from the Latin word for left 'sinister'*

Later, someone told me Robert sold his soul, bought a Gibson with the proceeds and went on to bigger and better things with Timothy J. steadfast at his side. Together they made it with another threesome that became known throughout the land as the Bob Roaches. His younger sibling Annabelle (who we all called wicked twister sister, for good reason), never forgave him for switching allegiances at the worst possible time. She however, ignored grievous family differences and the sudden dissolution of our ten member fan club and continued to give her unwavering support and romantic generosity for the sheer spite of it. Nick C, not one to hold a grudge or let the grass grow beneath his feet, didn't let the situation get him down one bit and after frantic weeks of searching through the forest for the trees, finally found a hole for his square peg. Relieved at the outcome, his brother Tommy blessed the stars of Mykonos and said, in the future running for lord mayor was a distinct possibility.

We might have lost our passion for notoriety and the burning neon of the big stage, but some good did come out of the debris we left behind. I passed my 11 Plus Examinations with flying colours and as a result, Doncaster Technical Grammar School beckoned.

A new year broke. Those familiar grey skies we had grown up with, returned once more to bite us. But by now no one really cared a cuckoo about clouds and colour palettes. We were too busy admiring the scenery.

Annabelle reluctantly joined the formidable ranks of the girl guides, won the Baden-Powell award for common sense, got a promotion big time and last I heard was still twisting the night away somewhere in the land of molasses and cotton. As for Tony, George, Trevor, Robert, Timothy, Jane and Andrea, sadly I never saw any of them again.

Although, for a long time afterwards, I dreamed about Andrea with the roving ruby red lips and strawberry blond hair.

And I never saw the future until it hit me between the eyes.

27

HEATHERBRAE

If you should chance to take a walk among the haystacks and the lonely swathes. Sometime soon in this golden summer. Then for a moment stop in soft repose, somewhere near the flowering lime and the ragged briar rose. There where the weary plough sweeps the patterned meadows of the moor. In the fleeting mist of morning you will catch me.

I will take your hand but for a short while, careful not to let you stray in purple bands of heather breaking. Far from these brooding, grey stone walls that run like scars upon a map. And if you tip toe between the crooked lane and hedgerow in search of buttercup and campion on the bloom, please keep to the line of clouds that hang above the ridge.

You will find there as you go, ambling all the way, the narrow trails of swallow and of ghost swift fading in the dying light of love's last day.

28

LONG JOURNEY SOUTH
(DRUMS OF THUNDER)

*Funny how I travel the same route. Pass the same
people again and again and the same places visited
come back to haunt me.*

In that instant, suspended in the half light, somewhere
between wide awake and lost in dreams, you sneezed
and brought me back to life. Gently touched my brow
with ice cold fingers that only minutes before had wiped
the condensation from the clouded glass. Almost at a loss
for words, you pointed at something unknown in the
distance, then said in a muffled voice that it was dark on
the outside. Too dark to make out anything of worth and
except for the occasional trace of red light from the trains
heading in another direction, I could distinguish nothing
at all. Still, you strained a casual smile that you had carried
across the sea grass fields and the bare, bleak woods left
behind. Saved just for me. At this place in time.

You shook your straggled hair loose from its pretty
pink ribbon, with a turn of the head that hinted of
better things to come. The small incandescent globe gave
off a dim yellow glow that flickered once or twice, then
crept into the corner of your eyes, a last glint that left
me craving the secret contours of your body. With all

the urgency of an excited schoolboy, I recalled how the moment held you there in its long summer dress, clinging to your hips like tightest glad wrap. True to those secretary days reborn, you stretched your legs and with a wave of your hand, tried to sketch out my other beginnings, even as they now shaped themselves to begin again.

The rattle of the empty cups and plates upon the table was the sound of ice tumbling into broken water.
The smell of home trapped in our suitcases was strong and binding.

Comforted in the valley of your cradled arms, protected from the outside world, I sensed that the many flowered meadows of youth had not changed in all the intervening years. Not even the miles that crept between the carriages could diminish that memory. Over and over again the image materialised. On our great sojourn together we drifted always above the same dull horizon. Seemingly at the same station of our lives. Slipped in and out of days without regret. Slipped like the soft caress of smoke and perfume on buffet cars that long ago had drawn to rest. We drifted until our noses pressed together and our sore eyes blinked. Drifted until there was nothing left to do but shrink away the hours in our reptile skins and drink to drown our sorrows. Dying ripples in a pond.

The rattle of the empty cups and plates upon the table was the sound of ice tumbling into broken water.

Taken by the cloak of night, the last shimmer from the old town disappeared, until it became a stardust ribbon behind us. Never to return.

Then you said, in a careless rush of words that pushed along the rivers to the sea, it was cold here in the arctic of our lives. For as long as you could remember it had always been that way.

You were so sure and certain.

Somehow your strength was the strength of thousands and the years we spent apart fell like a curtain on the real truth. For in truth or some sad irony I never could believe you.

So as if to mock the senses, it grew strangely colder by degrees. My teeth chattered and my lips grew numb and it didn't really matter how hard you rubbed our hands together, the fire, once inside our hearts, had gone.

And still we carried on. The smell of home trapped in our suitcases was strong and binding.

Outside, nothing had changed. A colourless landscape shifted into view and the stone wall tethered fields slipped away with each strum of wheels upon the metal rails. They clicked and counted off each mile with no regret.

A starless, jet black sky drew breath, threatening to take us in its creeping fingers.

The electric cables hummed and crackled in tune to a drum of thunder that seemed to rise from nowhere and follow us on our journey.

29

THE LAST OF THE RED HOT SPELLERS

The air was honey thick and the silence was golden. Unfortunately it didn't stay golden anywhere near long enough for us to enjoy. In the second last row, everyone's favourite peacemaker Alistair Lennox McBride gave Doreen a firm nudge in the ribs to stop her falling asleep on duty. While four seats across, ever annoying Maude the mouth, giggled. So loud even her teeth rattled. It was enough to raise the dead. To make matters worse, her partner in crime Edith couldn't resist the chance for stardom and tried to make rude noises with her armpit. That did it, this time they had gone one bridge too far. For sure and certain some pathetic plodder out there would pay. In sweat and tears.

At the sound of her booming vibrato, Ewan salivated and expecting to be the chosen one, dropped his pencil. Not to be outdone, Miss Ladybird dropped a bombshell. Yet again. Put simply, it was an overreaction. And for the second time this week. Of late her voices had become bad habits.

She threw out a few well directed knives to let him know she was coming and moved slowly to the right to get a better view of the situation. Came up alongside, so close he could feel her warm dragon breath and see the dimples on her chiselled chin. Then she turned diagonally to the left, did a Queen to Bishop 6 strategic move and by passed him completely, taking the strong scent of summer sweat with her. Fortunately, on this auspicious occasion Ewan had nothing to worry about. He crossed his heart and mumbled something foreign under his breath. Pity, the poor bugger who gets in her sights.

Between the aisles she tip toed with not a sound. Bean pole Albert whose recent growth spurt showed no signs of abating, let out a huge sigh of relief when she avoided him altogether. Thank goodness for small minds. She crept a couple of paces further, pirouetted three times on the spot then came to an abrupt halt. The game was up. There was nowhere to hide. At this distance, even with her poor marksmanship, she couldn't miss. Cedric shuddered, struck at point blank range by a mad glint that had sprung from her eyes. Things did not look promising. She coughed to confirm her intent, to give him time to say a prayer. Then a short excruciating pause, before "*Can you spell for me psychiatrist.*" The room spun around in reverse and you could hear the garden warblers warbling in the courtyard beneath the window. Fancy singing sonnets at this most inconvenient time.

Miss Ladybird's smile froze. The icebergs on her brow adjusted, ready for collision mode. It must have been the oats he'd eaten for breakfast or the bewildered look on his face that gave him away. So she helped move things along a little bit. "*In case anyone is wondering, a psychiatrist is a specialist in mental disorders.*" Now that was a great help. But it didn't stop the lump in his throat from growing to golf ball size. She meant business. Her syllables were clear and precise, but not precise enough to make him confident. He couldn't count his chickens yet.

Something clicked into overdrive and those wheels that were stuck solid when he left home this morning, began to turn. Thoughts formed deep inside that light and frosty head. Then revolted and went to jelly. *You have got to be kidding. Right.* He couldn't have been more *W R O N G.* With slow, perfect pronunciation she carefully repeated in the boldest and most emphatic way possible:

"P S Y C H I A T R I S T."

She didn't have to be so brazen. He had heard it the first time. Clear as a church bell in an empty steeple.

He accepted it would be a difficult assignment but this was ridiculous. Even his father who knew more than he would let on about Roget's Thesaurus and had been to more places than *S H E* could possibly imagine, would develop a serious ulcer over this one. Still, trying to look more intelligent than the rest of the class, he brushed himself down. Better to get it over and done with than fiddle around and be a Nero in his own lunch break.

Calming voices whispered '*KEEP CALM WHATEVER YOU DO. DO NOT PANIC. THE WORST THING TO DO IS PANIC.*' Spell it as it sounds. Easy as shelling peas he tried to convince himself. Science, sciatica and scimitar blades flashed through his mind. Immediately followed by encyclopaedia and a numb emptiness.

Gulp. Watch for any sudden movement on her part. Here goes….

"S-C-I-K-I-A-T-R-I-S-T." The letters just popped out. Not quite the way he expected. But firm and deliberate and not bad for a novice he thought, considering all the pressure he was under. His dad would be proud of that effort. Shame the teacher didn't share the same opinion.

"No toffee swirl caramels for you this week, dear boy."

Anyone would think it was the end of the world the way Miss Ladybird carried on. Blowing such a huge fuss over a silly word. Talk about making Everest out of a mole hill. Cedric's shoulders slumped. One of *those mental specialists* would come in handy right about now.

Clouds rustled by. The dust on the veldt settled. The lioness continued licking her lips. She had a taste for blood *"Mmm let's see, now who's next?"*

Poor Malcolm shifted uncomfortably on his creaky wooden chair, then put his sore head between his legs hoping she would pick on someone her own size. Lunchtime couldn't come soon enough. At the back Edith finally saw the serious side of her poor humour and you could hear a pin drop. Well almost. Even the garden warblers had shut up shop. And the silence was golden once again.

Everything was well with the world, at least for a brief, shining moment.

30

FAREWELL GOOD GEORGINA
(THE SIGN OF THE CROSS)

Little Bit Of Me * (8) 1971 Melanie from Gather
Me.

*Rainbows aren't easy to find and they don't come
cheap. Some days they never come at all.*

Dear grandmother Georgina Moss (nee Adams) died
from sheer hard work and a broken heart at the age
of 72. She was buried alongside her beloved Ernest and
other family members at Adwick Le Street Cemetery.

The men and women gathered at the graveside
brushing down their bombazine black. A bald headed
priest gave away the holy water and said a prayer, in a soft
voice that fluttered on the air like a thousand dancing
butterflies. I placed a bunch of white roses on her casket
and made a wish that I would see her again.

I can't remember what the weather was like that day.

My mother cried for weeks on end. She said they were
good tears shed for a good woman who deserved a much
better life than the one she had been given.

31

SONG OF THE DISAPPEARING HOMELAND

Welcome to Rossfire. Where there are no tree lined streets and no weathered branches rising up to greet us. No open windows, no smiling faces on familiar heads. No eyes of ice. No barking dogs for chasing happy tails. No loitering cats in search of church bound mice. No outstretched arms embrace. Here, there is no wind to feed the restless soul and there are no memories to erase.

Mother had been picking up vibrations since last Easter. Something in the air wasn't quite right. Long before anyone else had a clue, she was writing down instructions for those around to follow. She could read the signs and feel the tremors deep down in her bones. A sort of fifth sense that permeated every piece and part of her.

George had seen that wild look before. Too many times to mention. He ploughed on and just nodded his head in blind agreement. Caught up in the great arc and spark of the moment, he knew what those tea leaves in the bottom of his cup meant, better than most. Knew where the sun rose in the morning and where it went each and every night, but when it came to premonitions and tides of change, knew nothing whatsoever. Far better this way, to go with the flow and much less complicated. The last thing he wanted was to cause an argument. It was not in his nature and would be more prudent of him to stick to his usual and predictable routine. So he took his HB pencil and favourite newspaper and retired to his corner of the family room to fill out the daily dose of cryptic crossword puzzles. Life as it should be. Simple and carefree with no spanners to ruin the works.

Soon the change was there for all to see, like a breeze sifting through the long grass. Plain as the whisper in the branches of the trees, the ripples in the sand or the breaking waves upon a beach. Brighter than a comet's tail streaking through the sky. Then before we could catch our breath, the past had disappeared. Blown with the ashes of its feeble ghosts. Replaced by a new uncertain future. All consuming. Taking with it the faces and the sketches of our youth and the familiar places stopped at along the way. Relentless, it pushed everything into a ball. Never again to be unravelled. Progress came at such a cost. We were left counting pennies instead of memories.

This was a short and simple song of the disappearing homeland.

The old world had gone. Devoured in a whirlwind of modernism. Nothing would bring it back. Out went: the coals that burnt in the boilers of the steam trains. The painted canal barges drawn by horses fleet of foot. Picnics beside meandering crystal brooks. Barefoot walks through summer fields. Flying kites on lonely windswept moors. Childhood games of hide and seek among fresh cut golden haystacks. Strolls down narrow country lanes. Picking blackberries by the score. Eating them until we couldn't eat another morsel. Pink fairy floss, toffee apples and the smell of sawdust at the circus. The lion tamer with his whip and the lion with his mighty muffled roar. The leather clad rider on the wall of death. Weekend morning matinees with our nerves on edge, wondering if the price of admission was indeed worth the cost. Hoping never say die Flash Gordon would triumph in his battle against evil arch nemesis Ming the Merciless. Watching every single episode without fail. Watching our lives slip by in tired ripples on a pond.

No more seaside shows of Punch and Judy. No more cricket on the village green. Even the clock in the bell tower has fallen silent now.

All things gone the way of dust and atoms.

32

FACTORY GIRL

Nothing stays the same and nothing lasts forever.
Even the paper daisies you brought to me in a
moment of passionate weakness, have withered and
died.

Winter arrived with no warning. Some said, the coldest ever known. It raked across the purple heather and the stinging gorse. An angry beast amok. Hidden under a white whisper mist it crept down from the moors, licking its long tongue between the narrow country lanes and twisted avenues of stone and thorny hedgerow. There was nowhere to hide and there was nothing it did not touch and could not reach.

Clouds rolled in and with them the nameless ice wind that brought Margaret. No one knew from where she came and it was as if she was a thin shadow that carried no past.

Margaret was a spinster. She worked long tedious hours at a wooden bench in a dark, damp, brooding factory that stood upon the banks of a dirty river near the edge of the dirty town. The building was just like all the other forbidding buildings in the street. There were few windows and it had just one blue painted door recessed in a crooked granite frame. A high brick wall with broken glass embedded on the top, enclosed a simple cobbled courtyard. Where the light did not fall everything was grey and without life and no pretty flowers grew in its sad garden. In the middle, a tall, round chimney that appeared as though it had sprouted from the very ground below, sent its thick, viscous smoke plume high into the air. All day and all the long night, the black smoke brewed and billowed. Turning into choking ribbons. Some had the shape of harrowed faces. One was an old man with great flowing beard. Another, a woman carrying a child, their long tresses curling through the trees. Like twisted, sooty vines.

Margaret's fingers were small and nimble. Almost alabaster in appearance. She put intricate parts and pieces together into bombs, bullets and bright metal machines that grew wings and flew across the burning sky. But these were not birds. They brought only fire and brimstone, death and destruction.

Then one day filled with hard rain and painful memories, the restless wind came back. It had no hands, only a hollow voice that whistled as it blew the last of the primroses from the meadow.

The wind shook our bones and took away Margaret too.

33

AT THE CHURCH OF WHITE LIGHT

The old chair creaked every time you sat in it. All those long years now wasted the man said. Over and over until your head ached and your broken body tired of it. But still the chair creaked and the wind outside blew as sharp as arrows and as cold as ice. The wind blew your ghost away, never more here to reside. All those long years wasted he said, as a tear now gathered in the corner of his eye.

Between high vaulted ceilings, through stained glass, domes of white light shimmer and draw into familiar shape, guided by the fall of footsteps on the granite floor. In the central gallery a solitary figure plays out a solemn anthem to the echoes from our past. Sent here, to remind us of our sins. At this place where the long years' memories have been erased by winter fingers at the dark edge of the crumbling grave.

In a shadowed corner of the old church yard, where the awkward ivy climbs its way to heaven, far removed from godless prying eyes, a humble stone cross marks the spot.

Under heavy umbrellas, weighed down by a creeping sadness, young men in striped black suits and a woman's cherry lips of innocence, mourn your passing.

In stark contrast to the stains that will not fade, each one of them has scattered white roses on the muddy earth. Their crushed petals are all that remain of a last fitting carpet epitaph to human frailty.

Though far apart our lives as brothers and sisters have become, we drift together strong and undivided, soft as the velvet smoke that drips like honey from the sycamore trees. Faltering for a moment. Then settle, just in time to gather at the precipice and watch your ghost slip silently away.

34

BAREFOOT BOY WITH KITE

In each new life, I was there at your side when you fell.

Out in the fields above Horsehouse[1], CJ and I running together as fast as the wind could blow us. Heads crammed with nothing but simple dreams and plastic flowers and the smell of bacon cooking on the kitchen stove.

Jumping over walls and muddy puddles. There with our string and woven cloth stretched high above. Patchwork kites under heavy clouds encroaching.

Then just before the rain sets in, we take off our shoes and socks and rush through the tall whisper grass that snaps and stings against our legs. My metronome heart racing, beat by precious beat. You, such a sight. Nettle wild and pretty, yellow ribbon in your hair, coloured by the streaming light from a thousand eyes on fire. Drinking up the moment. Flying with the birds.

Wishing this day would never end.

---

1. *A tiny village in North Yorkshire nestled on the banks of the River Cover. So named because pack horses once fed and rested there.*

35

HOW TO BUILD A CRANE

Out of some obstinate pleasure of my trade, I stumbled at the heart of madness, anxious to explore the chemicals and pheromones of your smile.

My brand new *how to build a crane in ten foolproof steps* meccano set was scattered around the room ready for launch and the only material filling my head was snow covered Christmas trees and piles. Not the formidable type used for construction but the painful sort you would only read about in the latest edition of the British medical Journal. Filed under H for haemorrhoids, that most unmentionable of human afflictions of which I had scant knowledge.

Now it might have been an old wives' tale handed down across the generations or a comment taken out of context, but my grandmother sitting in her favourite chair minding her own business, sure made a whole house full of noise for someone who had never even heard of *The Dave Clarke Five*. She did not bat an eyelid as she warned me about taking her words of anatomical wisdom with a grain of salt. *"Of course I should know about such things"* she boasted, as if she were an expert on the matter. *"Take it from first hand experience... and in any case, I'm a lot older than you"!* It was easy to see where the dissertation was heading.

I soon found out that the cold, hard floor was not the most comfortable spot in the world to place one's posterior. And it most certainly did nothing to help the powers of concentration needed for the enormous task ahead. So I frantically searched about for a nice thick cushion to alleviate the numbness that had suddenly set in.

The paper in my hand tells me in no uncertain terms, part A attaches to part C via a long thin metal strip with no name but lots of wonderful holes and all that is required is a measurable degree of patience, a few nuts and bolts and a length of wire cable. Oh and of course some good old fashioned common sense. Easy. I had plenty of that. So far so good but then I realised this was only the first page on my epic journey and according to the manual the road would only get more difficult from here. Still, the temperature outside hovered at a balmy minus five degrees and the snow was plain miserable. Therefore I had plenty of time to get the job done right. Good boys deserve a challenge and after all a crane *sans* jib and counterbalance wasn't a crane by any stretch of the scientific imagination. Then an awful thought struck home. Like it or not, one cannot get from A to C without the help of B. Sifting through the mountain of colourful packaging I couldn't help but think that Frank Hornby had a great deal to answer for. Search high and low, I couldn't find the blessed beast and the instructions conveniently bypassed that critical component altogether.

There was only one solution. Aggressive retaliation. Furious, I shook the cardboard box until the seams fell apart. No sign of B. I squinted at the printing on the side of the lid. In small, inconspicuous type, the words said *Made in England.* Thank goodness, that was a great relief.

Land of Hope and Glory belted through the airwaves of my head. Finally something positive I thought, no way would they forget such a simple piece. I suddenly grew confident in the fact that never was an empire forged by leaving the most important boat behind. Sadly, the bright light at the end of the tunnel didn't last long. Minutes passed and the uneasy weight of failure drew from me blank stares that wouldn't go away. I began to sweat. A trickle at first, until doubt and morbid rumblings set in. Now where were those wheels, cogs and whatchamacallits I had a moment ago? I need those wheels and cogs to complete the exercise at hand otherwise my dreams of following in the footsteps of Isambard Kingdom Brunel would quickly be evaporated and anyway what excuse would I then make up for my engineering minded friends at school.

Some three excruciating hours later, the coal fire almost extinguished to the very point of no return and myself somewhat similarly indisposed, I decided to do what should have been done in the first place: try out the easy to assemble, one hundred percent guaranteed not to irritate, nigh on fail proof Marie Curie microscope kit for bashful beginners instead. This time there could be no excuses. At least no pieces were missing and of course everyone I knew liked to get up close and personal with amoebas, protozoas and other delicate organisms of infinitesimal scale.

Meanwhile in a cosy corner of the room, dear old grandmother continued to rock backwards and forwards, knitting and stitching in three four time. Still minding her own business. Ticking off the days until Swan Upping[1].

---

1. *The much revered annual ceremony of the counting of the swans, which takes place on the River Thames. A tradition dating back to the 12th century.*

36

TRAINS AND BOATS, SORRY NO PLANES

At light speed we have travelled, you and I. To another place and time. We have unravelled without sound, without shape, through the ink dark void of space. Suffused and bound by the sting of fire and ice we have carried on this journey. Like a curse that blinds, our thoughts blur into strange lines, transcribed from pole to pole. We have travelled here at reckless light speed. Never more to go home.

The horse we were on was going nowhere fast. At least that's how it seemed at the time. It was then, in a spiritual moment born out of sheer desperation, mother took a stand and said without a second thought: *"If at first blink, sweet things come undone and fall apart, then blink once more and think again and before you lose your mind, change horses in mid stride. You might have a better chance of winning".* Which apart from sounding splendidly Shakespearian and quaintly philosophical, was just plain good advice. They also turned out to be words of wisdom.

So in the cold, bleak November of '64 we changed horses. For better or for worse. Expecting rain and thunder squalls, we somehow got a soft summer breeze and in the shadows of the finishing post, we received the news we had all waited for: our official legal papers and a stamped letter of immigration approval from Australia House. In the Smith household, excitement ran at fever pitch. Five months, several medical tests, swabs and smallpox vaccinations later, George, Sylvia and I were on a train, south bound for foggy London. Suitcases in hand and our heads filled with the expectations a great adventure might bring.

Uncle Les drove his Jensen Interceptor down from Sheffield, met us on the banks of the Thames and then kindly escorted us to Southampton. The day was grey and overcast with more than a hint of rain about. With heavy hearts we embarked a very nice vessel the T.S.S Fairstar (previously named the Oxfordshire and recently overhauled and refurbished for the specific transport of migrants) and sailed for Australia.

Looking for a better place somewhere to plant our bed of roses. We were the iconic Ten Pound Poms complete with wide brimmed hats, sun cream lotion and our possessions packed up neat and tidily into three large tea chests.

It's funny but the song being played on the radio was *I'll Never Find Another You** (6) by The Seekers. Something about a new world and a promised land waiting just for us. Deep down it struck a chord.

As the ship pulled away from the quay and the anxious crowd waved and threw their streamers in the air[1], we couldn't help but smile. We smiled until their faces became so small we couldn't tell they were people any more.

---

1. *Drawing comparison to the picture perfect description of departing love in* Bonnie Please Don't Go* *(8) 1971 Kevin Johnson.*

Just smudges on the pale horizon. England's fair shores disappeared into the creeping ether of yesterday and a soft rain began to fall. A gentle drizzle that washed our past away. Perhaps it was a pious bird of good omen that called us.

37

LONG DISTANCE VOYAGERS

The strong wind did nothing to comfort us. It teased hard against our tattered sails then whipped shrapnel bursts of mist rain on our backs. Out of the north, dark the winter shadows came and dark the winter shadows passed. Steadfast under burning stars we ran, wild and head strong on the fetch. Storm and tempest on our trail, fast torn across these fading tracks. And still the winter shadows came and still those winter shadows passed.

Our maiden sea voyage, unlike that undertaken by those brave pioneers long before us, was very comfortable to say the least. And for the greater part, rather uneventful. We did not encounter mountainous icebergs, hidden reefs and sandbars nor treacherous seas. We were also spared the grave fate of falling into the clutches of mutineers and pirates and our encounters with natives of any kind, proved to be far less threatening and downright amicable. And of course to make the going easier, we had the added benefit of twentieth century technology and some special home comforts to assist us on our journey. One certain James Cook cramped up in his converted barque would have been envious.

Places came and went. Names rolled off the tongue. Names I had only read about in dusty old books, or seen in grainy pictures on the television news. The Bay of Biscay, Cadiz and the Spanish coast. Portugal, the Straits of Gibraltar, Morocco and Algiers. The bejewelled blue expanse of the Mediterranean Sea. The exotic realms of the distant east somewhere in a haze beyond. From the crowded games deck we watched the islands drift by. We could easily make out the majestic walled city of Valetta, its ancient houses perched precariously around the rocky harbour. Then on course for the sights of famous Alexandria and past the delta of the Nile.

Port Said was our stopover point in Egypt.

After some degree of difficulty, we docked at a half built pontoon and were greeted by a veritable armada of small boats and other craft which had suddenly appeared out of thin air. Each filled to the brim with men and children vying to sell fruit and vegetables to anyone who cared (or dared) to buy. For those who wanted a little more excitement or maybe just a keepsake souvenir, there were boxes of cigarettes, cigarette lighters, bottles of whiskey and rum, cheap jewellery, silk clothes of every description and even dubious electrical goods. All the way from America. Still in their original packaging. Complete with one hundred percent satisfaction or your money back guarantee. What could be better than that?

We hired a tall, wiry haired local guide by the name of Farouk (I think most Egyptians were called Rameses or Farouk), who took us to see the city sights in an old carriage with a wobbly wheel and drawn by an exhausted horse. I even think the poor old wretch had only one good eye.

The narrow streets teemed with cattle, goats, rats and all manner of creatures. Strange music danced along the twisting mud brick canyons where no sunshine could ever reach. Between nooks and niches where children sang in secret doorways. Where the sirens called the sailors home. Where the real kasbah sprang to life in a dazzling spectacle of colours and sounds.

Mother, unable to resist the temptation, bought some artisan trinkets and a pair of leather sandals from a vendor in a bustling bazaar. With great conviction the bearded man thanked us and said that his young, beautiful wife Nadir was on the same ancestral tree as Nefertiti and Hatshepsut and we should be most privileged to have met her. It seemed that everyone in that quarter of the city was somewhere along the way related to a pharaoh or his noble queen. George was suitably impressed with her impeccable background and said the road to Luxor was paved with golden intentions. Nadir however didn't quite see the funny side of his sarcasm.

Red, yellow and blue striped canvas awnings lined with curios and exotic objects, swayed above the heads of the people in the market stalls. A warm breeze and the strong aroma of Turkish coffee, juniper and spices drifted through the maze of alleyways. The place assaulted the senses until the mind spun. A not too subtle trader holding a cigar in a toothless mouth, put down the tattered National Geographic he had been reading and tried very hard to sell my father a fresh out of the box *genuine* Rolex. His long arms were festooned from wrist to shoulder with every kind and make of watch imaginable. This one he could do at a bargain basement price of five hundred piastres. A mere trifle by anyone's calculation. However, the deal was strictly non-negotiable and as things stood, surely a fruit worth eating. Especially for a novice, white faced tourist fresh out of the antipodes. He intimated one would need to travel to the ends of the earth to find a more accurate or reliable time piece. George got the message loud and clear. With a boyish grin and a Lincolnshire turn of phrase devoid of all humour, commented that's exactly where we were going and we needed to get there in a hurry.

Now agitated and in an odd dialect that was half pigeon English and half Arabic, Hazeem said he could sense our misgivings and was more than happy to swear on its authenticity. George was happy just to swear. The offer was kindly refused. Somehow we couldn't help but think that our persistent friend, had never heard of Wall Street or the New York Times. We left him in our wake, glancing more than once over our shoulders to make sure he was not in hot pursuit with an even more tempting proposition.

At dusk when the boisterous crowds had gone and the drone of giant insects had waned, we visited the shimmering mosque of Al Salam and a nearby cemetery.

A day later with little fanfare and not much to show for our sightseeing adventure we departed port in a rag tag convoy bound for Ismailia and the narrow stretches of the Suez Canal. For an escort, several Bedouin merchants perched atop their sturdy camels, scurried along the flat barren plains ahead of us. The sun reflecting from the rifles strapped around their shoulders. The heat shimmered in waves upon the burning sands.

These hirsute, hardy souls covered from head to toe in flowing white robes were traditional native tribesmen, bartering goods and oils across the broad sweep of the desert. It was like a frantic scene from a David Lean epic. But this was no mirage. And we were in no oasis.

Having negotiated safe passage through the Gulf of Suez we emerged into the rough, broad waters of the biblical Red Sea.

Moses and the Israelites were nowhere to be seen.

38

EARL GREY IN THE MARKET SQUARE / TANKS FOR THE MEMORIES

*I'm gonna take that beast and feed it, I'm gonna
stoke the fire that burns, I'm gonna pack my bags
and leave it and take away the heart that yearns..*

Being somewhat overawed and easily impressed by numbers and geographic statistics, I always thought the earth was too big for its own orbit. So big, one could not possibly imagine being able to navigate across its surface from one hemisphere to the next. Not in a thousand lifetimes. It turned out that in this department, I was very much wrong. We would achieve the feat in far less than eighty days, much faster than Phileas Fogg[1] could ever have hoped to contemplate. To my astonishment, I discovered almost overnight that the world had shrunk to Lilliputian proportions. And indeed, proved no less interesting a place than that great realm of fantasy devised by Jonathan Swift himself.

Through no fault of my own therefore, it was easy to overlook and disregard the many surprises the world had to offer. Culturally blinkered by circumstance beyond my control, it was a case of ignoring the ways and workings

---

1. *The main character from Jules Verne's classic novel* <u>*Around The World In Eighty Days*</u>

of others. Foreign lands by definition were not foreign without good reason.

It would come as no great surprise then, to realise the only stuff I knew about Aden was that it really did exist and was not just a figment of my imagination, its olive skinned inhabitants actually thrived and multiplied in that hot and arid land, that it issued postage stamps emblazoned with Queen Elizabeth's portrait and the main form of transport was by donkey or by dhow. In the vast scheme of cogs and wheels, I was of the strong opinion that this useless information would be more than enough to carry me through.

Situated near the southern tip of the Arabian Peninsula, it had been a Crown Colony until 1963, when it was formally reconstituted as the State of Aden. Military forces had been operating in the region for a number of years in order to counteract the Yemeni and other anti-British factions seeking autonomy. Needless to say, the government in Westminster and its blinkered imperial policy were none too popular with the red eyed local populace.

Thankfully our stay there would be brief.

Our Napolitan sea master was a short, pear shaped man with pearl white teeth and huge eyebrows that raised and lowered each time he spoke. So it was not difficult to listen with interest and follow his every expression as he glanced across the thin line of soldiers gathered in the courtyard. In his best Italian English, the instructions were quite clear. No one was to venture away from the confines of the port. From where we stood, it was obvious he meant business.

In the distance the treeless valleys filled with smoke. Above the craggy ridges, the sound of gunfire and the whistling drone of mortar shells could be heard. Fearing dire consequences we gladly obeyed the captain's stern directive. We would much rather have been stranded in the Sahara desert than here in this god forsaken outpost.

Surrounded by a dozen or so coughing tanks and in the elite company of a blind cattle dog that had been injured by an insurgent's stray bullet, we shared ice tea and stale scones with the Postmaster General and his wife. Left to our own devices we exchanged glances and ideas in the confines of a dingy grey brick structure in the centre of the market square. It was the only building for miles around that did not have its windows broken and was not riddled with the marks of war. A solitary date palm that looked unlike anything I imagined, shook and swayed its tattered fronds in the warm breeze. My father must have had his mind fixed on something completely different or the heat and humidity had affected his powers of thinking. He said it reminded him of an exotic dancer in some forbidden hareem. Not that he would know a hareem from a kibbutz without a map. But that didn't matter, at that moment I knew precisely what he was on about.

My mother smiled and grabbed my shoulder in a brave effort to reinforce the awkward sensation that everything would be alright. We were after all ensconced in the midst of an entire army regiment and a British one at that. Ironically, that did nothing to help dissolve the cold truth that at this point in time we languished an eternity from anywhere. Caught between a rock and a very hard place we might have been, but it was still thankfully the safest refuge in the whole of dusty Aden.

As the ship pulled from its mooring, there were no flags raised to wave farewell, no marching bands to reinforce the edict of old empire. The tug boat that had guided us out between the breakwaters, lurched to starboard, dropped its trembling cable and with one final blast of its feeble horn, disappeared into the thick, brown haze. It was as though we had never set foot in that odd land at all.

Standing on the promenade deck under a glowing afternoon sun, a thought occurred: I never did get to see Scheherazade in a dhow. Although for most of the other happy passengers sipping their lemon, lime and bitters that was the last thing on their minds.

On the final leg of our voyage, the Indian Ocean was anything but calm. Dark skies and stormy monsoon seas prevailed. For days on end, due to the inclement conditions, passengers were denied deck access. Sea sickness ran rampant and the entertainment rooms and cinema, as expected, were packed to the rafters.

Arriving in Fremantle on a hideous, wet late April evening, we decided to bypass Perth altogether. Melbourne too, with its friendly welcome docker's strike was given the cold shoulder. My mother just didn't like the look of the weather in those two cities and for the record, Melbourne appeared disarmingly very much like Manchester.

Reinforcing the idiom that *a nod's every bit as good as a wink to a blind horse*[2] it was with a huge sigh that Sydney got our seal of approval.

---

2. *A Nod's As Good As A Wink To A Blind Horse** (8) 1970 *The Faces*

39

THE BIRDS, THE BEES AND A
TROPICAL BREEZE

He had read about his journey in a book. Where and when, he was not quite sure. Perhaps it was in a dream he saw his road unravel. Over and over again laid out before him, until the lines blurred. Always cursed to travel the same stations in his life.

A bright, cool morning dawned, as our ship glided between the sandstone headlands into the wide, sheltering arms of Port Jackson. Red and white brick houses of every imaginable shape and size, clung against the steep, wooded hills that hugged the foreshore. Yachts bobbed lazily about on the cobalt blue water. The Opera House (under construction) on Bennelong Point and the iconic steel skeleton of Sydney Harbour Bridge awaited. It was early May and at that very moment, we knew exactly how those first settlers must have felt.

We cleared Customs at Circular Quay. My faithful guitar was still strapped across my shoulder. How it ever survived the arduous journey I'll never know. Like prime cattle, everyone was herded on board a bus that looked very much as if it had been extricated from a memorabilia museum. After what seemed an interminably long drive we arrived bottom sore and sorry at a remote colonial outpost somewhere at the edge of civilisation, officially known as the Commonwealth Villawood Migrant Hostel. Although it wasn't long after we had another name for it.

The manager dressed for the occasion in khaki shorts, Omo white knee socks and sandals greeted us with a warm wave of the arms. *"Welcome my friends to your humble abode... my name is Mr Smith"*. He stopped briefly to swat away the thick cloud of flies that had gathered around the group of puzzled onlookers. *"If you have any questions please do not hesitate to contact me... her majesty's staff and I wish you all the best in your endeavours"*. Short though it was, the speech was not exactly uplifting. Nor did it fill us with boundless joy or enthusiasm. Before we could catch our breath and scratch the itch that quickly afflicted us, we were whisked away to our accommodation. They were to be the last words we ever heard from our fearless leader.

The term hostel was a polite but dangerous misnomer. It gave the distinct impression of being a sort of faux sunny seaside resort complete with dark haired hula girls, frangipani flowers and tall trees swaying in a soothing breeze. A home away from home, a domicile of sparse but palatable mathematical dimensions. Somewhere to rest our tired legs.

The images we had conjured in our mind, were to say the least, flattering. However, we soon discovered nothing could be further from the truth. What we got was more of a horror halfway station torn straight from the pages of a disturbing Kafka novel. Our new residence turned out to be a place where the feng shui just wasn't quite up to scratch.

We were blessed with row upon row of half round rusting corrugated iron huts that stood like underworld guardians of the river Styx. All we needed now was a heavy handed platoon sergeant to prepare us for combat manoeuvres. We really did think we had been conscripted into the army.

The buildings were equally divided into two sections. A family allocated to each. The final result was something akin to sardines in a tin. The larger families found the going tough as space was at an absolute premium with no margin for error. For those with small families it was a strange blessing. At least there was some room to stretch out and unpack their meagre belongings.

There was no insulation and no cooking facilities inside. Paper thin walls did nothing to help with privacy. So needless to say, everything that happened in the neighbour's unit, could easily be heard on the other side. And I mean everything.

To shower it was the ritual daily march with towel and soap in hand. Across the road and down a winding bush track to the ablutions block. A very difficult assignment indeed, especially when raining and especially for the men who tried to drown their sorrows in a moderate glass of Johnny Walker.

Our first winter hit hard. Freezing cold conditions was the order and therefore best forgotten. But summer was an entirely different creature. With it came the lightning and the storms and the ear splitting sounds of the secretive cicada which I am sure hid in every single branch and hollow of the trees. And of course there were lots and lots of those. To compound matters, snakes, spiders and mosquitoes tormented us in epidemic numbers. We struggled to sleep at night and in the oppressive heat and humidity, huge cockroaches scurried like alien life forms across the ceiling. Grotesque puppets in a shadow play.

Eating facilities were very basic. In the centre of the compound, was a large cylindrical shaped mess hall with a line of broken louvre windows at each end. Inside, the floor was black and white linoleum that had seen much better days. Formica topped tables (each one apparently defaced by some rascal called Bill Briggs) with metal edge trims and wobbly chairs (most had only three good legs) were placed awkwardly around the room with little space left for manoeuvring. Especially while delicately trying to balance a dinner tray full of our evening's nutrition.

The menu which was scrawled on a chalk board in almost illegible English could by no means be called cuisine. Staple offerings consisted of saute kidney, fried liver, goulash and spaghetti bolognaise with an unpalatable, rubberised sago pudding for dessert. So enticing was the food, no one asked for doggy bags. Occasionally roast beef or roast pork would crop up on the dinner list. On those special warm days, ice cream with apple pie was available. I am sure these were the only culinary delights our large Hungarian chef could muster up. Being of good British stock we stuck solid to fish and chips with lots of vinegar to complement the taste. It was by far the safest option. The coffee was always strong but was at least palatable. Which is more than could be said for the thick, mud grade tea which gushed from the bowels of a giant metal urn. Fearing a gastro outbreak or some such scenario, most of the sensible migrants naturally abstained.

The hostel did however have its positive side. A rickety bus service ran past the main entrance once every hour or so and I was very close to school. Chester Hill High was a mere stone's throw from the main gates. There was also a large sports field for football (which had more dirt and rocks than good old fashioned grass), a half size basketball court and a lot of dense virgin bushland for exploring and catching lizards, which we gladly brought home to keep the rampant spiders in check. Blue Tongues were especially popular. Geckoes and bearded water dragons were common visitors, but much harder to catch. Pets were not allowed but just about every second person took care of a scraggy cat or canine of some description. Of course no one ever admitted animal ownership for fear of being run out of town.

Fortune somehow favoured those with short memories and elephant hides. Thankfully we were subjected to such a modest existence for a mere fourteen months. Many young families had been residents for years and were so entrenched in the system it looked as though they would stay until the cows came home. So we couldn't really complain. It was a whole new beginning for everyone.

One morning after the usual, ordinary breakfast fare my father had a bright idea and in his best north country dialect, snapped *"enuff is enuff"*. No one disagreed with his sentiment and so our cabbage days at Villawood came to an abrupt, but most welcome end. We promptly moved into a small but comfortable three bedroom home in nearby Guildford. Dad took on shift work at the local Ford factory in Homebush as an assembly line welder, but was made redundant a short time later.

He then accepted a position in a multinational company in Silverwater. Within the space of three years he was promoted to warehouse manager and stayed there until his retirement in 1992.

Mum also worked. In those days two wages was an absolute necessity. She found her first job at a company called Smith's Alarms in Granville. Poor dear lasted about three weeks until she couldn't take it anymore. Trapped amongst the springs and mechanisms of ordered punctuality, repetitive strain syndrome and menial labour took on a whole new meaning. Sylvia then tried her luck on the non-too popular graveyard shift at the post office headquarters in Redfern before taking on a supervisor role for the Australian Taxation Office. She remained there for many years until poor health brought about an early redundancy.

For all of us the beloved homeland was now just a distant shadow. Swallowed up inside the belly of the new machine we went about our busy lives with due diligence. Not quite knowing which way the cards would tumble or which way the road would turn. But certain of one thing, our world had changed forever.

A LITTLE SOMETHING TO PASS THE TIME AWAY 3

STRANGE PEOPLE WITH EVEN STRANGER NAMES

Happy Jack (7)	The Who	A Quick One
Captain Jack (6)	Billy Joel	Piano Man
Mean Mr Mustard (7)	The Beatles	Abbey Road
Ziggy Stardust (8)	David Bowie	Ziggy Stardust And The Spiders From Mars
Bungalow Bill (5)	The Beatles	The Beatles (White Album)

LET ME CHECK MY DIARY

Ruby Tuesday (9)	The Rolling Stones/ Melanie	Between The Buttons (U.S Version) Candles In The Rain
Wednesday Morning 3AM (6)	Simon And Garfunkle	Wednesday Morning 3 AM
Sunday Morning Coming Down (8)	Kris Kristofferson Johnny Cash	Kristofferson The Johnny Cash Show
Come Monday (6)	Jimmy Buffet	Living And Dying In 3 / 4 Time
Saturday In The Park (5)	Chicago	Chicago V

MY LITTLE COLOURING BOOK

Green Tambourine (6)	Lemon Pipers	Green Tambourine
My White Bicycle (7)	Tomorrow	Tomorrow
Mellow Yellow (8)	Donovan	Mellow yellow
Lily The Pink (5)	The Scaffold	Lily The Pink

| *Blue Jay Way* (8) | The Beatles | Magical Mystery Tour |

WHERE ARE WE GOING?

Los Angeles, I'm Yours (7)	The Decemberists	Her Majesty
Galveston (6)	Glenn Campbell	Galveston
Road To Birmingham (7)	Mott The Hoople	Mott The Hoople
London Calling (8)	The Clash	London Calling
Roads To Moscow (5)	Al Stewart	Past Present And Future

WHAT'S IN A NAME?

Wicked Annabella (5)	The Kinks	The Village Green Preservation Society
Sad Lisa (7)	Cat Stevens	Tea For The Tillerman
Suzanne (9)	Leonard Cohen	Songs Of Leonard Cohen
Naomi (7)	Ralph McTell	Right Side Up
Arms Of Mary (7)	Sutherland Brothers	Reach for the Sky

PRETTY WITH PIANO

Fire In The Hole (8)	Steely Dan	Can't Buy A Thrill
Where'er Ye Go (7)	Paul Weller	22 Dreams
The Way It Is (7)	Bruce Hornsby	The Way It Is
Against The Wind (9)	Bob Seger	Against The Wind
Wildfire (8)	Michael Murphy	Blue Sky Night Thunder

40

PAPERBACK RIDER
(HEY, THAT'S NO WAY TO MAKE A LIVING)

In my wildest dreams I could not wish for more.
I think I am a knight in shining armour. I ride
the clouds on a dancing, dappled pony named
Clarabelle Tea Biscuit.

The plain truth of the matter was I was bored and needed pocket money. Urgently. And a lot more than my parents were prepared to dispense. So I charmed and begged my way in a performance worthy of an academy award, convincing the local newsagent come entrepreneur Mr Hennessy that together with my trusty Raleigh bicycle I would make a most reliable and competent paper delivery boy. Although at the time I had no idea what I was getting myself in for. Payment was a meagre one dollar and thirty cents (plus gracious customer tips) for the morning round, but still, with thoughts of money-for-old-rope rattling around inside my head and with not much more than a pocket full of marbles for company, I set off on my great pilgrimage. Seeking fame and fortune somewhere along the winding road. The harsh reality however, soon hit home like a

Brickfield[1] buster. The hard work and balancing skills necessary to succeed were more than I had bargained for. It required a special person with almost herculean strength just to keep the damn bike in an upright position. Then of course came the most difficult part, steering the fully loaded, wild and inconsiderate beast. Encouraging it to go where it just wouldn't. Came off so many times it dented my ego. Which sort of matched the cuts and bruises on my legs.

Sometime of August 1966 I purchased my very first album, _Revolver_* (10). The year was a watershed moment in recording history. The Beatles managed to put down on record what no other artist/s had so far achieved. Furthering the previous innovative rumblings of _Rubber Soul_* (9), it was a great leap forward. One that perhaps for the first time delivered a truly artistic statement. Made up of a witches brew of strange and wonderful new songs. An eclectic array of instruments (sitar, cello, violin and harpsichord). _Eleanor Rigby_* (10), a pop song unlike any other and on which none of the Beatles actually played an instrument. Great studio techniques incorporating looped and overdubbed tapes. Music slowed down and music playing in reverse. The sounds of the mellotron.

John singing as if standing at the top of a mist shrouded mountain. Shouting through a megaphone the chant like drone of _Tomorrow Never Knows_* (10)[2]. The song included what on first hearing, appeared to be the

---

1. _The Brickfielder: a term commonly given to the hot, dry and dusty summer wind springing up from the south or south west and affecting Sydney and other eastern coastal regions. Today the word is rarely used._

2. _The song's interesting evolution has been directly attributed to John Lennon's morbid fascination for The Tibetan Book Of The Dead_

cacophony from a thousand screeching birds. Wonder what all the fuss was about? Then listen and be totally informed. This was the new direction the Beatles would have us take.

Two winters came and went. Then unexpected, my high flying life on the paper boy circuit came to a fortuitous end. I think the new proprietor couldn't stand the sight of blood and called the match off before any further damage could be done. How I ever stuck it out so long, I'll never know. Perhaps it all came down to sheer obstinacy and the power of mind over matter.

I was one of the lucky ones.

41

SOME THINGS JUST WORK OUT FINE

Long years past, this scene had textured meadows for a border and gardens filled to overflowing with trumpet flowers of ghostly hue.

I have it on very good authority, the year was 1967. Clear as if it were only yesterday. No ifs, no buts, no maybes. Much better than all the six's sixty six and without doubt far more hip, cultural and downright frenetic. The San Francisco flower scene was in full petal. Opened up in glorious panavision for everyone to see. We couldn't resist. Plenty caught the bug and those with any ounce of sense or appreciation for beauty, thought they were hopelessly in love with Lauro Nyro, Michelle Phillips or sultry Grace Slick and her elusive white rabbit. So much so that the mad hatters at the table swore Alice in Wonderland never looked so good. Who were we to argue the point?

In sleepy cut out cardboard town a whole world removed from the glitzy *what you see is what you get* doctrines of Haight Ashbury, I drifted in and out of normality with all the finesse of a Bolshoi ballet dancer in a Siberian gulag. It was hot and steamy in this jungle and there were no excuses for not running with the tide. Perhaps it was the puberty blues that took control of us or perhaps it was the moonlight dancing on the ocean waves.

Whatever the reason, it turned out to be the best year of our lives.

It started with a kiss somewhere behind the locker rooms. And things changed. Before I had any chance to protest my conscription into the ranks of the Ten Pin brigade we were the flavour on everybody's lips. The aptly named Ruminators pondering the unthinkable, shocked the sporting world and won the inaugural Fairfield under Fifteen AMF Bowling tournament by careful planning and default. The dogs of war barked long and loud and DW could feel it in the air. All week the hairs on the back of his neck had been giving him good vibrations. I called them palpitations. Then at the very last minute as if to reinforce his erratic behaviour, the god of checks and balances smiled upon us and out of nowhere a pestilence struck the other team down. We celebrated our marvellous victory with a lap of honour and a sermon on the mount.

Priscilla Pottinger appeared, straight out of the ravaged pages of a bikini model magazine. She was everybody's perfect body. With her fully inflated, wild accordion skirt that hovered about her hips like something from a National Geographic butterfly documentary and those extra-long legs that didn't know quite where to stop and quite where to begin. The girl that never took no for an answer especially on Mondays, always said we had a lot in common. A great deal it seemed. But somehow I refused to put a finger on it. Caught up in grandiose visions and youthful yearnings, the only picture I could see was green smoke and mirrors. And Priscilla being true to form, passed on by in a fog rolling over open water. She left behind a trail of sequins, sparks and breadcrumbs for anyone who cared to follow. Why I didn't take the hint I'll never know. I kicked myself for months until it hurt.

Fortunately young boys are thick skinned and have short memories and the pain thankfully did not last.

To cap it off, amidst the chaos and confusion the Beatles released Penny Lane and Strawberry Fields Forever and all traces of lust, longing and regret slipped peacefully away.

It ended on a sour note. Gaius Gracchus and his brother in crime Tiberius, by foul means put an end to the fortunes of the Ruminators and their brief time in the spotlight. The result was not pretty.

Summer arrived right on schedule, transformed itself from an ugly duckling into a feast of sights and sounds and I resigned myself to floating along a river under those endless blue, suburban skies. On the lookout for *that* silly fireman with an hour glass and the nurse selling poppies.

I never found them.

42

MISS MOODY'S GARDEN OF
SECRET DELIGHTS

With just a little imagination, I think most of us could picture her in a meter maid outfit. It wasn't that difficult. After all it was the swinging sixties. Inspired by Lovely Rita* (8) 1967 The Beatles from Sgt Pepper's Lonely Hearts Club Band

Helen Moody was one in a million. She also happened to be our favourite music teacher. Come to think of it she was the only music teacher we knew. But that didn't matter one precious iota. For those of us who cared not in the least about clefs and quavers or the finer arts, she was the best thing since donuts and sliced bread.

I was fourteen, young and susceptible to Freudian thoughts and other misguided concepts. With a head full of fluffy daydreams and little else, I had a rampant teenage crush on her. You might say more lust than love. It was that simple. Mind you I wasn't on my pat malone in that department. Most of the boys thought about Miss Moody. Perhaps way too much for their own sanity. It was difficult not to however, as she did not fit the typical teacher poster profile. Fortunately for us she was tall, Racquel Welch good looking and in possession of long, flame red hair that seemed to stretch all the way from her neck to California. You could say she was soft on the optic nerve. Furthermore, she had a god given gift for clavichord and cantata. To add the final chapter to this rollicking adolescent manuscript, the rest of her music taste was impeccable. Well that did it for me and those others amongst us smart enough to recognise a good thing when they saw it. And that's where the learning stopped and the real adventure began.

It wasn't very long before Miss Moody introduced me to a certain highly decorated Sgt. Pepper and his *anything but* Lonely Hearts Club Band. The whole kit and kaboodle. Which on further inspection proved to be a veritable carnival of Turkish delights. With all its bells and intricate whistles. Billy Shears soon became a close friend and my search for deep happiness and spiritual meaning became my holy grail. For the majority of the class, much valuable down time was spent in the crowded confines of the glorious music room. A virtual temple for the tortured soul, where over the coming weeks many a tale would be woven. Everyone was welcome. Almost on a daily basis, like mesmerised minions, as many as twenty or more of us would turn up to hear what all the critics had hailed as a modern masterpiece. Arguably the greatest recording of our lifetime.

For most lessons we would sit propped up against the piano, quivering sardines united in breathless anticipation. Waiting for that ring a ding moment when *she* walked into the room sporting a mini length skirt that somehow defied every preconceived notion of gravity yet at the same time managed to effortlessly hug her slender body. Fluorescent lights cavorted on her delicate tresses. Jaws dropped and knees trembled. Fireworks and cannons exploded in an overture of purple haze. Wayne got bad night sweats and thought he was coming down with the measles and as for

Robert, church bells rang in the convoluted confines of his head. Yes, Miss Moody had that sort of effect.

Even her smile gave away a sense of knowing that most young male eyes were keen to find out what secrets lay beneath that spurious article of clothing. We were smitten. So much so that in that instant it was difficult to concentrate on the real reason we were gathered there in the first place.

In a whimsical drawl she brought us quickly back to earth. "*Pay attention class.... I thought you might like to hear this new record. I like the Beatles.... I like the intricacies of lyric amalgamated with their unique sound. It is a magnum opus.... an aural feast indeed*". Our Miss Moody sure knew how to hit the right notes. Her pulsing violin could only play pizzicato.

At the much anticipated Year 4 formal I struck up enough courage to ask her for a dance. Tongue tied, I spluttered and muttered my words. They fell out of my mouth and on to the cold hard floor. Rather than hurt the feelings of a cherub faced dribbler who didn't know any better, she picked them up and put them in her handbag for safe keeping. *"Don't worry they're only words. That's all"*, she said. Then before I could count to ten, spinning beneath the bright neon stars in that Chubby Checker *Let's Twist Again**(5) before it's too late moment, I was transported to another place. Far removed from the madding crowd.

What started out with clouds and precipitation finished with a wild fire and by summer's end Miss Moody had departed, taking young hearts and adolescent desires with her. She had no intention of giving them back.

In a mere blink of an eye, the world I knew had changed forever.

Pimples and pomegranates were the last thing on my mind.

43

JUDITH IN DISGUISE
(JUST A SONG ON THE RADIO)

*Here she lies under the airwaves tonight. All arms
and legs, hair on fire, burning bright for me.
Calling out the captain of the dial, sending mixed
signals in the pale moon light. For everyone to see.*

High school wasn't such a drag after all. Contrary to
my expectations, it was a whole new adventure.
Gary Goodship was the first person I met upon arrival at
Chester Hill. The teacher insisted the pale, insipid looking
English boy with the weather beaten satchel, sit down
next to Gary who would duly look after him. Maybe share
his lunch and narrate some nautical tale or two. He sure
did. Good old Gary. Danny Stephens and Rob Stormont
were there too. Gary Smith, Dave Wakeling, Ron Murray,
Peter Williams and Zigmund J also lent a helping hand.
It was like some notorious bunch of shoot 'em up misfits
emerging from the pages of a Zane Grey western novel[1].
Heading out in a trail of smoke, ready to meet the
world head on. Come what may. For most it was simply
a case of *let the good times roll*. As for the rest, Engelbert
Humperdinck would suffice.

---

1. *No doubt I had The Riders of the Purple Sage in mind*

We tuned out to the vibes and bad karma generated by the press simply because Vashti Bunyan[2] told us it was the proper thing to do. We tuned in to Radio Station 2UE instead. Just to catch the mournful tones of Ward *Pally* Austin and *Long John* Laws. But best of all was the fun we had with the phantom top forty late night show host who took requests in a brave effort to keep himself and his indifferent audience awake.

Day after day in a seemingly endless cycle, we fiddled and twiddled and manipulated that dial until we couldn't take it anymore, until we reached the point where no one gave a monkeys. Then somehow it was always a strong cup of coffee and dunked shortbread biscuits that did the trick. Not to mention the same old song for the same invisible person. Trouble was she didn't have a clue. The only one on the planet who had no regard for the airwaves or the message it was trying to relay. The early bird had missed the worm. We figured it was her loss not ours and anyway we liked the sound of our own company. As the tides of change turned, we never bothered dear Miss Judy again. Now, if only someone out there would lend an ear and listen it sure would be one hell of a story to tell.

---

2. *Jennifer Vashti Bunyan: English singer / songwriter from the mid to late 1960's. Her first single was the Jagger / Richards penned 'Some Things Just Stick In Your Mind' which failed to make any lasting impression. It was the end of a sad love affair.*

44

REMEMBER ME TO MARION

Shoot first __then__ ask questions. That way you never lose. She couldn't have painted the picture any better, even if she wanted to. "And whatever you do always remember to join the dots", was her battle cry. So I carried out her instructions to the letter. But it didn't really help at all. Sentiment and salvation had nothing to do with politics.

Most nights I dreamed of coconut trees and pristine white sands on a Robinson Crusoe island somewhere at the edge of the world. What a carefree sailor's life for me! That is, until Marion came for dinner. Uninvited but by no means unwelcome. In the wink of an eye she straightened out my crooked thoughts and all of a sudden I just couldn't get enough of *Easy Rider* and that long black lonesome highway.

Marion, a tall sylvan maid of modest but desirable parts, liked me. She liked my guitar even better, said it suited her volatile gypsy temperament. Also gave her the chance to do things with those nimble itchy fingers, she never thought possible. Her mojo cranked up to overdrive and in a gesture of true kindness she grinned and in keeping with the Godfather made me an offer too good to refuse. Right then and there she lit up the night sky with a dazzling display of shooting stars and roman candles. So when she proclaimed even Robin Hood wouldn't find a better deal in a whole month of Sundays, I believed her right down to my boot laces. I sure knew the goose that laid the golden egg when I saw it.

And thus it came to pass, with a delicate push and a shove and more than a touch of sadness, I bade farewell to my faithful, old guitar. Capo, plectrum, Uncle Tom Cobly and all. Together with some other belongings, a few useless leftovers, my pet blue tongue lizard Albert and my prized collection of Marvel Comics. Marion however had a short fuse and an even shorter memory. Shorter than the straw I drew at the Boy Scout initiation ceremony. She soon forgot she had ever liked me and in a moment of weakness, burnt a lot of bridges and more than enough good rubber with a sizeable leather clad member of the local motor cycle chapter. The man with the chain mail teeth that shook every time he opened his mouth. I think she called him Django[1]. The smell of oil and diesel was enough to make me choke.

Her dangerous streak returned to haunt her. Deep down she couldn't resist Harley Davidson boys with bad attitudes, Mohican haircuts, nose rings and hypnotic tattoos that seemed to transform and jump to life every time you looked at them.[2] Of course Marion had to have one of those too.

A souvenir she could take with her. For good luck. Just to keep up with the in crowd, just to let them all know

---

1. *Rumour has it he was named in honour of the great guitarist Django Reinhardt. Though I believe this to be highly implausible. This Django could shake and rattle with the best of them but he certainly couldn't roll.*

2. *Now we all know how The Illustrated Man must have felt. Thank you Ray Bradbury. For dreams and nightmares.*

where she was coming from or where she was going. She couldn't go wrong if she had inked on her arm a giant red heart and a green two headed serpent wrapped around an arrow with words underneath that summed up the situation perfectly:

The road ahead is short and meaningless. Ride on asshole.

Well that was enough for me.

45

NO MILK TODAY

Through loves' great halls of madness, I have travelled to your door. Marched along this narrow road with a strength and passion undiminished. Turned myself inside out and back again, to be with you once more.

Tadeusz was the local milkman, a reluctant hero of the zombie waking hours whom I first met through a good school friend, Gary. Tad was the nearest thing to a rebel of imperfect pieces I had ever seen. He was of Polish descent, I think out of Gdansk and a nice enough fellow of sorts. Short and rather stocky in stature, almost as wide as he was tall. His blonde close cropped hair forever swept back with copious amounts of Brylcreem.

Most days he worked out in his converted garage lifting weights and heavy iron bells in a determined effort to become the next Mr Universe. Just like his muscle idol Arnold Schwarzenneger. Except poor Tad was no Arnold.

Tad had an older brother who like most inquisitive men of his age had absolutely no idea where he was going or how he was getting there. I am not quite sure what line of work he was in and I never dared to ask. Most sensible people steered well away from Vince who had become well known for his oddball photographic habits.

A hobby which kept him locked away for hours in his quirky little dark room foraging through a vast secret collection of girlie magazines. For want of a better name, we called him Copernicus as he was always gazing at the stars. Unfortunately they were not the kind that shone like diamonds in the night sky.

Sometime in March of nineteen sixty eight, Tad offered Gary and I casual work on his delivery run. He said it would be of great benefit to have some assistance and as it was lonely out there on the graveyard train, he certainly could use the company. We thought it was a novel idea and would be the perfect opportunity to earn a few brownie points for services rendered as well as some much needed cash. As it turned out, it was more a case of never blow a tuba in a rainstorm, than we expected. Out of bed well before sunrise. Wiping the cobwebs from our eyes and looking almost comatose in appearance. At the Dairy Farmers Fairfield depot by four thirty. Fully loaded and on the road before the clock struck five. Then back home, changed and ready for school by eight thirty. It was a killer job. Bloody hard work by any stretch of the imagination. But as Gary cleverly remarked some unlucky sod had to do it, so it might as well be us and after all we did get free helpings of chocolate milk and yoghurt. More than enough for ten summers. Still that didn't stop me wanting to punch him in the nose for his lopsided opinion.

Exactly how long we stayed together doing the sparrow rounds I am not sure, though it could be measured in mere weeks not months. Though the way things panned out it felt like months. Needless to say I dropped so many bottles tripping over vagrant cats and dogs or perhaps it was through sheer joy and enthusiasm my sweaty fingers let me down. Whatever the reason, Tad didn't see the funny side and neither did his bank account.

In his usual gruff and unflappable way he told me I wasn't cut from the right cloth to be a milk vendor. It took a certain unwavering mental constitution to succeed where countless others had failed. I didn't have the right DNA and that was that. Perhaps I should take up a plum position in the hospitality industry or better still run my own night carter business[1]. Maybe even something else that took my fancy, anything, he said with a belligerent wink and a nudge, that didn't involve the delivery of precious cargo. Words of wisdom they were and the best advice he ever gave. The choice was not difficult. I steered well away from the latter for the simple reason I had never heard of a happy latrine porter, let alone a wealthy one.

By year's end the fatted cow of animal kindness had turned sour and the chickens I had seen earlier on the open range came home to roost. I broke up with petite Jan Hughes (or perhaps it was the other way round) and all the radio stations were playing *I Started A Joke** (9). That's ironic I thought, wallowing in my own self pity. Feeling sorry for myself and anyone else who happened to cross paths with me.

Sympathy of course was the last thing on Jan's mind. The girl with the killer smile who never got the blues but sure could sing them, wouldn't let the current climate cause friction. She merely mused and meditated to get her bearings right, then got on with her life quick as I could say *O Sole Mio*.

Cruel, cruel world.

---

1. *In those days the notorious Night Carter collected the sewerage waste pans. His truck could often be heard bright and early on its regular weekly morning round.*

46

A STRANGE OBSESSION INDEED

It wasn't as if we had nothing to do. Or nothing worthwhile to aim for. Far from it. We were young and we were foolish and that kind of said it all. The sights and sounds of the occasion got the better of us and instead of resisting the urge, we simply gave way to the overwhelming temptation and took another sip of Martha Kringle's special formula juniper juice.

Whatever you could possibly wish for, you could find right there in Oscar Matthias Kringle's opportunity shop of hidden delights. Well most times anyway, especially on weekends and if you looked long and hard enough. Furthermore, one also had to be very meticulous and selective in their search, for the old building with the paint peeling façade and leaning walls that creaked when anyone walked by, contained more than its fair share of disposable junk.

Tucked away in some quiet cul-de-sac of suburbia, as shops go, it was not a large shop and it was certainly not Paris boutique. But what it lacked in size and status, it more than made up for in content and sheer confusion. There were wonky, wooden shelves stacked with unknown goods of unknown worth. Narrow aisles that twisted and turned in every direction. Once inside those shadowed corridors it was difficult to find a way out and then not without bumping headfirst into something that took your fancy and of course your hard earned money in the process. Boxes large and small, plain and decorative, covered every square inch of available floor space. Boxes stacked precariously on top of each other like plates perched upon a circus juggler's pole. Every last carton filled to the brim with knick knacks and various odds and sods accumulated from just about every continent and from every decade of Mr Kringle's abundant life.

Yes, there indeed, was a wondrous tale to tell.

Mr Kringle however, had a devious dark side. A shocking secret only his closest friends and immediate family knew about. Until of course those irritating, nosey neighbourhood kids happened to stumble upon him in a secluded corner of the shop, at a most inopportune moment. Literally catching him in the act, you might say. There he was, brushing away the cobwebs from their tattered ears and cleaning those brown beady glass eyes. Eyes that never blinked. Piercing eyes that gazed back at you from childhood dreams. Yet, Mr Kringle never made a sound, just packed them neatly away into padded containers, never more to see the golden sunlight. He did so with a nervous glance, to make sure no one was watching.

However this particular day, the ugly truth had finally been revealed. Bald headed Mr Kringle was not what one expected. No numismatist, lepidopterist or chronometrophile here. Heaven forbid, of all things great and small to collect, he plumped for Teddy Bears[1]. He was an expert of the highest garter on objects fat and furry, stuffed with the finest materials available and gathered from every realm on earth. It was a strange obsession, continued down over the generations but one borne from the heart and for that reason Mr Kringle was not perturbed. He was merely carrying on the family tradition. It was an institution cast in stone. Be it a Steiff or a Merrythought and Chad Valley, Mr Kringle could distinguish his cuddly Hugmee Bear from a Ting-a-Ling Golden Bruin. Which we all thought was pretty darn impressive. But somehow, that intimate knowledge seemed at best, to be totally wasted in the cut throat world of retail.

Mr Kringle tried hard to conceal his addiction, but the horse had well and truly bolted. To limit the damage and protect his good standing in the community, he resorted to bribery and plain old fashioned flattery to gain our silence. It worked.

We ventured home that very afternoon with a broad smile on our faces and our pockets stuffed with Violet Crumble bars[2] and other melting delicacies. Each one of us also given the latest hot off the press copy of Mad Magazine just to make sure we had received his message loud and clear and to put the icing on the cake, so to speak.

Mr Kringle didn't have to worry in that department, our collective lips were duly sealed.

---

1. *A person who collects Teddy Bears is called an Arctophile (derived from the Greek word arktos, meaning bear)*

2. *That most alluring morsel of Australian confectionary consisting of a honeycomb toffee interior coated with dark sensuous chocolate. It was originally manufactured by Hoadley and subsequently acquired by Rowntree and then later by Nestle.*

47

THE THIRD EYE

How the numbers fall and the dice tumble is anyone's guess. Which I suppose, is the real dilemma.

Nineteen sixty nine came and went. With little fanfare as it turned out. It was an ordinary year or at least most of us thought it was, as nothing much unusual and exciting had transpired. Except of course for Woodstock and the moon landing. We were still fighting a war of lost causes in faraway Vietnam. Politicians and world leaders were telling us the same old stories, with the same old smiles upon their faces and the news on television was the same news we had listened to the year before. But somehow, it got the pulses of a nation racing.

We did ordinary things and thought ordinary thoughts. For the most part we even had ordinary weather.

As a counterpoint to the mundane, someone in our midst hoping to win the coveted most popular student of the month award, had an Edison brainwave and brought a portable record player to school. This was permanently set up in the sanctity of the first floor Common Room and during lunchtimes and spare moments of sanity we could get to listen to our favourite music. The process of choosing which songs to play however was not entirely democratic.

More a case of first in best dressed. The occasional monetary bribe did not go to waste either.

Masters of the morose, Mick Dumbleton and Chris Reynolds insisted on subjecting everyone to radioactive doses of Creedence Clearwater Revival's _Green River_* (8) along with Tony Joe White's _Polk Salad Annie_* (6). The Stooges, Vanilla Fudge, The Velvet Underground and Moby Grape tested the patience of all but die hard fans. There was even some odd stuff by Captain Beefheart and Quicksilver Messenger Service thrown in for good measure. All the while Jefferson Airplane blossomed like the wild flowers on the common room wall.

Thank god the Beatles released _Abbey Road_* (10) and some form of normality prevailed.

Gary G. for the most part had a Jimi Hendrix vibe interspersed with a sprinkling of Donovan and Iron Butterfly to keep the mood in perspective. When others around were cruel, Gary S. was rather kind to Tiny Tim. Which was admirable really, as we were sick and tired of _tip toeing our way through all of those damn tulips...._ And that high pitched falsetto voice, well that was another matter altogether. David W. was what Simon and Garfunkle weren't and wished he could have had the role Dustin Hoffman played in the Graduate. Rob Stormont was, should I say, being true to form and continuing on his torrid relationship with the Beatles. Ron Murray believed in white temples, Hare Krishna and the Kamasutra, mystical meditation, T. Lobsang Rampa and the eternal flame of inner light. Just a phone call away the mysterious Third Eye watched over us. Our nerves twinged.

Somewhere not far away, the electric chords of Led Zeppelin sizzled down the narrow corridors of our education. With Jimmy Page at full throttle, it was a simple case of _Dazed and Confused*_ (7) or better still, be bedazzled. Take your pick.

As we searched among the cigarette ashes and the ruins of the _Gilded Palace Of Sin*_ (8) for answers, Frank Zappa offered anyone who cared to participate, a fresh off the shelf can of _Peaches En Regalia*_ (7). The paeans of Haight Ashbury and the flower power scene were in decline. The age of Aquarius had turned once more to water, leaving behind the sparkle but alas no wine. The gods of Olympus looked down from high above and all was well in our world. At least for the time being.

We called it our abracadabra year. The magic and the ecstasy. The year our voices broke.

A LITTLE SOMETHING TO PASS THE TIME AWAY 4

ORGAN RECITAL MOMENTS

Child In Time (9)	Deep Purple	In Rock
Big Boss Groove (8)	The Style Council	Home and Abroad
House Of The Rising Sun (10)	The Animals	Single Release only
Let It Be (10)	The Beatles	Let It Be
Reflections Of Charles Brown (7)	Rupert's People	Single Release only

BLOWING THEIR OWN TRUMPET

The Whole Of The Moon (8)	The Waterboys	This Is The Sea
Penny Lane (10)	The Beatles	1
Holding Back The Years (7)	Simply Red	Picture Book
Close To Me (7)	The Cure	The Head On The Door
Does Anybody Really Know What Time It Is (7)	Chicago	Chicago IV

FIDDLESTICKS

Hurricane (9)	Bob Dylan	Desire
Don't Pass Me By (7)	The Beatles	The Beatles (White Album)
The Lake Isle Of Innisfree (8)	The Waterboys	An Appointment With Mr Yeats

Come On Eileen (9)	Dexy's Midnight Runners	Too Rye Ay
Baba O' Riley (9)	The Who	Who's Next

WHERE ON EARTH DID THEY FIND THOSE LYRICS?

Bohemian Rhapsody (10)	Queen	A Night AT The Opera
You Can Call Me Al (9)	Paul Simon	Graceland
Stairway To Heaven (10)	Led Zeppelin	Led Zeppelin 4
Stuck Inside Of Mobile With The Memphis Blues Again (7)	Bob Dylan	Blonde On Blonde
I Am The Walrus (9)	The Beatles	Magical Mystery Tour

YOU COULD DO WORSE THAN LISTEN TO THESE

September 1913 (9)	The Waterboys	An Appointment With Mr Yeats
Cloudbusting (8)	Kate Bush	Hounds Of Love
Playing With Fire (9)	Brandon Flowers	Flamingo
The Last Of The Melting Snow (8)	Leisure Society	The Sleeper
When The War Is Over (8)	Cold Chisel	Circus Animals

SOMETHING TO EAT BEFORE BEDTIME

Savoy Truffle (8)	The Beatles	The Beatles (White Album)
Dixie Chicken (6)	Little Feat	Dixie Chicken
Red Apples (5)	Smog	Red Apple Falls
Soup Of The Day (6)	Chris Rea	Espresso Logic
Heinz Baked Beans (5)	The Who	The Who Sell Out

48

WELCOME TO THE MACHINE

The man who sold potions at the travelling show wanted our money and our undivided attention. Step up step up ladies and gentleman. Take your place alongside the stage. Let me reveal to you the secret of my youth. Only found here in this little box of human delights.

Our last year in high school although rather chaotic turned out to be our best. Sure, there were bumps and bruises along the way, which for the record proved to be a real pain in the backside. Yet it still brought a benefit or two and a special surprise. As turned out to be the case with our purchase of the best beverage brew maker this side of Norton Street, Leichhardt. The full colour brochure featuring the scantily clad girl from Ipanema, sold us on the first page. So after much sweat, toil and dogged negotiation, when we finally took possession of our wondrous state of the art coffee machine we thought we had a winner. It was a bargain, at least for the amount it cost. Or so we thought. However trouble lurked beneath those deceptive smooth waters and it soon became a proverbial albatross around our necks. You see, there was one slight hitch: no one ever wanted to undertake maintenance or clean out the reservoir when needed.

Of course, as any barista worth his salt would tell you, a good quality liquid is an essential component in the making of a drinkable cup of coffee.

It was not unexpected therefore, that due to neglect, strange creatures began to manifest themselves inside the deep, dark recesses of that tarnished urn.

Then one day, somebody whose nerve was greater than their wisdom decided to add a small but nevertheless troublesome amount of bi carbonate of soda to the mix and forgot to inform the rest of us. For three days solid the winds of change blew nobody any good.

From that point on the old machine got a health check-up and service on a regular basis.

The coin had finally dropped and the fire returned once more to our eyes.

And the coffee never tasted so damn good.

49

INCENSE WITH PEPPERMINT
(LIVING NEXT DOOR TO MALICE)

Goodtimes* _(8)_ _1967_ _Eric_ _Burdon_ _And_ _The_
Animals.

Whoever said, good times are wasted on the young,
didn't know what they were talking about.

It was a party, that's all. Nothing too exciting and
certainly no reason to get uptight. This was not a Lesley
Gore egocentric flavoured bash, but a rather ad hoc effort
at best. At worst it was a chance to clear the cobwebs and
remind ourselves of what we had missed out on along
the merry way. Communication strictly word of mouth,
no official invitations needed. No names, no tags and
definitely no numbers and no reason to worry about rowdy
gate crashers, they hadn't been invented yet. Then it struck.
What might happen if no one bothered to turn up. On a
scale of ten this would register as just an ordinary birthday.
Nothing special. So it came as great comfort that our
deepest fears were unfounded. Before the cuckoo could go
haywire in his little wooden box, everybody and anybody
of note duly arrived. Too many for the rather small house,
which not being accustomed to such grand functions,

bulged and creaked at every seam with boisterous activity and general rambunctiousness.

Bright eyed Darinka whose tresses bore an uncanny resemblance to Phar Lap's flashing tail, brought her older sister Yeles (who in turn brought Sally Saltwater) and then of course there was saucy Sue and spinning Jenny who never could stand still. Kathy, Yvonne, Ludka and Svetlana rounded out the rest of the group. It was like the United Nations of female friends past and present all gathered at the feast.

Cool and casual was definitely in. And so was just about anything else you could care to mention. Everyone wore the latest hip clothes. Levi jeans and acid etched denim legs. For the girls it was headbands, mosaic beads and long calico wrap around outfits or whatever else took their fancy. As for top of the pops Miss Kelly, she arrived attired as if she had been transported straight out of a *Laugh In* episode. Her baubles lit up like a Christmas tree on fire. Although Goldie Hawn she wasn't. Still we couldn't complain, she turned out to be the life of the party.

In a sign of the times, the boys were desperately trying to cultivate moustaches. The famous Che Guevara or Frank Zappa type but with little success. Except for Rob Stormont. His moustache and giant sideburns must have been genetically engineered. They were the envy of the entire sixth form.

Willie and the Poorboys echoed through the empty canyons and with the dense clouds of incense smoke refusing to go away, nobody could see a thing. And nobody cared. That is, until some bright spark called the fire brigade and Horace the neighbour with a mean streak as long as his memory, lodged a formal noise complaint.

50

THANK YOU VERY MUCH ALICE COOPER

Fountain Of Sorrow * (9) *Jackson Browne from Late For The Sky*

Petite Angela McTigue and fraulein Jutta Miller were late additions to school in that famous final stanza of educational excellence. Angela had a very pale complexion, which told everybody who cared to take note that she had not long since arrived from England's fair shores. On the other hand, the girl whose name we found difficult to get our tongue around, was Australian born, of German and Polish parents and had recently transferred from Our Lady of Mercy College, Parramatta.

Little did I know at the time, but that pretty lass in the drab brown uniform would a few years later become my dear wife.

Now it just so happened that the weeds in the garden where running rampant and the child of god had well and truly flown. Sandals, sarongs and semaphores in tow. Woodstock and those who sailed with her, at last became unstuck from our thoughts and those chemical charged ripples disappeared into the mists of hippy cult disintegration. Apollo 13 was aborted before moon orbit due to near disastrous consequences and the Vietnam War was quickly becoming a lost cause.

To lift the spirits, we listened with renewed optimism to Creedence, The Doors, Pink Floyd and the Rolling Stones.

And the saddest part of all hit home with the subtlety of a runaway freight train. The Beatles had packed up their cares and woe and gone on vacation to that most revered of places, Valhalla.

Still, we couldn't complain. Soon a whole new chapter would unfold and in the words of someone far wiser than any of us: *School was out of our minds forever.*

We raised our glasses and drank to that most sobering fact.

51

STUCK IN THE MIDDLE WITH NOTHING BUT A MOTLEY CREW

Only Heaven knows how we ever got there. But with a smile on our faces and the wind in our hair, somehow we made it.

Murphy's Law had struck again. With a vengeance. And this time we were unwilling participants. We found ourselves in the spotlight, trapped in a painful rerun of an old Keystone Cops episode. You know the one, grainy black and white, all slapstick and chaos. Plenty of fluff and nowhere near enough substance. Heading for its inevitable and fatal conclusion. Unfortunately, that's how the song would play out for us.

Someone in their wisdom (I am not sure who exactly), suggested this particular rainy morning to venture out on the estuary. To try out our inconsiderable navigation skills on the wide balmy reaches of the muddy river. Now we were not talking tales of Huckleberry Finn and the rambling Mississippi. No painted paddle steamers in sight. This was the plain and rather listless Hawkesbury. Although it did have its fair share of catfish and eels. Still, as we were soon to discover even ordinary rivers can pack a surprising punch.

It was also the same astute person who emphasised in no uncertain words that we should hire an aluminium run about with a canopy to guard against the elements. To play safe. No matter what might happen. No need therefore for any wet weather gear other than a light spray jacket. In theory it sounded great. Only trouble was the irritable young man at the boat hire kiosk in Brooklyn (who bore an uncanny resemblance to Lee Marvin – the one from that famous western movie, sitting half drunk and cockeyed on a horse)[1] didn't have any left with a rain cover. Just your average run of the mill, hard to manoeuvre at the best of times, four metre aluminium runabout with no fringe on top. It did however have a most reliable Mercury outboard, so we felt vindicated in our decision to continue on our merry way. We thought 'Ah what the Dickens', we were here, prepped and ready for the long haul and the day didn't look like it could possibly get any worse.

Mistake number one.

On board we packed the bare essentials, a large esky full of food and a thermos flask of black coffee. Enough to calm the nerves. Also threw in some thick newspapers as well. They would be useful to sit on and perhaps provide extra protection. From what, I was not quite certain. Of course, our meteorological expert who reported signs of breaking clouds and patches of blue, reiterated most confidently, such items would not be required. At this juncture we turned the other way, looking for a sign from above, hoping that somewhere out there, a bearded man in white robes was walking across the waves.

---

1. *Should anyone be interested in following up on this rather useless piece of information, the movie was* Cat Ballou

We filled up with fuel and thanked the attendant who looked even more so like *that other person* from the movies, than when first we met. The transformation in such a short time, was miraculous but unnerving. The rain coursed down his face and through his fox tail moustache which was now rapidly turning into a soggy broom. A noise came from deep down in his throat. *"Be careful boys, strange things can happen when they are least expected",* Mr Marvin gurgled. Was he in pain or was it twisted pleasure that drove him. *"Who knows, the weather might take a nasty turn yet".* He gurgled even more, just to make sure we were paying attention to the large albatross sat perched upon his shoulders. Now why we were not surprised and why he hadn't mentioned this before we had loaded up and paid our money, was anyone's guess.

Mr Marvin didn't hear our muffled curses as we slowly disappeared into the jaws of a howling gale.

Mistake number two.

Barely half an hour out from the safety of port our troubles began. Small problems at first. But like the proverbial snowball rolling down the hill, they soon got a whole lot bigger!

The Flying Goose (for that's what we subsequently decided to call our vessel), in a brave attempt to get up close and personal with a colony of oysters sound asleep in their beds, badly misjudged the channel clearance buoy, thereby being fated to meet with a huge rock protruding from the shallows. I might also add, it was the only piece of sandstone for miles around that could possibly do any damage. We felt privileged to have found it. The call came for all hands on deck, but to no avail.

At our breakneck speed we could not avert disaster. Our newly discovered rock put a hole in the hull just above the water line. Mind you, this was not a small you can barely see it hole even if you were blind, but a hole that would make a rabbit salivate. Poker faced David, cursed his fortune and our subtle protestations and flatly refused to emulate the brave boy who risked his digit in the leaking dyke. No matter how dire the predicament. So without further ado, we hastily resorted to rolled up sheets of paper and double strength PK chewing gum to fix the problem.

To add further insult to injury, at noon or thereabouts, under a leaden sky threatening to deluge, we were treated to an electrical display of awesome splendour. Putting two and two together, it didn't take long to realise the gravity of our situation. Everyone knew that the worst possible place to be during a violent thunderstorm was of course, in a boat out on the open water. Everyone that is except jolly Captain Pugwash[2], whose neon saucer eyes lit up at the very mention of the words *lightning kills.*

Third mistake.

Now the fate of our expedition took on a whole new twist. In our haste to find safe harbour, the famous foursome failed to notice the large mud bank that had miraculously sprung up out of nowhere. First it was on our starboard side and then to aft and then…..in a desperate attempt to avoid embarrassment and throwing caution to the sharks, we engaged the motor in full reverse. There was

---

2. *The much loved fictional Captain Pugwash, created by British author John Ryan, could not match the feats of ineptitude produced by our very own captain of chaos.*

a large puff of smoke, a splutter and a pop. And then it stopped altogether.

Too late, catastrophe struck. The Flying Goose, ran aground with a resonating thud that had enough force to lodge us firmly in the thick mire and at the same time, knock the thermos out of David's grasp. With an acrobatic lunge, more arms than legs, he tried in vain to scoop the container from its oozy abode. It was then that Peter calling on his vast historical knowledge pertaining to shipwrecks and motley personnel, referenced a certain infamous Dutch mariner, one Jeronimus Cornelisz[3] and his blood curdling deeds. How relevant those events we thought, when applied to the drama we found ourselves in. From this point on no one on the vessel was safe, least of all the bosun.

So it was that for two, long, excruciating hours we sat, hapless and helpless, stuck fast like flies in a honey pot. Cold and soaked to the marrow. Discontent rife and tempers brewing at an alarming rate. Grand mutiny itself, now a very distinct possibility. Until at last a change in wind direction and a rising tide shifted us from our resting place. And all thoughts of treachery and the remote Abrolhos Islands were put to sleep.

Suffering from near hypothermia and acute caffeine withdrawal we lurched back to the marina. Flag at half-mast and looking for Lee Marvin and a length of strong rope and a sturdy tree from which to hang him.

Yet still this story had one final sting left in the proverbial tail.

Anchored and secure at last, Captain Pugwash while clambering ashore, somehow managed to drop the car keys

---

3. *History remembers him for the gruesome part he played among the surviving members of the Dutch vessel Batavia, wrecked off the north west coast of Western Australia in June 1629.*

and other valuables into the bowels of that insatiable river. Never more to be seen by human eyes.

At six thirty five pm on the dot, the Vauxhall Cresta complete with broken side window and a missing door handle, limped slowly out of sleepy Brooklyn and into the pitch black void of night.

Lights flashed somewhere in the distance. Lights flashed in Peter's eyes. Leaning back into the cheap vinyl seat, I couldn't help but smile. Contemplating what should have been – if only I had stayed at home wrapped up in my nice warm woollen blanket.

Lost in dreams forever counting sheep.

52

JOHNNY WAS A SHOOTING STAR

I am the Eye in the Sky Corporation. Circling high above the home world, connecting wires for a simple living. Cables and copper cords, ancient motherboards, whirly gigs and weather satellites. For what logical reason, I wouldn't have a clue. Although they tell me in good faith, it's the stuff of dreams and birthday cake. What better way to eradicate the blues.

One thing was for sure, Alison Stockhausen was ahead of her time. She could see which way the cards would fall or which way the dice would tumble. How the poem and couplets rhymed. How the winter wind would blow and how cities rise and how cities crumble. Alison knew all this and more.

She could unlock the permutations. Read the future from the past, predict the pattern of the planets drifting through the sky. That is how she knew deep down that Johnny was a rocket. No ordinary fly as you may, regular rocket, but a wild and fiery comet. Blazing its trail far and away from here. Where darkness has no bounds.

Johnny was not tethered nor restrained like the others Alison had known. He was always travelling in a different orbit to the rest. At the very best one step in front, but mostly two steps behind. That was poor old Johnny to a fault. That's what it would come down to in the end.

Alison had lived knowing what she did for most a lifetime. Understanding the whys and wherefores. When to push when thoughts of failure prevailed. When to pull down the flags and beat the retreat or when to beat the drum. Somehow managing to balance on a knife edge, the best of all possible worlds. Her world and his. In her mind they could never be the same and would remain that way forever.

Alison had a sixth sense when it came to matters of the heart. Knew his quirks and qualms and how much he missed her when apart. How he would run into her open arms. How he chased the sunshine into his pockets, saving it up for that one rainy day. Then Johnny up and left for the bright lights, said that the sad lights of her eyes would somehow bring him back. Like a tired moth drawn to a flickering flame by some great god electric. Before she knew it, he would return sometime soon before the moon changed gibbous. When mellow May ran headlong into mellow June and black pipers played their mournful tune. He would not have it any other way. Said he would open that suitcase full of rainbows and diamonds. Just for her. He knew how much she loved rainbows. They reminded her of candy floss afternoons and striped lollipops on sticks.

Memory set on overdrive, Alison smiled. Of late it had become second nature. She couldn't help herself. Johnny was just a dreamer. A bold schemer of many things, who no matter how hard he tried, could never hide from the fact that somehow those spoons he thought were silver turned out to be just plain old copper instead.

He went, leaving behind some little part of himself and taking a piece of her away. Forever.

In a circus of pure white he rides, where the great star horses glide. Foaming as they pass on by.

He won't be coming home tonight.

53

DANGLING CONVERSATIONS

Standing in the doorway of a second hand bookshop, waiting for the rain to stop, waiting for the girl with the champagne eyes. To my dismay she blew away the cobwebs from the shelves and with a twisted smile, said in a soft voice "You're not the one I'm thinking of".

How we ever got here in one piece was anyone's guess. Fortunately the tide of good omens fell upon the brave and we couldn't be held back a moment longer. Time was at a premium and we were moving at the speed of light in search of ordinary people living in extraordinary new worlds. Worlds that didn't exist twelve months ago. To help find direction, we were reading Lord of the Rings, A Clockwork Orange, Catch 22, Slaughterhouse 5 and Sons and Lovers. Fine literary material without doubt. Although a few of us preferred the erotic implications and textual nuances of Portnoy's Complaint or the Decameron. Some (who cared to admit it) even became indoctrinated by good Chairman Mao's *Little Red Book*. It was the hottest thing going around. Though God only knows why?

Seeking fame and favour from anyone who might be kind enough to dispense it, my once close band of school comrades soon scattered with the breeze. I too was about to take a special sojourn over the seas, when as luck would have it, I fell quite by accident into my first *real* job. It was with a man named Bruce who also happened to be an architect.

Although the first eight months of nineteen seventy one were spent as a storeman packer working with my father, I did not consider this to be ground breaking employment of any great substance. August Schleck the imperious but keen as mustard personnel officer sitting behind the see through desk thought I was a soft touch and rostered me on the dreaded graveyard shift. Simply because no one in their right mind wanted a bar of it. It turned out to be more of an occupational hazard than anything else. Still, the money was good and the job introduced me to earth shattering experiences: such as learning to master the difficult task of trolley manoeuvring between skyscraper aisles of shelving or seeking out the best places to sit down amongst the cartons and the boxes to keep look out for the renegade union delegate. We had all heard the glowing reports about the giant of a fellow who feared nothing and no one and whose ignominious reputation preceded him. He was Scottish. Born in Dumfries. I think his name was Jack or Jock. But ignorant of his Celtic roots, he never once wore a kilt or tossed a caber. The staff were thankful for small mercies.

Those with an ounce of humour and a sadistic streak had to laugh. Out of frustration we called him Wild Bill Hiccup. Probably because he fancied himself as the last of the cowboy kind, on the prowl and more than ready for an old fashioned gun fight in the local saloon. And also for the fact he liked to partake in the occasional drink or two. Chivas Regal of course. Straight up with no ice. Nothing else would he allow to touch his fervid lips.

By hook or by crook (he wasn't fussed which), he made it an extreme art form to gently coerce the workers in his flock to join the faithful cause. To this end he was a devoted disciple of the nth degree and somewhere far beyond.

It came as no great surprise that my father was a much smarter and wiser man than I and knew all the loopholes and get out clauses. He had been around long enough to know trouble when he saw it. Charles Darwin would have been impressed with his survival instincts. George's people maps were right up to date and meticulously drawn. He was a fully paid up member of the union and as goods receiving manager, he therefore avoided the perils and pitfalls that befell the unfortunate minority. He also kept well clear of Jock at all costs. Diplomacy and a troublesome knee was the much better part of George's valour.

Then just when I was beginning to think that Jock had put a curse on me, my leaf turned and I received a welcome phone call offering a junior position in a small architectural practice in western Sydney. Eager not to waste this golden opportunity, I put away my trusty yellow Crown pallet loader and left the cornflakes packets and other cardboard memories far behind. I rode off into the dusty sunset, never more to cross paths with Wild Bill. Although I am sure others would not have been so lucky.

In hindsight, my brief time as a storeman taught me a whole lot about human nature and how best to avoid falling foul of restless gunfighters with bad haircuts and bad attitudes.

Salad days and sunshine lay spread out upon the freshly made table. I couldn't wait to get stuck in. I rubbed my hands with glee and shut the door behind me.

Bruce was a short and one might say rather distinguished looking gentleman of local renown, who had served his secondary education days at a very famous private school before gaining a scholarship to attend university. He ran the firm with an iron fist wrapped in a velvet glove to sort of soften the impact he frequently made upon the furniture and other miscellaneous office items.

His good natured, military minded wife, whom we all referred to with the discreet moniker Madame Hardback, simply because she never showed her mellow side, owned a popular nearby bookshop. A special hang out of the goateed café latte Bohemian set who had never heard of The Velvet Underground and Greenwich Village.

Madame Hardback a Gemini of no particular political persuasion, was a connoisseur of all fine things literary and otherwise and could converse with great conviction on just about any topic of note. You name it and without hesitation like the best magician, she could pluck the details out of thin air. From Puccini to Machu Picchu, from Aldous Huxley to Winnie the Pooh she painted beautiful pictures with gay abandon. Some more elaborate than others.

She was particularly interested in the migration habits of North American bison and the history and origins of Canadian Indian totem poles. Her favourite piece was the decorative and strangely named Thunderbird House Post. I shuddered at the very thought and never brought up the subject again.

Madame Hardback also fine-tuned her card playing skills in the local Bridge club of which she was an honorary life member. Although she was no great fan of Omar Sharif. She never could quite get over the fact that the handsome figure from Dr. Zhivago (the moustachioed man she never got to marry) had the nerve to play such an illustrious game.

The tiny but quaint shop would not have been out of place in Dickensian London with its bottle glass windows, intricate patterned ceilings and poor lighting. The heavy entry door was carved oak, adorned with the finest antique hardware and had a huge bronze bell hanging above that Quasimodo would have been proud to ring. It was the sort of place one could spend endless idle hours sifting through the collection of leather bound masterpieces housed upon the shelves. Or better yet, scouring for that rarest of first edition books. Could even buy the cheaper paperback copies if one so desired. One could of course do all these things. Except I didn't. Only went there in order to peruse the new sales assistant. Lithe and sensuous Yvonne with her wild, windswept hair that teased as if she were forever running barefoot along a golden beach somewhere in the Caribbean. The same Yvonne who had once served with distinction behind the counter at the local St. Vincent De Paul Society and who held a bizarre fascination for Mae West, Buster Keaton and George Orwell. She took great pleasure in reminding me ad nauseum that nineteen eighty four was fast approaching and Big Brother and his eye in the sky would soon be the way of all things. I felt almost embarrassed to admit it, but the only Big Brother I knew was the one that Janis Joplin sang with.

Apart from the fact that she was as Australian as Aeroplane jelly and just as tasty (that is the only remote comparison between the two) Yvonne passed very well for a Scandinavian bombshell. A sort of Britt Ekland lookalike, but with a little less curvature and far more curls. And unlike her counterpart, she couldn't speak a word of Swedish. Which was perhaps for the better because I certainly couldn't.

With devious intent and to get into Yvonne's good books so to speak I fastidiously nurtured my secret *bibliophile* alter ego, even going so far as to purchase multiple copies of D.H. Lawrence, Ray Bradbury, J.P. Donleavy, Edmund Cooper and Joseph Conrad. If it achieved nothing else they would at least give me something to spruik about at the boring end of year work functions. Having thought long and hard about it, they might even open doors to other rooms. Then, if that course of action failed, I would be in a very strong position to start my own book repository.

Striking up a conversation for the first time with the girl from Kingswood Country[1], I blurted out in what must have appeared at that very moment to be pigeon English *"Let me guess, you must be an avid Pink Floyd listener. I can deduce that by the way you dress"*. Finishing with a broad smile, confident I had struck the magic chord. *"No"* she replied curtly, perhaps offended by my ridiculous remarks *"actually I prefer the Rolling Stones.[2] For better or worse they somehow bring out the devil in me."* I had never before been tongue tied by such a pretty Beelzebub. A large lump that proved very hard to dislodge, grew in my throat. So that was it I thought, believing I had ruined every possible chance of a meaningful relationship. *The end was here, before it even had a chance to start.*

On the contrary the opposite proved to be true. My profound words must have been the tonic the

---

1. *Also the name of an iconic Australian television sitcom starring Ross Higgins and Judi Farr*

2. *As Chris Rea was later to discover: only special girls from special places could possibly love the Rolling Stones. Stainsby Girls on* Shamrock Diaries* (9)

doctor ordered, for a few short days later she accepted my invitation to attend a Ross Ryan concert at the old Hordern Pavilion. I was a big fan of Ross Wilson, formerly of Daddy Cool fame and she secretly admired handsome thespian Ryan O'Neill, so Ross Ryan and his flying horse Pegasus was the almost perfect compromise.

However, my total infatuation with her charm and vital statistics was regrettably short lived. An impromptu meeting with her reckless, wanderlust family did not go down well at all and as I departed the claustrophobic corridors of Bruce and his associates for the wide open spaces and greener pastures, Yvonne took her magazines, her Mum roll on deodorant and melting marzipan moments and left Sydney far behind for the sunshine and surf life of the Capricorn Coast. A whole new world away. Too far at least for this bird to fly. I suppose it was her destiny.

Never heard from Yvonne again, except for a rough paper note pinned on the door:

Who knows where the time goes, where the future lies and who knows where the butterflies? Sent not with love and kisses, but only kind regards. The girl with the hazel eyes and broken lantern.

Nothing more no less. Nothing ventured nothing gained.

A LITTLE SOMETHING TO PASS THE TIME AWAY 5

IN WITH A SPORTING CHANCE

The Boxer (10)	Simon and Garfunkle	Bridge Over Troubled Water
We Are The Champions (7)	Queen	News Of The World
Tennis (5)	Chris Rea	Tennis
Speedway At Nazareth (7)	Mark Knopfler	Sailing To Philadelphia
Turn Of A Friendly Card (7)	Alan Parsons Project	Turn Of A Friendly Card

JUST AN OLD FASHIONED LOVE SONG

4th July Asbury Park (Sandy) (9)	Bruce Springsteen	Greetings From Asbury Park. N.J
Hollies	Another Saturday Night	
Here, There And Everywhere (10)	The Beatles	Revolver
Just Like A Woman (10)	Bob Dylan	Blonde On Blonde
The Air That I Breathe (9)	Albert Hammond	It Never Rains In Southern California
God Only Knows (10)	The Beach Boys	Pet Sounds

LET'S COVER THAT AND MAKE LOTS OF MONEY

Black Magic Woman (9)	Santana	Abraxas
Blinded By The Light (7)	Manfred Mann	The Roaring Silence

Without You (9)	Nilsson	Nilsson Schmilsson
Me And Bobby McGee (10)	Janis Joplin	Pearl
All Along The Watchtower (9)	Jimi Hendrix	Electric Ladyland

WHAT ABOUT THE ORIGINAL?

Black Magic Woman (7)	Fleetwood Mac	English Rose
Blinded By The Light (6)	Bruce Springsteen	Greetings From Asbury Park N.J.
Without You (8)	Badfinger	No Dice
Me And Bobby McGee (8)	Kris Kristofferson	Me And Bobby McGee
All Along The Watchtower (5)	Bob Dylan	John Wesley Harding

A BALLAD BORN OUT OF BETTER DAYS

The Weight (8)	The Band	Music From Big Pink
Man Of The World (9)	Fleetwood Mac	Original Single release
Ruby Over Diamonds (7)	Kashmir	Zitilites
Love Hurts (8)	Nazareth	Hair Of The Dog
I Want To Know What Love Is (8)	Foreigner	Agent Provocateur

WELCOME TO GUITAR CITY

| *Classical Gas* (9) | Mason Williams | The Mason Williams Phonograph Record |
| *My Old School* (9) | Steely Dan | Countdown To Ecstasy |

Layla (8)	Derek And The Dominoes	Layla & Other Assorted Love Songs
The Curse Of The Traveller (8)	Chris Rea	Dancing With Strangers
Private Investigations (9)	Dire Straits	Love Over Gold

54

BRIGHT RED LUCY
(GENTLEMEN, PLEASE START YOUR ENGINES)

Fumbling hands grope for sand in pockets, while somewhere overhead, rockets explode. We meet on the street where the lingering heat of long-legged girls in short skirts takes our fancy. Parading wares with a casual air and a come on look of disdain. Pick up your feet, better pick up your feet and move to the rhythm and groove. Baby said, you've just got to move to the rhythm and groove and dance to the beat of the drum.

Silly as it sounds, it was a car that struck my fancy and played havoc with my circadian rhythms. I might further add, not just any run of the mill car. No sir. This one was different. From the very moment we bumped into each other, it was love at first sight. I called her Red Lucy for want of a better name and at that particular point in time, caught in her mesmerising headlights and somehow thinking of the most tangerine of trees and marmalade painted skies[1] it seemed to be the perfect fit.

---

1. *Recalling that most psychedelic of Beatles songs* <u>Lucy In The Sky With Diamonds</u>* (9) *1967*

Mother, seeing the twinkle in my eyes and knowing where that just might lead me, said that it was an ill wind that blew nobody any good and really what was the point, as never was a car made that deserved the love of a man over that for a pretty woman. Now that thought alone made me a tad uncomfortable. Not one to hold a grudge, I squirmed momentarily, then smiled, content with the fact that to all great beliefs, there are indeed notable exceptions.

Lucy was a classic Studebaker Avanti. I think circa 1962 model. Built in the great American automobile tradition out of South Bend, Indiana. The finest pedigree. Vermillion red with a chassis to die for. A jaw dropping sleek metallic marvel embellished with silver dashboard, artificial leather seats and bright chrome wheels that glistened like diamonds in the dappled light. I had heard of such a clean machine[2] but had never before set eyes upon one.

Sparks flew from her vibrato twin exhausts every time she spoke. That was it. I could just picture myself cruising down the highway, wind at my back, radio turned up full volume playing palatable doses of Bachman Turner Overdrive or the dogged strains of Canned Heat. Where was that polaroid instant camera when you needed it ?

Baby, I'm a rich man in a poor man's suit was all I could mutter, trying hard to convince myself that this Lucy was indeed the genuine article. One hundred percent bona fide. The sentiment however overpowering, was sublime and warm as a woollen glove on a winter's morning. Then and there I knew where I was going and what I had to do. All I needed was a little time, spare money and a touch of providence to clinch the deal.

---

2. *Of course we all know about that fire engine in* _Penny Lane_* (10) *1967*

Hans Dieter Kaufmann, the thick bearded man with the bad Ted Mulry haircut and strong southern dialect, had giant hands. He was also the local mechanic, the right go to fellow, who knew about cars and other mechanical devices of note. Like most Germans before him it was in his blood. Indeed, somewhere along the ancestral lineage he may have had strong connections with Karl Benz or Rudolf Diesel. Maybe even Mr 57 Varieties, Henry Heinz himself. Nothing would surprise.

With a slight lisp that made it difficult for me to keep a straight face, he said it had (under the lid) one of the *finetht enginth* he had ever had the *pleathure* to have known[3]. In the same breath, he also mentioned something about cubic capacity and horse power that was meant to impress, but all it did was confuse the issue even further. But whichever way you turned the book and looked at it, the numbers sure sounded good. To add magic to the mystery he promised he would hold onto dear Miss Lucy, put her in cotton wool until I found enough cash for the deposit.

It was the best of possible offers and I believed him.

When I returned two weeks later she was gone, sold ingloriously to someone else who came up with the dollars sooner than I could. Never forgave Hans for that. And of course Lucy had slipped through my fingers and rolled into the mists of night. It was an abrupt end to what could have been a beautiful friendship.

That did it for me. I hoped Hans' haircut would come back to haunt him. I hoped whoever took Red Lucy gave her a good, safe garage to live in. After all, she deserved it.

---

3. *Similarities can be easily made with the barber in the corner shop, also referred to in* Penny Lane* (10) *1967 The Beatles*

My worst fears however were well founded, _Born To Be Wild_* (8)[4] had played out as a mere figment of my imagination. I guess I wasn't cut out for a nomadic life on the wide open road. But then again not many are.

By the way as a matter of public record, my first car was a stomach churning green 1963 Holden EJ sedan, 3 Speed Hydramatic transmission, single pipe exhaust, well-worn seats and white wall tyres.

Not much to get excited about and not exactly in the same league as Lucy.

---

4. _The classic highway drive time song by Steppenwolf. Music to an entire generation. Soundtrack to the movie Easy Rider_

55

ABSINTHE MAKES THE HEART GROW FONDER

Herbie, said Miles, it's time to let go, pack up our bags and run. Play me that jazz and I'll play you those rhythm and blues. Just put on your shoes and pull up your socks and shuffle along the road. I'll let you down easy, if you let me down slow. Yes everyone knows there's no place like home. And we've nothing to lose but our hearts and our souls.

M r Stardust[1] groaned and twisted my arm. He was an old friend with a screwed up sense of humour and said it hurt him more than it hurt me. I knew he wasn't joking, but from where I stood, I didn't believe a single word. Then he twisted a little more just to make sure he had my full attention. And when he conveniently mentioned something about song birds having flown, a species of duck named after a remote equatorial island and his favourite flavour of the month, my mind went into overdrive. How could anyone resist such a tempting treat? How could I resist? Then and there I had cinemascope visions. Thinking we were in for a marvellous culinary experience and great night out, the sort of Saturday

---

1. *This was my nickname for school friend and confidante Ziggy. Not to be confused with Alvin Stardust. Inspired by the David Bowie landmark album Ziggy Stardust and the Spiders from Mars*[*] (10) 1972

fare we had lately become accustomed to, I meekly surrendered. Enough said. He couldn't help but smile at my reaction.

It turned out I was half right. Well almost, anyway. Little did I know. And nothing whatsoever about the finer points of jazz or blues. Except for what I had casually scanned across in dust filled books. Or heard about along the notorious grapevine.

I had once worked with a man of many faces called Gregarious Greg who loved chewing gum, had a soft spot for dovetail joints and listened to Herbie Hancock, wild eyed Miles Davis and Thelonius Monk in his spare time. His favourite record was *Bitches Brew** (9). Which said a whole lot about the fellow. He also sang bawdy bar room ballads, played saxophone, piano and had a dextrous hand for mean honky tonk blues. But in the overall scheme of things, that counted for very little substance. Especially where I was concerned. My ignorance in all departments, knew no bounds. For sure and certain. That's where I came unstuck. That's where Mr Stardust came to the rescue.

I was soon to discover that he was not referring to a cosy, seductive kind of restaurant as such, even though Galapagos Duck was high on the evening menu. As were Dizzie Gillespie, Vince Jones and a host of other celebrities. This was quite a line up I countered and sure to keep the turnstiles spinning but where in the world was reliable Donovan Leitch when needed the most. Why had he not be given the keys to commence proceedings? Totally bemused, a whispered voice beside me responded, that by an accident of oversight he was not on the short list and probably never would be. Which perhaps given the nature of the establishment, was for the better.

By now, Mr Stardust's paint by number pictures had become much clearer, augmented by his hands and feet which were moving in rapid time to highlight his frustration at my total lack of integrity. It was he insisted, *nothing like* a folk club and there were *no long haired folk singers* on the agenda. I soon got the message. In triplicate.

You see, these were no ordinary times and this was no ordinary place. It was the Basement and we were fortunate enough to be there for its official birth year in 1972. In such a short space of time it had become the craziest jazz ticket in all of town. And virtual home to a who's who of A list high flyers who got their kicks not on dusty Route 66, but rather from an intoxicating brew of Monkberry Moon Delight[2].

The premises were by no stretch of the imagination large, so to describe the venue as bursting at the seams would be an understatement. The entrance was from street level via a flight of stairs that led down into what once must have been an old, illicit rum cellar or opium den. Kegs, barrels, hoops and pegs, as well as half-filled bottles and casks were lined up in neat rows along a stone rampart that formed part of the buildings original foundations. The entire lower floor had been converted into a veritable kaleidoscope of colour and sound. It turned out to be a claustrophobic music bowl complete with Beale Street appeal, lavish wall murals, stage in the round, café and bar. And lots and lots of smoke.

It was as close to Memphis as we had ever been.

---

2. *What this strange brew is I don't really know, but you can find some of your very own to taste test on the Paul McCartney album* Ram

The small, incongruous electric sign above the doorway should have read, *all who enter here, do so at their own peril,* for once inside that nicotine charged establishment, it was each man for himself. Which was fine if one chose to get up close and personal with a complete stranger of the opposite sex. Then it really was a case of consumer beware.

We however, were the lucky ones. Somehow by the sheer good fortune of knowing *King Pin* Kevin the jovial door bouncer and his nefarious crew, along with the promise of a few drinks thrown in for the special occasion, we managed to secure a small table in a tight corner next to the podium. Nothing too flash, but nevertheless, not far from where the live action was. And of course the Bewlay Brothers[3] were nowhere in sight.

After that and as for the rest of the night's events, I am afraid I cannot recall too much. People came and went. People famous and people salubrious and those trying to be somewhere in between. There were perfect caped crusaders with Cheshire cat grins, balancing trays between acts. Glow in the dark hour glass waitresses in nylon outfits that displayed all their finer points, flitted like nervous Bogong moths around the room. Caught on the summer breeze.

Our imaginations ran fast and wild and our bodies ran with them.

The time passed by in a haze of cocktail conversations, pristine pools of pina coladas and an overall frenzy of convivial music repertoire. Galapagos Duck took centre stage and an hour later departed, roasted to perfection and a lot thinner than when they arrived. What more could anyone ask?

---

3. *From Hunky Dory* (9) *David Bowie*

Perhaps Mr Stardust has better memories. Though from where I sat, somehow I doubt it. We left those dark recesses behind us, knowing Charlie Parker's secret was in no danger. At least not until our next scheduled visit to that wonderful underground palace of pleasure.

56

MEA CULPA

The funny girl in the raincoat with the sun bleached hair and a face full of freckles said, close your eyes and make believe I'm Marlene Dietrich. If you like I'll make believe you're Elvis. Well that suited me fine, but when she brought white roses and whisky instead of red wine, poor Marlene turned into sweet Caroline. Now she's no friend of mine and Elvis is dead.

Suffice it to say, I once had the pleasure to work for a brave band of merry men, in a fictional concrete forest, many long years ago. Please excuse me for some liberties taken and a little judicious sprinkling of poetic license added to the mix. But the truth is out there somewhere in the void and the characters depicted here are very real.

So it was my fledgling, formative years came and went in rapid succession, happily spent in the honourable company of H F. A and Wicks, a medium sized firm of Architects who occupied two large offices on the twelfth floor of an old Art Deco building in an imaginary city not too far from here. Diminutive patriarch Hector C. Fotheringay (who had changed his name by deed poll) was the founding figure behind the business venture that began way back in the mid nineteen forties or so. His ancestors were shrouded in tittle tattle and whispers and his legacy was now hidden in the shadowy mists of time. Whatever happened to Hector no one quite seemed to know, or for the better part of discretion they simply would not tell. He proved to be as enigmatic as Edwin Drood[1] and twice as interesting, but the subject though fascinating, was never mentioned again.

Larry Ignatius Annan, a mountain of a man and a college by the river old boy was the current principal and his esteemed partner was flamboyant Vivian Wicks. How they came to have met exactly, was uncertain, for the two were much like chalk and cheese and poles apart. In the office they kept their distance by tape measure and discretion and each knew the precise moment when to talk and when not to. Whatever the perception one had of the pair, their actions however skewed, seemed to work to the distinct benefit of the company. Perhaps that is the reason they never had a bad word to say about the other. In a who's who guide Larry could best be described as the cautious, silent type. Brooding and with a slight touch of ambivalence that no one seemed to mind. A well-read scholar and a traveller, who in his early days had visited the iconic institutions of Oxford and Cambridge as well as the Sorbonne in Paris. He had a certain Tibetan monk aura about his persona, a trait that was the envy of most. Whether it was the bald head or his perpetual inquisitive nature that made him seem so clichéd Kathmandu, no one could be quite sure.

He was much older than the other associates. Almost to the point one could say retirement would be a

---

1. *Published in 1870, The Mystery of Edwin Drood was the final novel by Charles Dickens.*

reasonable option. But Larry never contemplated such an absurd idea. Even at this late hour in his working life, he had much to offer his younger compatriots. His mind was sharp and precise when it came to buildings and modern architecture and his crossword solving feats unbounded. Larry was no one trick pony.

For hours he would wander around the office with reading glasses perched precariously on top of his head and ask to our great amusement, if anyone had taken them from his desk. He had a bad habit also, of misplacing them either on the handle of the kettle or even in the remote corners of the refrigerator. Some of the staff occasionally took great satisfaction in hanging them from the ceiling on giant rubber bands.

The office brouhaha did not detract from the obvious truth that everyone liked Larry and of course, Larry always generously reciprocated.

Never one to play second fiddle, especially around the women folk, Mr Wicks or Vee Dub as he preferred to be called, was always perfectly dressed. I think the Kinks must have had Vivian foremost in mind to provide inspiration to their song lyrics, as he was most definitely *A Dedicated Follower Of Fashion** (7) and a real, livewire north shore *Dandy** (6). Beau Brummel he may not have been, but there was a quaint, yet magnetic quality, something comparable to the bright spark of high heeled boys about him.[2] Nothing was ever in the wrong place, or looked as though it didn't belong. Not even his hair could be criticised. His preference in clothes was superior to most of his peers. He had a soft spot for Harris Tweed jackets or double breasted suits worn with light blue pin

2. *The Low Spark of High Heeled Boys** (9) *Traffic*

striped shirt, sterling silver cuff links and yellow bow tie. Occasionally he would surprise everyone and go for red, especially on those summer days spent supervising on site under the baking sun when the colour somehow matched his inquisitive face. He also preferred to wear thick horn rimmed spectacles, which we thought infused him with a certain Buddy Holly charisma. However unlike good old Larry's, they remained firmly affixed to his nose and ears via a long gold chain. Yes, Vivian could quite easily have fitted into the well-oiled, eccentric lifestyle of an English country lord.

Sadly, Vee Dub's (the obvious association with that famous German name garnered great attention among the more observant office staff) car appreciation and motoring expertise, did not equate to his immaculate taste in clothes. Not by a long shot. Strictly speaking when it came to engines, cams and drive shafts, he had no remote idea which side was up and which was down. Nor which was front or back. While careful as she goes, but always reliable Patrick Larke saw bright stars and drove around in the latest model Toyota Celica, complete with pop up headlights and leather seats, Vivian couldn't do much better than purchase the current motor vehicle sensation of its day. The car that was on everyone's lips, for all the right or wrong reasons. The car that promised the world and more. A brand spanking new Leyland P76. Fresh off the production line. Destined for glory or doomed to catastrophic failure.

Unfortunately it proved to be a lethal case of the latter. Vivian had bought himself a genuine one hundred percent stinker from the bottom of the box. A special piece of engineered fruit that drove and handled not unlike a government bus with square wheels and ultimately proved to have no intrinsic value whatsoever. Within a short twelve months or so the P76 was duly terminated, consigned to the gigantic scrapheap of automobile history. Pandora had spilled out its hideous contents. Try as he may, Vee Dub couldn't get them back in.

Larry on the other hand didn't have a flash motor car. He had more sense than that. *Anyway, never had any need for one* he said. Far more trouble than they were beneficial. So day in and day out, come rain, hail or shine, he caught the seven forty five am train to work. Sat in the same tattered seat at the same dirty window and read the Sydney Morning Herald without fail. A habit which to Larry just happened to be the safest and cheapest option of them all. That bugged Vee Dub no end.

In his spare time (of which there seemed to be a great deal) and for strictly therapeutic purposes, Vivian was a devoted cricket enthusiast always taking days off work or leaving the office early, whenever a test match was being played at the SCG. I am sure he would have much preferred to have had the life of a professional cricketer than that of an architect. At least that way, he would get to travel the world.

His favourite player was W.G. Grace, but for what apparent reason no one was ever quite sure. Perhaps it had something to do with the man's long beard and the colourful striped attire that appealed, or the fact that Mr Grace was a doctor with a wild, slashing blade made of willow instead of steel.

Vee Dub had a razor sharp wit and the eye of a hawk. Especially for the pretty, young ladies that always congregated around the tables at the annual architectural convention for excellence.

He would argue until blue in the face, that in business above all other things, it was only common sense to employ a stunning, well-formed distraction to occupy the front reception desk. Fingers crossed, one who could welcome his important clients with a broad smile and casual flutter of the eye. The kind who would take your breath away but give it back at the end of a glorious day. To reinforce the idea he drew 3D sketches in the air, articulating delicately about a large stone lioness gracing the entrance to a fine French museum. Imagine that, such a sight for all to see.

It was essential the secretary also wear the shortest skirt possible so that everyone entering the office couldn't help but notice such a great pair of legs. With more than a little input from his friend this of course would make our visitors keen to be the proud recipient of a home designed exclusively by Vivian W. We couldn't wait to get our order in.

You have to hand it to Vee Dub. He knew which side his morning toast was buttered. And of course the clever analogy with the lioness did not go unnoticed by those of us who thought we understood exactly what he meant. So to begin with, it was a simple choice really. A case of lights, camera then action and that's where Carol came into the frame. In all her technicolour glory.

Vivian rubbed his hands together. He could see the dollars rolling in like waves on Bronte beach. But he was oblivious to the bluebottles that came in with them.

Carol was about twenty two years of age and as beautiful a creature as ever walked this fair earth. She possessed little in the way of creative, think for yourself administration skills (though to be absolutely fair she was a good typist) or business acumen but what she lacked in diligence and expertise, she more than made up for in lucid gossip and exotic flair. With a subtle flick back of her auburn hair, she could sure muster up the numbers. The ones that really counted. Those customers that desperately wanted that exclusive one off design dwelling by the sea. Her endless talents in that department were unchallenged.

Why she didn't have a boyfriend was as perplexing a mystery as that of the Mary Celeste. God only knows how that could be humanly possible. Someone was missing out that was for sure and certain. Terry T. never backwards when it came to being forward, offered many times to take up the slack and fill the vacant role, but was always politely ignored. Opportunity never knocked again for hapless Terry. Unlucky for some we thought and lucky for the rest of us prepared to take a chance. Sadly no one ever did.

To add petrol to the office pyrotechnics, there was polaroid Rick, the man who dreamed two days ahead of anyone else without considering the consequences. Black and white photography was his specialty. He even thought of himself as somewhat of an Ansel Adams protégé minus the accent and the hat. Except of course, Rickety Split's mouth-watering landscapes were of a slightly different kind. They put a whole new spin on shapes, forms and function.

He was no accountant but it didn't take him long to do the sums and figure out the assets from the liabilities. Yes sir, Carol had the goods. If only he could get her over her indifference to deliver them. Out of desperation, he even promised a front page spread on the cover of *that* glossy men's magazine. He would make her a star he said and for a mere ten percent management fee. Which was a real bargain basement price when you come to think about it.

Carol was stunned at Rick's chutzpah. Not being the least bit concerned, Terry just smiled. He had seen and heard it all before and knew that Carol in addition to her curvaceous manifest, was not a girl easily led down the garden path. Rick's efforts to convert her to a *lifetime membership of the Hugh Heffner bunny association* hit a proverbial brick wall. The *Hit Where It Hurts, Promise Them Diamonds* theory failed to deliver when it counted the most. Needless to say, she never uttered a word to reckless Rick again.

Later that same month, Rick traded his faithful Minolta camera for a brand spanking new Leica, thinking it would bring about a well-deserved change of fortune. Somehow it didn't change a thing other than the weather. From that point on, a dark cloud seemed to hang perpetually above his head. A little worse for wear and suffering from a bad dose of goodtime Charlie blues[3], Rick promptly resigned from his job to search over the fence for greener pastures. In a moment of reflection, the rest of us breathed a huge sigh of relief.

Terry was our chief draftsman and more than a talented artist and designer. He had a unique way with pens and pencils, which sometimes bordered on the downright bizarre. Terry could fold sheets of paper into Origami artwork as quickly as you could say *Oh Carol*. By an unexplainable twist of genetics he also happened to be Peter Sarstedt's[4] doppelganger. Tall and solidly built, with head of thick black hair, large heavy moustache (that gave the impression it was glued on tightly above his lip) and to add the finishing touches he chose only the finest label seersucker ties to compliment his range of satin shirts.

---

3. *Danny O'Keefe* Goodtime Charlie's Got The *Blues* (7) 1972 from the album* O'Keefe

4. *Peter Sarstedt had a huge worldwide bestseller in 1969 with* Where Do You Go To (My Lovely) ?* (8)

One morning still carrying a hangover from Carol's rejection of his innocent advances and in a light bulb moment that refused to dim, Terry stepped forward, fists clenched tight like Moses on the mount and said with great conviction *"that girl is dangeroussss...."* His words trailing away into the distance. Red necks and retribution had brought it down to this. Even V. Dub, no matter how hard he turned the cheek the other way, had lately come to realise that most obvious of facts. The girl who once had been the angelic messiah had suddenly transformed into deadly Delilah Nightshade with a capital D.

Carol was just way too hot for her own good. I might add, a view not shared by the many wide eyed clients that continued to march through the front door in an incessant parade of passion and self-delusion. Only those who had to put up with her shortcomings and lack of enthusiasm for the job, had an axe to grind. Put bluntly, Carol was bored. She was bored after the first month of meeting, greeting and seating. After the second month it was nigh on catastrophic.

Once the phones stopped ringing and the typing was completed it was a case of read a book or write a novel. Or better still, come strutting into the drawing office to have a talk to the lads. Whenever that happened not a great deal of work got done. So it was no surprise that the long haired, boys are back in town collective often prayed for the old telephone switchboard to go on the blink. In order to get a glimpse of Carol, however fleeting, in her tight fitting Paisley print jumper and matching mini skirt that must have belonged to her younger sister. You could easily paint a picture. We certainly did. And therein was the nub. We had accumulated more than enough modern art to hang on the walls of the Tate gallery.

Everyone agreed that something had to be done to right the ship. The danger had to be eliminated at all costs. So Vivian, Larry and Patrick put on their best dinner suits along with their diplomat faces, then hummed and harred and plotted many a long hour between them. Even called a think tank meeting for the sake of it. How best to be discreet, without being obvious? They scratched heads and wondered, transfixed by the light of their blue lagoon, until a toss of a coin, further debate and procrastination decided the issue once and for all. At last the penny dropped and in true democratic process they bid *hasta manana* Carol and *bonjour* Sally Sermon. A change would be as good as any Roman holiday. This in itself was no bad thing. However, the total dissimilarity between the two was difficult to comprehend. Yet Sally's unfortunate surname said it like nothing else could. From that moment on, the place never quite had the contagious vibe and recklessness again. They disappeared as quickly as the scented fragrance of Carol's Chanel No.5.

I was fortunate enough to celebrate my twenty first birthday whilst still with the company. Put on a good old fashioned party for the occasion, to be held at a family friends place in Campsie. Eileen and Sam organised the seating and the catered food. I took care of the more important things such as the marquis, music and the alcohol. Sally came with her Gideon's Bible and logistics register to keep the entire proceedings on the straight and narrow. And who better to bring along than her lawyer boyfriend for good measure. The office larrikin was Max, a tall suntanned Queenslander from Townsville who had a bite far worse than his bark. Not known for his subtlety or non-invasive wit, Max whose fond nickname was

Meteor (a description borne in honour of the heavens, not the band) was totally unaware of Sally's prudent background and mild disposition. He decided to cordially invite just about everyone and anyone who wanted to sample the fine Johnny Walker and best bourbon that was on offer. This was a volatile mix that did not auger well for the guests.

In vivid scenes reminiscent of a take from West Side Story, the evening finished with strained vocal chords, broken windows and a badly broken nose. As for Max himself, he ended up at the local police station trying his very best to explain the night's sordid events. After some harsh words and a little subtle coercion from the duty sergeant, he agreed to pay for all the damages. No questions asked.

Weeks later, Max took everyone by surprise and without so much as a wink or a word, headed far north in his battered orange Kombi van, back to the sunshine high life and surf beaches he longed for. He was a dead set sucker for Norgen Vaaz, California girls and buxom Gold Coast meter maids.

I stayed with H.F. A and Wicks for twelve more months until the writing was well and truly on the bathroom wall. Difficult economic times forced an internal restructure and like myself most of the crew moved on..... perhaps hoping to one day bump into Carol somewhere on their journey to the promised land. What happened to the others I am not quite sure. Although Patrick I am reliably informed became a proud grandfather. In his spare time he bounced the children on his knees and told them bedtime stories about a jovial man, with a sharp wit who once owned a fabled motor car and travelled the world over in search of peace and love.

Larry retired, happy and content in the fact that he never purchased a lemon in his life. He took his myopia, drawings and mantra with him and headed back once more across the seven stormy seas.

As for convivial Vivian Wicks, perhaps he still watches his beloved game of cricket from the Bradman Stand perched high above the hallowed turf of the SCG, enjoying strawberries with cream and a glass of fine Burgundy Pinot Noir. Dreaming of that girl with the Colgate teeth no one could quite forget.

To that I say, three cheers to the good and generous Doctor Grace, wherever he may roam.

Hip hip hooray.

57

THE RIGHT PLACE BUT THE WRONG TIME

With a wink and a nudge he said for old times' sake, 'please kiss me quick, it's getting late. Soon it will be too late to stay'. Sitting here with the cold wind on my shoulders, wondering which way the road goes and which way the road turns. And will it ever lead me back where I belong? Just a town somewhere, someplace I've never been, where the neon gods stand and wait. Another song on the jukebox and fifteen minutes of fame is all it ever takes.

Long before Dexy and his Midnight Runners, even before the strident battle cries of Star Wars and The Empire Strikes Back, there was a certain wondrous, young lady who owned a black pair of lycra, Lolita leotards. A girl with plenty to offer except the kitchen sink, who didn't like James Bond action movies but adored pretty foxgloves, vibrant marigolds, butterflies and brain teasers. She married a handsome, swarthy prince, who worked long hours as a banker by day and sang in a blues band at night. Just to earn enough money to meet her high standards of discretionary spending. They resided in a big house together but she lived in a galaxy, far, far away. And yet it was as though

Mrs Vandenrocket had been here all along. Hiding in the shadows. Waiting for her special moment to shine.

Funny when you think about it, how some things in life never change. Even if you wanted them to. No matter how hard you push and pull. Some wishes just never come true.

Call it kismet, karma, déjà vu or call it down right plain ironic. Before we first set eyes on her, we had somehow managed to procure front row tickets to Neil Diamond's one and only sensational open air Sydney concert. The critics raved and said it was set to rival in intensity, his off the cuff performance in Los Angeles some years earlier. Unfortunately for those in the know, *come along and see me sometime at Moore Park* did not have the same grand appeal about it as Live at the Greek Theatre. Still, it was the best we could manage and for that we were forever thankful. Under threat of thunderstorms and rain it became our Hot August Night special interlude on the grass and the man who wanted to be Noah Kaminsky[1] but thankfully declined, turned out to be our best friend in more ways than one.

It was quite by accident, we happened upon petite Prudence Vandenrocket, resident of leafy north side Pymble via leafless downtown Hurstville. Bubbly and effervescent, Prudence was not your average, leave alone stay at home suburban housewife. God forbid, she was not in the least bit like the typical young newlyweds of her ilk who had nothing to say, precious little to do and too much time to do it in. Far from it. She was a firecracker of the highest order, had an insatiable bucket thirst for Veuve Clicquot, a taste for camembert cheese as long as it was

---

1. *Neil Leslie Diamond was born in New York City in 1941. He seriously considered using the alias Noah Kaminsky.*

from the south of France and to cap it off, talent to burn. More than enough pop and fizz to go around and who, just as a side interest, happened to have a fascination for none other than Mr Diamond out of the *Big Apple*.

Can you believe it, when we were introduced to Prudence, it was as if all our Christmas's had materialised at once. We had stumbled across a rose in a field of giant nettles.

However the situation at hand was no ordinary box of beer and skittles. We had a job to do. Sent at the eleventh hour on a hit and run reconnaissance mission to take measurements and pretty polaroids of the old sandstone house and its sprawling English garden. You see the Vandenrockets were keen to keep up with the Jones's and whoever else of importance and undertake some badly needed renovation and refurbishment work of their own. Only trouble was, Mr Vandenrocket had neglected to duly inform his wife of our imminent arrival that particular morning. Which was a shame really, as embarrassment and red faces all round might well have been avoided. Perhaps.

She was dressed (I use the word most loosely) for the occasion in a body hugging outfit that left nothing to the imagination. Particularly ours.

Apparently Prudence was a newly inducted member of the local fitness fraternity, though who she was instructing at that hour of the day, was anyone's guess. She was a sight to behold. Diligently practising her formidable breakfast routine. Without missing a single beat. One, two, three high kick, repeat, then twist, turn and genuflect. All at the same time. Which said a lot for Prudence. She certainly had a talent when it came to aerobics and acrobatics.

The tuneful strains of Crunchy Granola Suite*(8) reverberated around the rooms like an echo in an empty canyon. At that very moment we became frozen in our own minds. Mesmerised and mellow to the core, trapped in a dense fog not of our own making.

Outside, birds sang in the trees and the street dogs were baying for someone's blood. We looked at each other and decided then and there that it couldn't get any crunchier than this.

In hindsight, perhaps Prudence should have changed her name to Brandy, Candy or Cracklin' Rose. It seemed much more appropriate at the time.

After a long day under a cloudless sky, we packed up our protractors and book of logarithms and in the golden hours of the late afternoon, left that place less focused than when we first arrived and considering the difficulties encountered, more than satisfied that our assignment had been completed with great success. Prudence, oblivious to her surroundings, was still stuck in that galaxy far away, singing her lungs out and devoting heart and soul to Soolaimon*(8) and Brother Love's Travelling Salvation Show*(7). As for us, we were suffering from a severe case of traumatic work disorder. Vivid colours and images flashed before our eyes and we couldn't help but wonder where were the illusive Californian tree people when you needed them the most? Deep down, dear Prudence knew. So did Noah Kaminsky. Mr. Vandenrocket however, just didn't have a clue.

A few days later and a thousand light years from home, we were inducted into the office hall of fame and awarded the special Charlie Bronson medal for good conduct and bravery under extreme fire.

Without blinking an eyelid, in a gesture befitting Andy Warhol himself, we gratefully accepted.

After all, we deserved our fifteen minutes in the sun.

A LITTLE SOMETHING TO PASS THE TIME AWAY 6

THE WORD IS THE MESSAGE

Universal Soldier (7)	Donovan	Single Release and EP only
The Eve Of Destruction (7)	Barry Mcquire	Eve Of Destruction
With God On Our Side (6)	Manfred Mann	My Little Red Book Of Winners
It's Good News Week (5)	Hedgehoppers Anonymous	Jonathan King/ Hedgehoppers Anonymous
7 O'Clock News/Silent Night (5)	Simon and Garfunkle	Parsley, Sage, Rosemary and Thyme

INCIDENTAL INSTRUMENTAL

Albatross (7)	Fleetwood Mac	English Rose
Funeral For A Friend (7)	Elton John	Goodbye Yellow Brick Road
Flying (5)	The Beatles	Magical Mystery Tour
The Big Sleep In Search Of Hades (7)	Tangerine Dream	Stratos Fear
Telstar (8)	The Tornados	

POLITICAL PROSE AND POINTED BARBS

Hurricane (9)	Bob Dylan	Desire
Letter From America (6)	The Proclaimers	This Is The Story
Biko (6)	Peter Gabriel	Peter Gabriel

Shipbuilding (7)	Elvis Costello	Punch The Clock
Between The Wars (6)	Billy Bragg	Between The Wars (EP)

ROOMS WITH A VIEW IF NOTHING ELSE

Hotel Yorba (8)	White Stripes	White Blood Cells
Grand Hotel (7)	Procul Harum	Grand Hotel
Hotel Arizona (8)	Wilco	Being There
Chelsea Hotel No.2 (7)	Leonard Cohen	New Skin For The Old ceremony
Pentecost Hotel (7)	Nirvana*	Single Release

ONE HIT WONDERS

Driver's Seat (8)	Sniff N' The Tears	Fickle Heart
Radar Love (8)	Golden Earring	Moontan
Spirit In The Sky (9)	Norman Greenbaum	Spirit In The Sky
My Sharona (8)	The Knack	Get The Knack
Love Grows (Where My Rosemary Goes) (8)	Edison Lighthouse	Single Release

DARING ADVENTURES IN TRAIN SPOTTING FOR THOSE WHO PREFER CARS

Marrakesh Express (8)	Crosby,Stills and Nash	Déjà vu
Trans-Europe Express (7)	Kraftwerk	Trans-Europe Express
Last Train To Clarksville (7)	The Monkees	The Monkees
Rock Island Line (8)	Lonnie Donegan	Single Release
City Of New Orleans (8)	Arlo Guthrie	Hobo's Lullaby

IMAGES OF THE CITY

Summer In The City (7)	The Lovin Spoonful	Hums Of The Lovin' Spoonful
Waterloo Sunset (9)	The Kinks	Something Else
The Road To Hell Pts 1 and 2 (9)	Chris Rea	Road To Hell
Distant Lights (7)	Burial	Burial
The Suburbs (7)	Arcade Fire	The Suburbs

58

YOU PICKED A FINE TIME TO
LEAVE ME IRENE

I have walked each corner of this room without you. I have watched red sunsets dip and wane through softly faded curtains and counted the countless mountains on the moon. I have held the tethered trails of stars at night, within my trembling hands and kept the turning seas at bay. I have waved back these moments much too soon and listened to every heartbeat slip away. Then die alone. Without you.

Back then things were different. I was a fresh faced Don Quixote without horse, trying to find my way in the world. Straight out of high school, I was soon to find out that the next few years would test out the very frailties of mice and men. In short one could only describe them as a metaphysical haze. A bit like smoke covering troubled waters. Somewhere along the way old friendships diminished. New friendships and challenges landed on the doorstep. Normally sane people in a spasm of weakness, ravelled and just as quickly unravelled. The piece of string we had been holding on to suddenly got knotted. Danny married Anne who was a close friend of Wendy. Gary married Wendy. Gary got divorced then remarried.

Wendy moved on to settle down with a shoe salesman, have lots of kids and live happily ever after. That was the last we heard from her. Peter W went on to marry Kerry and they would have enough kids to form a platoon. Mary came and disappeared like a spring breeze blown across a melting glacier and Norm dated so many girls I lost count, until he met and subsequently said his vows to Judy. It got so complicated that by comparison, Rubik's pesky cube of many colours was easier to solve than the sticky mess we found ourselves in. Confusion became the vast new order and the new order took no prisoners.

Out of a grey smudge on the far horizon, Irenka dropped into my field of vision and suddenly things became a whole lot clearer. Of impeccable Polish stock with questionable ancestral roots going all the way back to Kadlubek[1], she was bright, slim, attractive and to further complement these assets, she also turned out to be a great cook. Her European cuisine was simply irresistible. Especially the slow cooked, giant dumplings that simmered like moon rocks in the pan and the powerful borscht brew with mushrooms that once eaten became a case of twice shy.

I was lucky enough to meet Irene on my daily commute into the big smoke. We caught the same train every morning. It seemed almost inevitable that from such humble beginnings we would strike up a relationship that in hindsight was as straight and narrow as the railway tracks we rode each day.

Irene worked as a secretary for a large law firm and had a discreet but ill fated menage a trois with the fine arts. It might have been because of her heady days spent at the

---

1. *Wincenty Kadlubek was elected Bishop of Krakow in the year 1207.*

Conservatorium of Music that she did not like her job and was somehow forever caught up in grandiose dreams of strutting the light fantastic on some stage in London or New York. Drama or musical productions would be fine, whichever one, Irene was not fussed. I came to the obvious conclusion she should have taken up a career as a performer at the Moulin Rouge. It was criminal to see her long legs were wasted sitting behind an office desk.

When it came to interests and hobbies, there was a total lack of commitment on her part. She could not fire up her engines for just anything. Except maybe for ballroom dancing and old romantic movies. The sort grandmother would get teared up over. Her favourite was _Casablanca_, which she had already seen more times than I cared to remember. What on earth she liked about it she never did say. Although I suspect it may have had something to do with female hormones or perhaps a secret unhealthy desire for Humphrey Bogart in his overcoat and hat. She also had a chronic Robert Redford fixation, so _The Sting_ was high on her top one thousand bucket list. As for Irene's Broadway taste, Stephen Sondheim was flavour of the month. Which was probably as good a reason as any to catch up on the terrific production of _A Little Night Music_, showing at the newly opened Her Majesty's Theatre. A few days later it was my turn to reciprocate. With some amount of trepidation, Irene agreed to go along and see the very talented Reginald Livermore perform his highly controversial one man destruction act, _Betty Blockbuster Follies_ at the Balmain Bijou. Never could get over the sight of Mr Livermore, fitted out in black nylon stockings and floral cleaner's cap, swinging precariously on a trapeze high above the auditorium. That rascal _Captain Jack_* (8)[2] was never quite the same again. Neither was Irene.

Things were good while they lasted, but I think Irene and I had oblique hemisphere interests. Hers were firmly trapped in the icy polar north, mine were aimlessly wandering the vast oceans of the south, in search of hidden treasures under a wide blue sky. We were at opposite ends of the spectrum. I wondered was my fashion sense really at fault? Had the wide, bell bottomed trousers and Elton John platform soled shoes I insisted on wearing, created a rift? The chasm just kept getting wider and wider. Until I fell into my own grand canyon. Perhaps it was written in the tea leaves or someone, somewhere along the way had given me the wrong road map.

I was too young or she was too old. Maybe I wasn't cut out for a simple village life with Polish sausage and dangerous vodka on the menu. And there were far too many ifs, buts and maybes to consider. Too many for comfort. Then to complicate matters further, along came a tall, handsome stranger. Straight out of some parallel nightmare universe to sweep her off her size six feet, who promised his best summer wine and a suitcase lined with stars. Enough to match those that twinkled in her eyes. Sounded promising enough. Instead all she got was Kentucky moonshine and a barrel full of rainy days and Mondays. They might have shared the same short back and curly hairstyle, but his was a different wavelength. Irene deserved better.

The last I saw, she was heavily pregnant standing on Central Railway Station, waiting for that train to come

---

2. _For those readers unfamiliar with the works of Billy Joel, Captain Jack can be found on his excellent second album The Piano Man* (8)_

along and whisk her away to god knows only where. In search of that elusive rainbow's end. That tall, dark stranger who had taken her heart and a whole lot more, now but a fading memory in the distance. As the lights cascaded from her narrow shoulders and the arrival clock clicked over two pm, she disappeared in a cloud of smoke that had whipped up out of the shadows. Nearby, a familiar lament cut a swathe through the open door of a small sidewalk café. Across the rain drenched streets, the ghost of Janis Joplin assaulted my senses. The words of _Me and Bobby McGee_[3] seemed to rise and resonate in sad irony. Those windscreen wipers working overtime.

I hope Irene avoided Baton Rouge. I hope Irene found that pot of gold.

---

3. _Me and Bobby McGee_* (10) 1971 _Janis Joplin. Original words and music by Kris Kristofferson_

59

THE PLOUGHMAN BRINGS GREAT PROVIDENCE

I often think of mushrooms growing in the pines,
scented flowers on the vine and sweet, red wine.
The taste of summer on your lips, the soft caress
of fingertips and you beside me in the purple sun
kissed meadow.

How we spent hours toiling in those green, furrowed fields. So many, I think I lost count along the way. Too many long hours in the sunshine measured at a cost. And all because of strawberries. The fat juicy kind that demanded a great deal of loving care and constant attention. The very same that were destined for market or at the very least to be consumed by our voracious appetites. Verushka's only daughter Anna played havoc with our hormones. She might have garnered all our naughty thoughts and flights of fantasy, however it was those good old strawberries that got our blood, sweat and tears and then some. But boy it was worth it.

True to her proud heritage, Verushka proved herself a hard taskmaster. She had to be I suppose, having grown up in a small isolated village (whose name I cannot begin to pronounce) somewhere in the vast expanses of the Ukraine. At one time long ago, she was young and carefree. The special, blue eyed girl with tussled hazel hair, which was as wild as the cold breeze blowing out of the Urals. Now, the hard life and the passing of the years had taken their toll and battered her fragile beauty, but never once dimmed her spirit.

At sixteen she had run away and married a handsome Red Army Officer from Minsk (almost twenty years her senior), who had served his country during the siege of Stalingrad. Grainy photographs of *tato* (as we fondly called him) decorated the walls and nooks of the cosy sitting room. Complete in uniform with medals proudly displayed on his jacket, his smile captivated any audience.

In his native Belorussia and before his enlistment, Tato had been a cobbler's apprentice. After the war he immigrated with his young bride to Australia in search of a better life and found a job as a fitter and boilermaker on the New South Wales railways. This required him to work long and arduous hours, yet still somehow he managed to maintain a shoe repair business, which he operated out of a cramped but never the less comfortable garage. It contained a plethora of metal tools and other strange implements which he said were essential to his trade. Large saws and scythes hung on the walls and clattered each time the wind blew through the open door.

I suppose they came in handy for something. Though for what exactly I was never quite sure. Tato often remarked they kept the wrong type of people away. "*In business*" he often said, "*there is no such thing as trust, only bad behaviour and consequence*".

Tato stored his very own pickles and onions. Hundreds of them fermenting in jars of every shape and size. Lined up in neat little packages on splintered wooden shelves. There was enough fine picklery contained within those walls to feed a small platoon.

Mamochka Vera was the brains trust and kinetic force of their symbiotic partnership. Everyone except Tato knew who wore the pants. She persisted and insisted and then hounded him more like a rampant boar than a beloved wife, until he finally agreed that they should buy a farm holding (twenty five acres of prime real estate) on the outskirts of Sydney. After that, he always bragged it was his brilliant idea to purchase a special parcel of dirt from which they could make some revenue on the side. Vera crossed her heart and gritted her teeth and dug in for the long haul.

They would build a new home, with four spatial bedrooms instead of three and enjoy their idyllic pastoral years together. Arguing side by side as only the happiest of couples do.

Vera pencilled in dairy cattle. Sure it was the sensible thing to do. Tato cursed. He liked lamb roast and thick wool and therefore fancied sheep. So in true Russian democratic process, Tato drew Vera's short straw, thereby avoiding all out conflict and cattle it was. Good stock too. Mostly fatted up Friesians for the quality of their milk.

To sweeten the final piece of the pie, it was essential to have some vegetables and other desirable produce to sell to the local market. Tato in his wisdom, declared potatoes and tomatoes (which reminded him of the good old days before the war) were the way to go. Stubborn Vera much preferred pumpkins, cabbages and lettuce along with bright red strawberries in lots and lots of pretty rows.

So it came as no surprise that Vera got her way once again and strawberries they grew. Tato was convinced a despicable conspiracy had taken place and said the Bible was to blame.

On the first day God fell out of bed in a fine mood. A bright idea hit him.

So in his wisdom he made the heavens and the earth and said it was good.

And god made the cattle and the strawberries and also said it was good.

Then God smiled upon the market gardeners.

God liked strawberries. Which was more than enough encouragement for Vera.

God however, no matter how clever, had nothing to do with the huge shed that miraculously seemed to sprout up in the middle of the paddock almost overnight. The eighth wonder of the world. By anyone's imagination, a most splendid wooden and iron palace with plenty of room for all the machinery and other items of equipment. Plus, eleven pigs, two goats, one Shetland pony and four fat cows. More than enough space for those creatures great and small.

Vera had us to thank for that masterpiece of human engineering.

Going home at sunset, tired and weary to the bone, we could hear the words of our dear atom heart mother ringing in our ears, *'just work hard each day and then the rest of your life is but a soothing breeze'.* Believe me she would know.

Then before we had time to crank up the 8 track cartridge player, before the next new harvest fell, somewhere between lust and bravado, Anna resisted temptation and finished her dental studies with a distinction and honourable mention from her boss.

And not one among us ever stooped so low as to pick those bright red berries again.

60

DRIVER IN WHITE SEDAN

She waits for me in wine dark open waters

There was no moon and the high beam of the car skipped along the gravel road. Through the cold crisp air the halogen lights cut sharp as steel through butter. At first there was nothing. Then out of the darkness that stretched far ahead, they came half blurred and silent, as if from nowhere. Rising slowly to meet us, entwined in the fingers of a white, insidious fog. And all the while in the black night sky high above, the great star fires that had burned so brightly, extinguished themselves. Each one by precious one, until just before the dawn had sketched its morning colours over the landscape, they were gone.

We yawned. Tired and stretched almost to the point of exhaustion.

With nowhere else to go we sat motionless, waiting for a sign.

Then they came marching onward, hanging on the slight breeze that blew from the west. Stayed there in the rear view mirror but for a brief moment only to disappear before returning to somehow rearrange themselves in strange glowing patterns.

Those same unknown ghost faces that had haunted us all along.

Until at our journey's end, transfixed beyond further distraction, we became attached to each other in time, between two single points. Strung along a line with no beginning and no end.

We knew then, as the red tail lights we had been following now began to fade, our minds would surely come to balance on some phantom edge in that other lonely place.

In that last twinkling space between dimensions.

61

ALL WE EVER WANTED
(WAS TO MAKE MOVIES)

The sidewalk cafes swim in the summer heat. Bare chested Latin lovers with their slick back hair and pointed shoes, don't miss a beat as they strut past. Side by side, they effortlessly glide with nothing to hide but their souls. Then in the wink of an eye, they're gone and we are left behind to pick up the pieces.

Not that anyone was counting, but as best I can recall it was nineteen hundred and seventy five as that old reliable black crow flies and great things were expected from us. One Zigmund J and myself that is. Together with a few other notable associates who had their minds firmly set on becoming celluloid heroes. Or at least would go down fighting in the attempt.

It was the end of a wet and most forgettable summer and the start of a brand new journey to an as yet undetermined destination. I had just turned twenty three and was a victim of my own imagination. Caught in a sort of monochrome limbo halfway between here, there and the remote stretches of the Kalahari, I was on the prowl, searching for bright ideas and a whole new direction. And not much else it seems.

So it transpired that unforeseen events and the alignment of the planets brought us together. For better or for worse. And not one of us gave a damn.

Without warning, Ziggy's once deep and spiritual partnership with his first true sweetheart had deteriorated to the point of no return. He soon found himself in a state of flux. Caught betwixt a pebble and a hard place. This was no situation for the fainthearted. Then, harsh reality hit home like a hammer on a walnut and somehow through the mayhem, _The First Time Ever I Saw Your Face_* (7) took on a new meaning, even though the images of _Play Misty For Me_[1] had long since vanished into the sunset. Ziggy was determined to prevent a repeat of those tragic events and rather than be a subject of the movies, he turned to making them instead. His intentions were both honourable and admirable. The stuff of dreams and castles in the air. All fluffy cotton clouds with dollar linings and harbouring aspirations to be recognised alongside such Hollywood luminaries as Victor Fleming, Samuel Goldwyn and Stanley Kubrick. If only he could be that lucky. But as it turned out, luck didn't have a say in it.

Also Sprach Zarathustra was never far from Ziggy's mind set and at this point in time, it seemed as if we were cut adrift in an endless vacuum, stuck somewhere among a myriad stars. Rocket men from Mars come home to roost. Elton John and good old Hal the computer sure had a lot to answer for.

Like a badly drawn tattoo on someone else's arm our motto was inked in blood. _Children of the revolution the world over, stand up and be counted. For tomorrow might be too late._

---

1. _The 1971 Clint Eastwood movie_

That then is the beginning of this story. Or the final act. The denouement. Whichever you may care to believe.

Ross winged it as a big corporate wheel in Sydney's famous North Shore social circles and had (so we were informed) a reliable contact high up in the ABC hierarchy. It subsequently came to light that the television network was on the lookout for local talent to produce and direct authentic Australiana movie dramas. Something in the vein of *Rush*[2] or the much acclaimed early period piece *For The Term Of His Natural Life*. Anything worthwhile that could whip up a storm and get the cash registers ringing. All proposals would be welcome.

Ziggy was right in the moment. With the chance to be caught in the spotlight. Steadfast and stoic in his *I want to be as good as Francis Ford Coppola* moment and experimenting with Super 8mm film and collage techniques like Timothy Leary on a bad trip. He was ready and primed to develop and direct a story which could be turned into a veritable blockbuster. A stepping stone to the walk of fame boulevard. Such was his confidence.

He was determined to shoot footage with amateur and professional actors alike in the rugged bushranger country of New South Wales. Forbes and Grenfell he said would be ideal. Gary S. with his fascination and predisposition for collecting antique firearms was to be a major player along with Gary G. and a few other slick stalwarts and hangers on. The road crew, actors, costumes and locations were prepared and set. To get the show underway all that was needed was a working title, adaptable screen play and good management to help expedite proceedings.

---

2. *ABC Television series produced between 1974-1976 (26 episodes in total). Set during the Victorian Gold Rush of the 1850's*

It was then, *greased lightning* John, who unfortunately would turn out to be more grease than lightning, materialised almost out of nowhere. As if he had been especially sent to earth for this occasion. He had known Ziggy from his early university days. Like a barnacle to a boat he stuck at what he knew best, emitting large volumes of hot air. Now he was Ziggy's right hand man. The front seat driver of this machine. A still slightly green behind the ears numbers player and fund raiser of some repute. In the cut throat, dog eat dog entertainment world, he did however know who was who and what was what and where the cream rose to the top. He was also keen to show off his special aptitude for media PR, particularly to impresario Ross. So when John, whose knockout sister was dating a cameraman from Channel Two, suggested we could preview our film at a cocktail party function he would organise strictly to impress the powers that be, we thought the odds were definitely stacked in our favour.

By a simple process of deduction, mathematical probability and a round of darts we came to the inevitable conclusion that only six degrees separated us from Ross and everyone else on the entire planet. How much more up close and personal could one possibly get without being related to the man himself, was too frightening to even contemplate.

We placed a lot on our assumption that nepotism and narcissism was the magic key to our success. We just had to sign, seal and deliver the genuine article. Surely not a difficult assignment. That's where I came on board. Brash and bold, full of stars and trumpets and eager to make a mark far bigger than any ordinary blemish.

A few months earlier, I had put the finishing touches to a modest short story of fiction, which upon further scrutiny had the possibilities of being turned into a screen play for an amateur movie project. Ziggy with director's cap planted firmly on his head, jumped at the idea and even more importantly John (who was a major shaker in the entire process) thought it had potential. It should therefore be adapted to suit Ziggy's plans and put into production as soon as possible. Thus it came about, *A Long Way To Fall* was born. We marked our spot on the map with an X and headed off in search of hidden gold.

The evening started well enough, disguising what was yet to come. To fix the mood, fireworks exploded in a cloudless sky. Isabelle said she had an itchy palm, which we all mistook for an omen of overblown proportions. In the packed gallery, a four piece Muscovite ensemble played a musical smorgasbord incorporating the very best of Bach, Beethoven and Liszt. To make things interesting and add a little spice to the proceedings, a bikini clad girl with a tattoo of a moon and star just above her naval, appeared from a large ice topped cake like a startled white rabbit from some cheap magician's hat. Canapés and camembert passed around on an endless parade of plates, as the guests mingled and jingled on the terraces. They drifted in and out of the enormous rooms, clutching crocodile leather handbags and Ralph Lauren wallets, making all the right noises in all the wrong places. So far so good. That is, until several gin slings and margaritas later and not long after the clock struck nine, events began to turn sour. And when Ross did an unexpected backflip and failed to show, we knew we were in big trouble. To compound matters even further, our distinguished MC who looked a dead ringer for W.C. Fields the morning after the night before, took on a bad case of laryngitis and just at the most interesting part, when the roar of the crowd subsided to a whisper, the movie reel jammed, refusing to cooperate any further.

It was breakneck speed downhill from that point. We were on board the Titanic and sinking fast. Not even the brave band and the swinging hipsters could save us now.

Our dreams evaporated into the mists of embarrassment before a blow could be struck.

A Long Way To Fall suddenly turned into *a nightmare place to crawl,* taking on a chilling scenario that would never see the light of day. Red faced, drained of every ounce of enthusiasm and hope, we hurriedly departed the scene as even then amidst the turmoil, Frank Sinatra crooned something about being twenty one and having a very good year. If only there was some truth in his wild ramblings.

The irate guests and dignitaries demanded a full refund and Ziggy was left contemplating what might have been if only… and where on earth *greased lightning* John had gone in our special hour of need. I think he must have caught the early train.

As for me, all these years later I'm still the king of wishful thinking, hoping someone with a good eye and sympathetic streak will take on board my forgotten screen play. Fingers crossed.

Steven Spielberg would be nice.

62

ONE SPARK DOES NOT A BONFIRE MAKE

4ᵗʰ July, Asbury Park (Sandy)* (9) 1973 Bruce Springsteen / The Hollies (Cover Version)

Her old man said. Sat her on his knee. Listen to these words sweet child or you'll make a fool of me. You've gotta give it what you've got and if you don't have a lot to give, then you've sure got a lot to love. It made sense.

Up and down the long business corridors of mirth and corporate good will, everyone referred to *L* as *Le Opal* because he was a real gem and extremely difficult to find. Especially when needed the most. *Le Opal* the man from Hong Kong, with fire in his eyes, a haystack hairdo and belly to match, who had a real flair for disappearing at the wrong time also happened to be *A's* younger brother, which sort of gave him a kick start when it came to discussions about the fairer sex.

Thanks to a matter of good fortune, Sue Strangelove didn't work for *A.C.* But *L* wished she did. He wished every morning and he wished every night. Pleading to Confucious for words of wisdom in his desperate hour of need. He did whatever he could to make the impossible happen, always trying to dangle a carrot she couldn't possibly refuse. *A* had seen and heard enough, mildly remonstrated and said she was way out of their league. In other words it came down to the hard facts of simple economics-they couldn't afford her. And that should be the end of the story, full stop. Which was a real shame and as good an excuse as any. *L* never forgave *A* for being such a cheap skate and of course *A* with his usual, unflappable charm didn't give an owl's hoot. Brotherly love is a strange creature.

Sue held a cushy job with an industrial accountancy firm on the floor below and thought it was a blessing in disguise. Expatriate Jon English, long since removed from the old dart, had regular liaisons with some theatrical high fliers two levels up. He too thought it a sign from the heavens and with humble reverence promptly accepted the plumb part of Judas Iscariot in the latest production of Jesus Christ Superstar. He soon left the building and its memories far behind and never once looked back in anger.

It was a keen observation on my part that Sue had an acute fashion sense and was always impeccably attired, befitting her status. She was also extremely well endowed in the physical attribute department and the envy of all the other, less fortunate *Twiggy built girls with lucky legs* who happened to work on the same floor. Jealousy was a curse and those who knew her gave her the odious nickname Perky Parton. Which I always thought was a little harsh and somewhat unkind. Dolly Parton really didn't have much to worry about in those stakes.

Everybody wanted Sue to be their exclusive secretary. *L* had no secretary, just a few filing cabinets left to gather dust in the corner of the room, a broken Swiss clock he bought from a one eyed Cantonese celebrity in China Town, a rusted army knife with a missing corkscrew and a pilot's license recently attained with honours plus bar from the local aeronautical school for daredevil practitioners of the unstable kind. This latter feat sat well with most of the young ladies who seemed suitably impressed by joysticks and cockpits. But unfortunately not Sue. Sue was difficult to please at the best of times and never could see rhyme or reason why anyone should want to fly in a large passenger airplane with two pilots, let alone rush themselves around in a flimsy single engine Piper Cherokee. When you look at it that way, it made for a sound argument.

It was no secret, I liked Sue. A lot. Enough to be a distraction, but not enough to be considered dangerous. It was difficult not to be impressed with her demeanour and precocious talent. In addition, her stenographic credentials were first class. She was kind, generous to a fault, a very proficient violin player and a flash hand when it came to keeping cryptic notes and diaries. As such, Samuel Pepys had nothing on Sue. She had a diary for almost every possible occasion and circumstance. One for shoes, one for clothes and yet another put aside for friends and special affiliations. She also had a brown belt in martial arts. As well as a huge male companion, who was proud of the fact he himself had acquired a number of black belts from Gucci, for good measure.

This pleased Sue no end. And of course the boyfriend looked after Sue very well. But mostly it was she who took care of Robert. That suited most people fine, but funnily enough not L.

L was in a right state and lingered an awful long time for Sue, never quite sure what to do or what to say. He was forever tongue tied for words. But the more the man lingered, the more things stayed the same. Somehow without even trying he could always find lumps in his porridge. *L* also longed a lean time for Sue. The greater he longed the greater she leaned. You see Sue was smart as much as she was honest and said her only wish was to be stranded on a desert island with nothing but a straw skirt, coconuts and Robert. But not with *L*. Who it might be said missed out big time. One could say *L* got the run around from Sue. We could all read the signs, the raw prawn needed cooking but somehow *L* got lost in the trees. Those acrobatic displays of dash and daring consigned to the waste bin of human kindness. Sue was so far out of reach like a planet in someone else's orbit, she may as well have been an extra-terrestrial from Venus with impaired vision and green skin.

So it was to be, that never the twain would meet.

L collected all sorts of wonderful things, giant and minute, square and round and was a hoarder of some notoriety. He had two cars, a fine stallion of a horse and an Old English Sheep dog that never answered back and had not the faintest idea if it was coming or going. A bit like *L*. However it was a small white Nissan motor van that took pride of place in the *A* and *L* household. You know the type. Japanese built. All components in their rightful place. Very light weight. Long from front to back and higher than it was wide. In a strange way it sort of complemented their mind set. The vehicle unfortunately, proved unstable at the best of times but more so when fully loaded with bales of hay and other extraneous goods. And especially when going around corners at the speed *L* drove at. *A* could only close his eyes, cross his legs and pray for small mercies. Only ever went in the thing when it was absolutely necessary and then only after ensuring his insurances were fully paid.

A never did quite understand how the hell *L* ever managed to buy a plane let alone fly a plane. *L* just laughed. He must have had the controls on auto pilot.

A and *L* played ping pong. Although I think they preferred to call it the subtle art of complex aerial manoeuvres. There was something about that white plastic ball that drew them both in. I am sure that sooner or later if they had kept at it, they would have represented the Chinese Olympic Team.

On most weekends the brothers hosted the Mah-jong Club knockout tournament. Trouble was, *A* and *L* refused to stick steadfast to the gentleman's rules and regulations, which as to be expected caused great angst and panic amongst the other participants. Sadly, the club was short lived.

They also liked to visit the famous tea houses and apothecaries in down town Dixon Street and dine at the exclusive M Club where *A* was an honorary life member. For some inexplicable reason *L* was never allowed to join. *L* was not happy with his lot and said prejudices were the bane of the world and refused to believe it might have had something to do with the herbal medicine or the Tarot cards he used.

After taking care of business with *A, L*, Ken and Lee for a couple of months I realised that the only thing Chinese that agreed with me was fireworks. Especially on New Year's Eve. Catherine Wheels were my favourite, perhaps because they made a whooshing noise and moved in bright, pretty circles and never really went anywhere.

Somewhere along the telegraph wire, I heard *L* was still on the lookout for that bright elusive butterfly of love. But not one called Sue. That was a bridge too far.

A LITTLE SOMETHING TO PASS THE TIME AWAY 7

TRY THESE AS A LAXATIVE

Just A Little (8)	Beau Brummels	Introducing The Beau Brummels
Treat Her Right (8)	Roy Head	A Letter From Vietnam
Save My Soul (7)	Wimple Winch	
A Well Respected Man (8)	The Kinks	Picture Book
She Comes In Colors (7)	Love	Da Capo

THE BEAST (NOT THE BEST) OF THE BEE GEES BEFORE DISCO

How Can You Mend A Broken Heart (9)
I Started A Joke (10)
Massachusetts (9)
New York Mining Disaster 1941 (8)
World (7)

EVEN (CAT) STEVENS

Hard Headed Woman (7)
Lady D'Arbanville (8)
Father And Son (10)
Sitting (8)
Oh Very Young (6)

THE STRANGE CASE OF SIMON MINUS GARFUNKLE

Fifty Ways To Leave Your Lover (7)
Mother And Child Reunion (9)
You Can Call Me Al (8)
Take Me To The Mardi Gras (7)
Graceland (8)

NOT SO CLEAR WATER AS CREEDENCE IF YOU LIKE

Suzie Q (7)

Sailor's Lament (8)

Molina (8)

I Put A Spell On You (8)

Run Through The Jungle (8)

THEY CALLED HIM MISTER DWIGHT (BUT THAT JUST MAKES ME GLAD HE CHANGED HIS NAME)

Blues For My Baby And Me (10)

Daniel (8)

Mona Lisas And Mad Hatters (8)

Rocket Man (9)

Don't Let The Sun Go Down On Me (8)

MARK KNOPFLER'S FAMOUS HEAD BAND ANONYMOUS

Cannibals (6)

Sailing To Philadelphia (8)

El Macho (7)

Speedway At Nazareth (7)

Postcards From Paraguay (5)

63

THE OLD WORLD AND THE NEW WORLD

How I miss you in the morning. The way you smile, the way your pretty hair falls across your face. The little things most of all. That count. The way you shiver when it's cold. The way you hold your grace. It's just the little things. But most of all, I miss you in the morning light.

On the day he died she cried no tears of loss. Elizabeth had no deep remorse and she vowed there would be no sad farewells. Nor angel trumpets blown. She knew that soon it would be time to leave the old world and the old lifestyle behind forever. Never more to be revisited. To be carried along by a new breeze that even now was blowing through her bones like an unfamiliar ghost.

This would be a restart. Another beginning of her heart and soul.

In that death moment unfurled. That struck not with the clean precision of a surgeon's knife, but with the impact of a hammer. One that merely dulled the senses and brought a soft ache inside. As if the dense invisible fog that had attached itself to her and been a part of her all her life, had now been stripped away. Layer by single layer like the silver skin of an onion.

She closed the door and stepped outside into a different kind of light. For the very first time, alone without him.

It was early December and it was snowing. The soft flakes brushed against her cheeks. She could hear something breathing through the branches of the skeleton trees. It was cold and getting colder by the minute. But she did not care. There was an overpowering certainty about the whiteness that stretched far and away, further than the narrow avenue of street lights with their strange glow and piercing neon eyes that permeated the darkness.

Elizabeth stopped to inhale and consume the moment.

A vibrant world beckoned and opened itself and promised her its endless wealth and riches.

In return she whipped up her winds into a raging storm that carried her to places she had never seen before. Then suffused and exhausted, gladly gave all her parts to it.

64

OBSCURUM AND DIVINE INTERVENTION
(FOR LOVELY RITA)

You sure look pretty tonight. Ruby lips, high cut velvet jeans so tight. Let me take you out. We can paint the town and turn up those neon city lights. You sure do look pretty tonight. Take in the sights, the music's playing way too loud, so we'll put the pedal down and find our own little cloud, way up where the moon is high and the stars are bright. Baby sure looks pretty tonight.

Long legged Rita Coolidge was no stranger to fame. The girl from Lafayette who made it in the big league, had a lot going for her. As it happened, she also turned out to be a very good singer. Which was just as well, because neither of us was too sure quite what to expect. Would she have a hangover from the good old days with Kris Kristofferson? If so would she take out her marital frustrations on the audience? Did she really think that love would lift us *Higher and Higher** (7)[1] and would she have enough matches left to light our fire?

---

1. *Original version recorded by Jackie Wilson. Has also been recorded by numerous other artists including Jimmy Barnes.*

We caught her one off headline act at the rather obscure and exotically named Sydney Motor Club. Although what on earth Rolls Royce had to do with aerial ballet and petite pop stars was anyone's guess. From street level, the old sandstone building gave one the distinct impression of some raucus *speakeasy joint* or a clever front for a brazen Brazilian cocktail party. Located on the second floor the venue could only be accessed via a poorly lit narrow flight of stairs. At the top, barely visible in the shadows, a large wooden door with a viewing panel in the centre, blocked the corridor. A rotund, heavy set doorman dressed in a badly creased suit and wearing the most perfect white spats, eyed us up and down. Checking out our credentials with the careful scrutiny of an S.S. guard. Lucky for us we had all the right answers and an extra bob or two for emergencies.

Inside, it became a whole new secret world. The walls, painted pink from top to bottom, were decorated with Max Dupain photographs. We could have quite easily been somewhere back in the nineteen twenties in the discrete company of F. Scott Fitzgerald and his Folies Bergère entourage. For the moment at least, the golden age of prohibition had been resurrected. In the middle of the parquetry floor stood a half built replica of a roman amphitheatre in which semi naked male and female dancers cavorted beneath blazing banks of neon and curtains of falling water. To add more spice to the mix, amazon tall and topless waitresses brought drinks and winks to the tables. Their satin G strings aglow in the dark like bright stars in the southern constellation. Just the perfect tonic to soothe the bloodshot eyes before Miss C. appeared.

Then as the glissando beats from the orchestra died out and the lights slowly dimmed, we couldn't help but wonder. Did she really sing those plaintive backing vocals for Eric Clapton and his other friends[2]?

Could she still zip it out with the best? Could this Delta lady ever sing the blues? Was she indeed the owner of those wonderful legs? Soon all our questions would be answered.

She did. She could. Without doubt she was.

---

2. *Refers specifically to Delaney and Bonnie (Bramlet)*

65

THE MOON RESTS OVER AN OPEN FIELD

The Whole Of The Moon* (8) 1985 The Waterboys

And it never ceases to amaze how quickly time erases what the heart desires and how minds can meet in the strangest places.

The good old tent just wouldn't go up. Not at the first attempt anyway. Not even at the second. There were a few important pieces missing, which didn't help. Nor (did) the giant swarm of insects that gathered around the campsite like moths to an open flame. On the third attempt and in the fast fading light, we somehow managed to get it half erect but nowhere near in the correct alignment. It sort of stood there semi dressed in a most awkward fashion and leaning slightly down slope. This of course made it rather difficult for us to settle down in the customary comfortable position. But at least the long thick grass was soft beneath our bed rolls and blankets. Now all we needed was a clear starry night, a full moon and a drink to warm our hearts. We were so tired, we fell asleep as if we had been wrapped in a cotton wool meadow.

At day break, a feeble sun pierced through a thin layer of mist that all but filled the narrow clearing. It was very cold. Overnight, temperatures had dipped to below freezing. The ashes from the fire had burnt numerous small holes in the side walls of the tent. From a distance the canvas sheet looked like some famous Jackson Pollock painting. A lone kookaburra perched high in the branches of a gnarled eucalypt at least saw something funny in our predicament. The waters of the Boyd had overnight ceased babbling and for our morning wash and freshen up, we were greeted by a layer of thick ice that proved difficult to break through. After a heavy breakfast of sizzling bacon, eggs and toast, we decided to proceed with our plans to navigate the wide reaches of the famous Kowmung trail and the almost forgotten Gingra stock route.

Undaunted and determined to prevail, we sheathed our knives, secured our heavy packs, puffed out our chests and proud as peacocks, headed south east along the broken ridge line. At least that's the direction the ordinance map pointed us in. Hats firmly on heads and faces painted vivid white with zinc cream, we were intrepid explorers on a mission.

Hours later after hacking through the dense, prickly undergrowth with nothing more than a penknife and following what must have been the lost footprints of Blaxland, Lawson and Wentworth, we found ourselves teetering on the edge of a giant sandstone precipice. Close by we could hear the thunderous roar of water as it plummeted over the escarpment and into the dark abyss below. Somehow able to retrace our tracks and more through good luck than management, we returned safely to our point of origin. Compass in hand and each of us none the wiser as to how we had got here. Egos bruised into submission. Knees and arms scratched and scraped. Tails between our legs.

The three peaks of Rip, Rack, Roar and Rumble[1] stood defiant. Hidden in shadow, Mt. Cloudmaker far beyond still beckoned. Undisturbed.

We put out the last of the dying embers that had been burning in their stone circle and loaded the equipment into the station wagon. Then, as if with a sense of awe, we stood transfixed momentarily to gather our thoughts. Watched the wind whip its way through the long dry tussocks of the kangaroo fields. Tall river she oaks and twisted paper barks whispered in plaintive song as fat hairy nosed wombats heading for their burrows wombled idly by[2]. With not a care in the world.

Heavy clouds gathered in the distance and a storm shook and tumbled like smoke over silent waters.

In unison we breathed a sigh of relief and turned the car for home. The headlights struck upon the open road and the wheels hummed and drummed to the music on the radio. Clickety clack. Don't look back. Human hearts called. Something about time and a word[3]. Clickety clickety clack. We sang until our voices cracked.

Yes, it's right for us too.

Jutta never went on the wild side again.

---

1. *These are the pleasant sounding names of the famous four peaks in the Kanangra Boyd National Park NSW.*

2. *Just like the Wombles of Wimbledon (from the British TV series* The Wombles*)*

3. Time And A Word* *(9) 1970 Yes from the album Time and a Word.*

66

THE TREE

*For days we ran on under a storm of broken light,
beneath dark skies enclosing. On and on we went
in pursuit of our golden fleece, until exhausted we
could go no further.*

Alice had pestered the old man for what seemed an
eternity. He didn't listen. He never did. She nagged
him over and over until her head hurt and her throat
threatened to catch on fire. Scolded him more times
than she could remember about the straggly tree with the
strange botanical name, that grew in the little patch of
nemesia outside their bedroom window. How it rubbed
its branches against the glass each and every time the
wind blew. How it bent and moaned when winter came
along and how it sighed through summer and summer's
unforgiving rain. It was dangerous and would need to go.
Still he didn't listen.

That was twenty years ago or more. Half a lifetime to
most.

Alice had almost forgotten. Put it out of her head
altogether. Consigned it to the dark recesses, until by
surprise, one grey morning over coffee Harold quipped
"*That old tree you like so much won't see the end of the week*".
Clenched his fists in defiance and gritted his teeth. "*You

mark my words, missy", he huffed, not wishing to make light of his promise. Arrows flew as if to mock his words and Alice smiled, then thinking better of it, put her smile away to save for another day. She thought it unlike Harold.

That evening dusk came and went. But Harold never came home.

Dressed in black, Alice slowly stepped out of the long limousine with its bright silver wheels, tinted windows and discreet red curtains draped across the back. Covered from tip to toe, no light could reach Alice.

It was hot and humid and she was not in the mood for eulogies or empty sermons. In the dappled shade of the wide veranda, the fragrance from the jasmine growing on the vine was strong and overpowering. A moth startled by her presence, fluttered overhead, then quickly disappeared into a cloud of pink and yellow blossoms hanging from the wooden beams. She turned the door key and paused for a moment. Listening for his voice or his familiar footsteps close behind her. Waiting for his breath to catch upon her cheeks. But there was no sound and the air turned heavy. Even the cicadas that had greeted her arrival, had fallen silent.

Alice looked up. A thick ribbon of nimbus clouds crossed the horizon. It would rain this afternoon.

She had not noticed anything different or out of place, but then something drew her, like the last rays of sunlight creeping through brooding waters. An ache deep inside bubbled to the surface. Numbed her withered arms. Her bag dropped to the floor, its meagre contents spilling out upon the weathered floorboards.

A whiteness brushed over her and all colours drained away. Frozen to the spot, she couldn't move. The large birch tree lay stretched across the ground, split asunder, as though struck down by the fierce blade of a woodman's axe. In the far corner of the garden the shed door hung slightly ajar. It creaked in the breeze that had sprung up from nowhere. Her senses rose and fell in waves upon an empty beach and a broken voice beside her whispered. Nothing and everything. Then from the corner of her eye, she thought she saw the flash of a shadow rise above the roof. Whistling as it went.

On Sunday the bells rang out and for the first time in her life Alice Chapin went to church.

67

AFTER THE GOLD RUSH
(SHE WAS A MINER FORTY NINER)

The Weight (9) 1968 The Band from Music From
Big Pink*

Unlike her more illustrious namesake, she was far less than quizzical and had never studied pataphysical science[1] in her life. Nor did she have a burning desire to do so. Neither was she any danger to society and she certainly didn't go to the movies. Especially romantic sad ones with no intermission and an unpredictable ending. The sort that make you sniffle and cry.

Joan Beatrice Angus was a prospector in her own mind. A woman who loved digging in the dirt. Getting her manicured hands filthy in mountains of wonderful soil and detritus. Giving the worms a run for their money. And that was just for starters. She came all the way from the motherland to find her fame and fortune. At least that's what she told us when she arrived with her maps, Nikon camera and suitcase full of floral pattern Bermuda shorts.

Joan had been introduced to the art of lapidary some years earlier after catching a short documentary

---

1. *Maxwell's Silver Hammer** (9) *1969 The Beatles from the album Abbey Road*

highlighting the New South Wales Gold Rush. The seed of eternal thirst had been sown. Then and there, she decided to give away gastronomy. From now on prospecting was to be her holy grail and worth a try at the very least. After all, what was the worst that could happen?

Putting things into perspective I declared without prejudice or reservation *"Now that's one thing we have more than an abundance of, rocks and minerals and nuggets of gold. Not to mention flies, termites, mosquitoes and dangerous snakes".* Not that they would be a problem at this time of the year. With an air of confidence, we assured her there would be no difficulty encountering such tempting geological bits and pieces and with a little luck and help from mother nature, would perhaps even unearth some precious stones. Maybe even diamonds. It was the least we could do to kindle her flame. That was the Australian way.

It was late into autumn. The weather to date had been kind and the warm side of mild. With total conviction therefore, we suggested it would be a great time for fossicking in the remote and rugged wilds west of the Great Divide. Far from the usual annoying crowds and weekend shoppers. It remained obliging until the actual day we had arranged to venture out on our safari.

At dawn, a strong front pushed up from the south, sneaking out of a leaden purple sky that spelled *trouble.* The rain started. At first just a light drizzle. Enough to wet the skin but not our enthusiasm. Nothing inconvenient, or so we thought. But by the time we reached the last loop on Victoria Pass, it had become a torrent. With a hint of sarcasm, a faint voice from the seat behind whispered *"let's turn back now before my makeup washes away, it doesn't look too good out there".*

That was an understatement deserving of no response. Sylvia put her reliable wellingtons[2] on and grimaced. She didn't want to worry anyone, least of all the irate driver. But she was prepared for any backlash of consequence. Ashen faced George unable to hide the fact that he was a hair's breadth away from demanding a sick bag, groaned as the Torana[3] lurched around another bend. Joan however (still stuck in the bygone days of British Empire) merely ignored his pleas for mercy, clenched her fists and more determined than ever, elected to continue with the quest. Otherwise what stories would there be to tell the grandchildren? And she had after all brought along her heavy duty bag and specimen jars to hold anything valuable she might dig up.

So on we went. The wheels on the car going round and round and the crew on board going up and down, trying very hard to keep up their brave faces. Each one hoping that the weather would take pity on them. It was like being deployed _In Search Of The Lost Chord_* (8), only far less glamorous. The radio crackled and hissed in an effort to maintain good reception. Across the airwaves the afternoon _heavy music for careful drivers show_ somehow managed to squeeze out _When The Levee Breaks_* (8). The timing was impeccable. It was an ominous sign of things to come.

We crossed the raging Duckmaloi (usually barely a trickle at this time of year) in almost zero visibility, before soon after entering the little township of Oberon. Population 1800 give or take a few. Sleepy at the best of times, but today decidedly comatose. The streets silent and

---

2. _Gumboots, gumbies or gummies, depending on how you were brought up._

3. _The famous Holden Torana was a most reliable model of car manufactured by GMH in Australia._

almost void of human life. Then sure enough, to mock our thoughts, the weather turned for the worse and the snow began to tumble. Sarcasm and not much wit bubbled to the surface-it really couldn't get any better than this.

A warm, country lunch beckoned, fresh made potato pies and croissants from the local bakery and a strong cup of tea or two for Joan (who by now was frothing at the mouth). It was the only place open apart from the reliable Royal Hotel, whose blackboard message *sit by the fire, warm your toes,* at this particular point in time seemed rather optimistic. Especially as those hardy inhabitants with any modicum of intelligence had retired themselves into early hibernation.

The woman who served us, thought it very strange that any city folk in their right mind, would be out in this part of the world on such a god forsaken day. We thought it strange too.

Twelve large gates, four oil drum mailboxes and several cattle crossings later and with the car hidden under a layer of thick red mud, we came to a sudden halt somewhere on the bonny banks of Native Dog Creek. The very name induced fits of laughter. However, there were no ferocious canines to greet us and the only wildlife encountered was a lethargic murder of crows that had gathered on the broken fence like ducks lined up in a shooting gallery. But no one was in the mood for target practice.

The snow now fell heavier than before, forming a thick blanket of white that stretched away into the distance. Until the horizon blended with the sky and the shadows blurred. Overhead, the she oaks sang as the wind rustled through the branches. Even the sheep wrapped up in their fleecy woollen coats had more sense than us. They headed home for warmth and shelter.

That was the straw that broke the camel's back. We turned the car around put the gear shift into cruise mode and wished for some piping hot minestrone soup, the real stuff only the genuine Italians can make. Anything to take our minds off our frozen bodies.

Joan never did get her precious vial of gold flakes nor her good luck amethyst and as for the rest of the rocks, well we convinced her they would still be out there waiting for the next time she cared to visit. *"I think perhaps I would much prefer the warmer islands of Fiji"* she retorted with a twisted smile.

From somewhere in the rear the muffled voice of Maxwell Edison muttered in agreement.

Bang. Bang.

A LITTLE SOMETHING TO PASS THE TIME AWAY 8

JOHN (CAN'T SEEM TO MAKE UP HIS MIND) MELLENCAMP OR IS THAT COUGAR?

Jackie Brown (8)

Rain On The Scarecrow (7)

Human Wheels (9)

When Jesus Left Birmingham (7)

Cherry Bomb (7)

ANYTHING BUT CONVENTIONAL FAIRPORT FOR BEGGARS AND BEGINNERS

Farewell, Farewell (8)

A Sailor's Life (8)

Morning Glory (7)

Matty Groves (7)

Reynaldine (7)

ELO ELO THEY SAID

Mr Blue Sky (9)

Last Train To London (6)

Telephone Line (6)

Can't Get It Out Of My Head (7)

Living Thing (7)

THE DECEMBERISTS I PRESUME

Annan Water (7)

We Both Go Down Together (7)

Shanty For The Arethusa (7)

Dear Avery (7)

This Is Why We Fight (8)

WHERE EAGLES DARE

Desperado (7)
One Of These Nights (8)
Hotel California (9)
Lyin' Eyes (7)
Get Over It (7)

EVERYTHING IS JUST HUNKY DORY FOR DAVID

Andy Warhol (8)
Starman (9)
Changes (8)
Rebel Rebel (8)
Space Oddity (9)

PLEASE DON'T BRAGG BILLY

St Swithin's Day (7)
She's Got A New Spell (7)
Valentine's Day Is Over (7)
Between The Wars (8)
The Milkman Of Human Kindness (7)

68

TOMMY THE FAMOUS CARCOAR COCKATOO

Against The Wind * (9) 1980 Bob Seger and The
Silver Bullet Band from Against The Wind*

Screeeeechhhhhhhhh was the word. If you could
call it that. From somewhere close behind us it
compounded into something sinister. At first high pitched
and ear piercing. Enough to shock the cows into milk
production. A rowdy, raucous squawk befitting a bird of
such great standing. Soon after came more of the awful
same. Like the sound of long finger nails scratched across a
blackboard. It was as if it had appeared from nowhere just
to annoy the bloody daylights out of us. Then we heard
it again. No mistake this time "*Tommy want a cracker...
Tommy want a cracker. Fat Tommy is a pretty boy then.
Pretty, pretty Tommy boy. Arrrrrrrrr....*" echoed around the
room. In anger, the long, vivid comb on the top of his
scrawny head stood upright. And just in case we didn't
get the message loud and clear, it glowed bright yellow for
danger. So we kept our distance for fear of losing a finger
or some other vital appendage.

It became the standard, round the table talking point
for years to come. Our first comical encounter with the
Carcoar cockatoo. The bird that was a legend in his own
lunch time. The conversation piece that always kept

everyone amused. Great adventures and tall tales of Tommy, spoken about in the same breath as all those other great heroes of captivity. The man in the iron mask immediately sprang to mind. More than once, we had to pinch ourselves. *"My God can you really believe that this poor bird is nigh on eighty years old".* That's right. Methinks of Methuselah magnitude. Four score years and going strong. Eighty endless summer's long. More than a lifetime to most people. More than some people can even count. Still in the same battered cage (that had seen the light of better days), in the same old house in the same old mid western town. A million miles from anywhere. Stuck with the same little lady that had rescued him aeons ago and put him in the damn cage in the first place. Tommy certainly had a huge axe to grind. We smiled. It was difficult not to get caught up in the importance of the occasion.

A local cattle farmer related the tale. Said Mary (I am sure that was her name) first crossed paths with the young sulphur crested cockatoo when she was just six years old. Found the scrawny fledgling beneath a large gum tree on the banks of the Belubula River. From all accounts fallen from his nest. Took Tommy in and gave him a good home in an oversized bright silver aviary that had a nice gnarled branch for a perch, a water trough deep enough to scuba dive, a bell that didn't ring and a mirror that made Tommy look twice his real size. Occasionally Mary would show her soft side and let him out on the weekends or on those days he had been a particularly good boy cocky. But then only with a long chain tether which she tied to his thin leg. Otherwise Tommy would have shot the coup. Most sure and certain.

Nowadays Mary watches her pretty garden grow and sips on camomile tea. Twinings brand of course. Drinks it because that is what real country ladies do. And in any case, the doctor swears it's a great relief for heartburn and flatulence. For that Tommy is forever grateful.

To keep herself amused she recites verbatim Mulga Bill's Bicycle as well as anybody alive and kicking and judging by those well-worn rubber boots near the kitchen door she's still as fit as a Mallee bull.

Poor, poor Tommy.

Screeeechhhhhh.........

69

INSECT SECRET LIFE IN UNKNOWN GARDEN

It began as an afterthought and soon turned into an obsession

<u>Carolina In My Mind</u>* (8) 1968 James Taylor

The last of the cold night air stung the skin and made our nostrils flare. The lights of the Southern Cross danced high above, stretching like a diamond encrusted map in the great dark void of everything. Across the blue fringed, ragged ranges, we followed in the footsteps of the early pioneers.

Where the convict road cut the Great Divide. Up, beyond pleasant Hartley Vale and Little Hampton we ran. The wind streaming fast as mercury behind us. Comets in our hair and red dust in our shoes and pockets.

On some special day we wandered. Just as the sun rose early above bright fields of fire that hung with mist and pretty carpet blossoms, all pink and pearly white. Somewhere between the folded hills and sunlit ridges where the silver river turned its course, we stumbled into the great pine tree woods.

At that moment we became unblinded. As if a curtain had been lifted from our eyes.

The seasons passed us by like beads drawn along a wire and the siren voices called. Growing louder until they drowned out everything else.

Caught in the wondrous Babylon of our simple garden. Under heavy mackerel skies, filled with the scent of turpentine and smoke ash, we drew deep breath and painted images in our heads no artist could ever put to canvas. A smorgasbord gallery of sights and sounds that knew no earthly bounds.

Ahead, almost hidden in the shadows, protected from the whistling axe of progress and the machines that groaned and bellowed as they moved, a whole new insect secret life unfolded.

70

FOXTROT 2 TANGOBLUE
(IN RARE AIR)

They say you're out there somewhere, drifting in a sea of clouds. With your white scarf flowing and your heart on fire. You never will be lost.

Everyone wishes they knew somebody like Allan. You can easily picture the stereotype: popular, Clark Gable handsome to a fault, wide eyed and bushy tailed. The life of the party and the centre of attention for the female set, especially the blonde, good looking ones of unattached persuasion seeking meaningful connection with single alpha male. Well Allan was all of these things, except for the latter. In this regard, he was happily married with a pretty wife and young family. But this fact did not diminish in the least from the strange magnetism that somehow surrounded him like a basket of white light.

In any another time, perhaps he would have been called a lothario, cad or a bounder. Or better still a philanthropist of the highest order. Even an eccentric of sorts. Yes Allan was the complete package, a man for all seasons. Summer and winter rolled into one energetic bundle.

I first had the pleasure of crossing paths with Allan in the summer of nineteen hundred and seventy six. He was the newly appointed CEO for a profitable western Sydney project home builder. It had apparently been a startling transformation and rapid rise through the company ranks, considering he had started a mere twelve months earlier. No one seemed to know exactly where he had come from or what his credentials and qualifications were, but salesmanship and self-confidence would sit high amongst them. His close circle of friends included politicians, physicians and professors. You see Allan was liked by all. Those who met him couldn't help themselves. It was as if a strong current drew them into his complex persona. And of course to those lucky enough to strike Allan's fancy, this brought its own rewards and benefits. The motto was, stick to Allan and usually things happened and most times for the better.

The attraction in part, no doubt came from the fact that he had been a Canberra bomber pilot who had served in Saigon at the height of the Vietnam War. He had displayed exceptional courage and valour whilst on tactical and reconnaissance missions. When questioned about the details, Allan remarked that it was in another life, long, long ago.

Now discharged and firmly set in the civilian way, he had turned to flying part time mail and other cargo services out of Bankstown, running the gauntlet to Broken Hill and the remote far west towns of Queensland.

More than once on lazy non-productive days, he found the need to crank up those flying juices that coursed through his veins. So by reliable democratic process or the order of the short pretzel, he would choose a select few (although some might say unlucky) to participate in scenic joy flights over the Blue Mountains and along the South

Coast. Where he performed aerial manoeuvres devoid of common sense but requiring absolute precision. However nothing too daring for the fainthearted among us. Of course the loop the loop and the kamikaze dive were forbidden.

All this undertaken, not in a state of the art jet fighter but in a rather uncomfortable four seater single engine Cessna. When he scrambled into that cockpit, you would swear his eyes caught fire every time that old engine coughed and spluttered to life. Right then and there, Allan took on a whole new identity.

He caressed the buttons on the glowing console like ivory keys on a grand piano, until the Liberace within took control. Then taxiing along the runway, the wing flaps slowly retracted into position and with all systems go the sky above turned the deepest aqua blue.

Isn't it funny how for some inexplicable reason, people are mesmerised by tales of battle from days of yore and exotic places they have never been. Allan could capture the imagination with a simple word and a wave of his hand. He could charm as easily as a mediaeval jester in the court of the king, or a world weary Marco Polo describing his Chinese travels.

In a twinkling his narrative could take wings like the very machines he flew.

Sadly, Allan did not last as CEO. It might have been a *Simple Twist Of Fate** (8) that forced his hand or the fact he'd had enough of a life spent along the straight and narrow. A proud airman's lot no doubt difficult to purge. Or perhaps somewhere amongst his vast network of secret connections, someone made him a better offer. One he couldn't refuse.

Allan moved on like a prairie wind blown out of a vast Kansas flat land.

I can see him now, flying solo across that wide endless horizon. Head lost in the clouds, joystick at full throttle. Chasing those rainbows he always dreamed about.

71

THE LIGHTHOUSE ON THE CAPE

When the wind turned to a long drawn whisper
and the soft amber glow of the lightbulb had died,
I looked around and you were gone.

The door slammed shut behind them blocking out the last of the sun painted images on the wall of the cedar bungalow. It was late and things were not running to schedule. Maeve found herself in no mood for reminiscing or conversation and in any case she had wanted to make sure her pretty hair was perfect. Totally bemused, the short, fat man in the driver's seat, said *there was nothing to worry about. After all, he liked pigtails and coloured silk ribbons, especially pink ones.* His neatly groomed Salvador Dali moustache glistened in the half light. Distracting her momentarily from what it was that had brought her to this place. Doubt began to surface. There was something about him that almost compelled her to turn the other way and forget about their secret plans. Until thinking better of it, she fixed her thoughts on the baby cradled in her arms and started to cry.

The heavy traffic made the going slow, so by the time they reached the turnpike that took them out of town, darkness had already settled over the bay and the last of the fluffy ghost clouds now scurried home to bed.

In silence they drove along the broken line of the coast road that wound its way between the hills and the mud banks of the grey river. Until out of a sudden cross mist of rain that caught them by surprise, the rickety iron bridge loomed up ahead. The skeleton arches rising like dinosaur bones from a prehistoric graveyard. It was then, they became strangers lost in their own numbed senses. Where nothing else mattered. No use turning back now, they were far beyond the point of no return. There could be no regrets.

The numerals on the dashboard clock glowed nine fifteen pm. The radio hissed out of its quiet slumber and sprang to life in a defiant blaze of glory just in time to catch the jukebox Saturday Late show. It played out some almost forgotten love song sung when first they had met. Long, long ago somewhere in the crinkled stations of his mind.

Skimming over the cobblestones, the headlights cast strange patterns as they passed between a stand of giant paperbarks. The shadows moved and changed shape, transporting them from one world into the next. Then back again to emerge unscathed on the other side, at last freed from their secret past. She smiled at the thought that the miles traversed no longer would divide. The short man ignored her.

Wiping one hand across the cold glass, he could barely make out the lighthouse that stood silhouetted between the black cliff face and starless sky.

A rough breeze brushed the evening tide, defying the contours of the land stuck hard against the shore. The rush of air pushed through the branches of the trees that suddenly transformed, bent and folded into weather beaten soldiers marching on the sawtooth ridge.

The car shuddered to a halt. Overhead a noisy fruit bat glided from view.

A sliver of crescent moon hung above the city skyline while somewhere out at sea lightning cracked.

72

HANG ON A MINUTE WAS ALL SHE COULD SAY

The Wall Of Death* (8) 1982 Richard and Linda
Thompson from Shoot Out The Lights

The large, yellow sign on the leaning post we had
passed minutes earlier, indicated the gravel road
ahead was rough and very narrow. We thought, nothing
to be alarmed about. Nothing we had not encountered on
previous travels into parts unknown. And of course we had
done plenty of those. Slippery when wet and not suitable
for heavy loads and caravans, it also warned.

In the heat of the moment we couldn't help but laugh,
for someone in their frustration had taken the liberty
to shoot a lot of bullets through the thing. They were
obviously either illiterate or worse still, misguided souls
with poor eyesight. We were one hundred percent wrong
in both departments.

Leaving the last stretch of bitumen behind us, we
braced ourselves for a bumpy ride. We did not have long
to wait. Barely half an hour had gone when suddenly our
vehicle lurched across a cattle grid, then veered sharply to
avoid a large pothole. Patting ourselves on the back at our
success in avoiding disaster, we failed to negotiate an even
larger hole that materialised out of the dappled shadows of
the hill. After the first tremendous thump, I suddenly got

the urge to write a stern letter of complaint to the Roads and Traffic Authority. After the second, my mouth was in serious need of an orthodontist. However, in true epic style, the pothole saga was to be the least of our worries, for just around the next sweeping bend, things took a mighty turn for the worse.

The angelic voice came out of the blue. *"You're as white as a ghost"* she stuttered, interrupting my concentration. That did it, then and there I had to put my sandwich on her lap for safe keeping. It was difficult to eat whenever someone passed comments about one's complexion. *"And you're delirious"* she further added with a sarcastic touch. The words slapped hard against my face, then echoed long, as if they were trapped in an endless tunnel, with nowhere to go.

Here we were in the Wollondilly wilds, plain sailing and carefree. Or so it seemed. That is, until most unexpectedly, we encountered a huge boulder that had somehow dislodged itself from the steep slope above and come to rest in the middle of the road. That it happened to be on a precarious section of the mountain side, barely wide enough to accommodate a few sheep let alone an immovable giant rock and a car, merely added to our predicament. *"Can you believe our luck?"* I howled. I don't think anyone heard me.

Unable to move, we sat there uncomfortably numb and transfixed in the moment. As if time itself had stopped. A warm, fuzzy sensation swept over us. If only it could stay that way. If only we could press fast reverse and disappear out of the situation we found ourselves in. We hadn't passed so much as a stray cow or rampant kangaroo for hours and now this. And of all places, we have to perform a treacherous quadruple manoeuvre under adverse conditions. Easier said than done. What we needed was a stick of dynamite and a long fuse.

Rugged high cliffs towered on our left side cutting out the sun. To the right an almost sheer drop. The scene was both breathtaking and vomit inducing. We could even see the river twisting its way along the valley floor far below. No safety barriers. No margin for error. No place for the faint hearted that was for sure.

You can guess which side we were stuck on.

It was then, in a reflective mood more befitting a church sermon than a casual weekend drive, I thought we should have taken another route. The one that said *Stop at Joe's Café de Crème. What have you got to lose?* Better to be anywhere other than here, literally teetering on the edge and just a delicate snow flake away from oblivion. Joe's coffee would sure taste good right now.

"You're still as white as a ghost" she reiterated, with far more urgency than before. The sweat was now building on her furrowed brow and the tremor on her round, red lips was ready to turn into a full blown quake. She was trying hard to look relaxed, but the pattern on her face sketched an altogether different story. *"I know dear, but at least I've got my fingers crossed and my eyes closed."* I was almost at breaking point and my words didn't do much to help matters. They made her more irritable. She shuffled in her seat, quickly swallowed what was left of my pastrami and rye bread sandwich, then pinched hard on my quivering legs in a desperate attempt to inject an ampule of courage through my frozen veins. It must have worked, for soon not only was I even more delirious, I also couldn't feel a thing.

Hours later and grateful for small mercies, we arrived at our destination. Short circuited almost, nerves frazzled and requiring a double dose of tequila to calm us down.

Funny, but we never ever went close to the edge again. Stick to the straight highway from now on became our decree. As for that weather beaten sign, it suddenly hit me why it had been the victim of exuberant target practice.

Oh and by the way, her fingernails left marks on my thighs for weeks.

73

NEXUS IS PERPLEXUS

My Back Pages * (10) 1964 Bob Dylan.

In life, sometimes it pays to take a risk. Even a toss of the coin or throw of a dice might be enough to do the trick. And then, if all else fails there is always statistics and plain old common sense to get you through to the other side.

74

FAREWELL MISS GRACE

Elegy: <u>Funeral For A Friend</u> (9) 1973 Elton John
from Goodbye Yellow Brick Road*

For an hour or more we pushed along a narrow, stone trail overgrown with weeds of every size and description. To this last forgotten place. At rest somewhere in the heart of the great divide.

The wooden board had seen better days. It leaned at a slight angle against the slope. The words read *Miss Grace the Tailor*, but unlike most of the other signs and markers that still stood upright and intact, the large letters were faded and barely visible in the dimming light.

Grace died long ago, consumed by typhoid and wild fever and was buried next to her father and mother in a small, now neglected family plot on the side of the barren hill. In spring, silver daisies and white alpine heath bloomed across the length and breadth of that broad meadow.

A low, dark stone wall ran between the gravel road and the stippled, tree lined ridge. In the lower field, partially blocked from this wind swept point, a stream coursed over broken rocks, then disappeared into the distance.

We left the weathered gravestone, treading softly so as not to leave any footprints behind us in the heavy soil. The rain had now set in and was driving up a staccato flurry from the south. A band of thick low clouds stretched like streaks of oil between the broken mountain peaks. We watched as the patterns changed shape before our very eyes. Some became old men with twisted beards, riding giant stallions on the foamy brine. Others transformed into beasts with tails of ice.

It turned cold. Soon the same clouds would bring snow.

Below us, half hidden in the tall tussock grass and bed of purple thistles, a rusted stamp battery and bucket dredge were all that remained of the once thriving gold town.

The buildings and the people long since turned to dust and memories.

Only ghosts now roam the silent hillside.

75

THE HOTEL TOTAL FUTURISTIC

Tomorrow will turn out to be a better day than any of us can imagine.

It is with us now. A soft shadow in the doorway. A smudge on the pencil thin horizon. I think it's always been this way. Suitably absorbed and stored for all the generations. A sort of trial and error overview that plots the very course to take. Then once there to make of it what you will.

The predicament materialises out of some cloudy, restless sleep, twists and turns in helical abundance and deep beneath the surface is anything other than it seems.

We are trapped in cognitive chambers of exponential growth. Spiralling out of control its Malthusian coefficients jump into overload. Then mingled with our genes and molecules, flashes but once in a fish eyed world and unravels moebius like in all its forms.

Life indeed is but a process of simplification or elimination.

For sure and certain it is the falling curtain of our destiny or an image projected upon a wall. From binary system dialogue entering another phase to adjusting the alignment of the planets with a wave of the hand. Simple as placing pieces in a puzzle, we shall forever play gods without borders.

We stand where the new world and the old world collide, side by side exchanging fluids and ideas. There stripped back for all to see. Sustenance to the senses.

Picture this somewhere deep inside your head. A scenario sublime. If you can in your wildest dreams imagine being forever greeted by machines that have no feelings and ageless women without breasts. Cocooned in a place where our bodies rest in soft marigolds on the ocean floor.

Welcome to the hotel total futuristic.

Please take a seat and wait until your number is called.

76

JEREMIAH WAS A BULLDOG, SOME CALLED HIM BARKING MAD

Stairway To Heaven* *(10) 1971 Led Zeppelin from Led Zeppelin IV.*

I can see the blue campfire smoke as it threads its way through the trees.

The merry Masons lived on the other side of town a mere stone's throw away from a large reserve of woodland that bounded the old racecourse. We would often visit them on public holidays or any other special occasion whenever the chance arose.

My father and Eric had been staunch friends for many years. They first met whilst in service training for the Territorial Army Unit based at Catterick Garrison, North Yorkshire. Driving trucks and tanks for love of queen and country. All for the great and just cause of long lost empire.

The two storey house was neat and unassuming: a quaint, semi-detached new build surrounded by a fairy-tale perfect picket fence and a pastiche of a garden that bloomed with the most fragrant roses in the springtime. A drab concrete path zig zagged to the front door where a large bell salvaged from a sunken clipper, hung from a projecting beam above the portico. Even in the lightest breeze it resonated with the loudest din. The rear was full of wallflowers, snapdragons, dahlias, sweet peas and had a scented jasmine vine that climbed tenaciously about a broken trellis. There was also a greenhouse with a metal framed door that creaked when opened. The neighbours affectionately called it his majesty's crystal palace. Inside, grew juicy tomatoes and other prized vegetables together with a rare collection of cymbidium orchids purchased from an old horticultural colleague. Eric always said the flowers made him think of sunshine and rainbows. Even on the greyest of days.

It would have been the almost idyllic setting except for the fact that it backed onto the railway line. Once a week a goods train carrying its cargo of heavy freight to who knows where, would sound its whistle when it hurtled past. Which was just as well for those poor souls who happened to reside right alongside, for when that train came by, everyone ran for cover. The thunderous roar of the engine was enough to shake the houses to their very foundations.

Now to Jeremiah, this was no ordinary disturbance and it annoyed him a great deal. Especially as the wooden kennel was the closest thing by far to the source of everyone's displeasure. Each Saturday afternoon around three, he would stand defiant, hidden among the burdock and the dandelions, put his head down for a moment, growl and then release a blood curdling howl. The stubborn train driver who must have thought he was a long lost relative of Casey Jones, didn't help matters by pulling on the siren cord. Not once, but twice in extended bursts. Just for the fun of it. And just to rub salt into Jeremiah's wounds. The absolute nerve of the man.

Jeremiah was a bulldog. *No take care as you go fellow, watch out for the teeth* in this dog. That would have been an insult. He was but purest breed and of finest British stock. There was not a bad hair on his short, stocky frame and to cap it off a certain distinguished trademark stance made him irresistible. There was that familiar dark circular patch around his left eye and a mouth that drooped to one side and seemed to be forever blowing bubbles. His little bowed legs (well) disguising the fact that he was by anyone's account one hell of a canine for chasing the hare and badger that freely roamed the wilderness on the other side of the tracks. But harm them he never did, for his bothersome bark was far worse than his bite.

On bright summer days when god's creatures great and otherwise rustled and bustled through the tall grass near the edge of the lake, Christine, Jeremiah and I would wriggle under the wire fence and disappear for hours on end in search of hedgehogs and other wondrous things. Never coming home before dark, or not until we had at least explored the vast labyrinth of trails and hollows.

Eric always said Jeremiah should have been a bloodhound. The kind used to search for truffles or hunt down escaped prisoners on the run. After all, he certainly had the temperament, if not quite the physique. Jeremiah thought Eric should have known better. He was more than happy with his lot and besides, his ears though acutely sensitive, were much too small and his flat nose far too refined for that caper.

When he died, Jeremiah was given full military honours and a twelve candle salute. With his rubber bone and studded name collar, he was buried alongside a patch of bluebells near a little stream that burbled where it ran past his favourite warren.

Whenever the wind rushed and rippled through that sylvan glade, when the moon pushed hard through the fluffy cotton clouds high above, you would swear those pretty flowers played out a symphony to good old Jeremiah.

A LITTLE SOMETHING TO PASS THE TIME AWAY 9

THE HOUSE OF STEWART (ROD THAT IS, NOT JIMMY)

Gasoline Alley (7)

Mandolin Wind (8)

Reason To Believe (7)

Sailing (7)

Rhythm Of My Heart (6)

THE SITUATION IS SLIGHTLY MORE THAN DIRE

Sultans Of Swing (8)

Private Investigations (8)

Brothers In Arms (8)

Romeo And Juliet (7)

Walk OF Life (6)

STILL ROLLING AFTER ALL THESE YEARS

2000 Light Years From Home (8)

Sympathy For The Devil (8)

Honky Tonk Women (8)

Wild Horses (9)

Jumpin' Jack Flash (9)

I FEEL LIKE FRED ASTAIRE

Funky Town (8)	Lipps Inc.
Twistin' The Night Away (7)	Sam Cooke / Rod Stewart
Funky Cold Medina (8)	Tone Loc
You Should Be Dancing (8)	Bee Gees
Dancing Queen (7)	Abba

SONGS FROM THE HEARTBREAK HOTEL

How Can You Mend A Broken Heart (9)	Al Green / Bee Gees
Mrs Bartolozzi (8)	Kate Bush
So This Is Goodbye (7)	Stina Nordenstam
Old Friends (8)	Simon and Garfunkle
Go Now (7)	Moody Blues

PAINTING BY STARS

Star Child (8)	Junior's Eyes
The Boy With The Moon And Star On	
His Head (8)	Cat Stevens
Searching For Satellites (7)	Wishbone Ash
Supermassive Black Hole (7)	Muse
Supernova (8)	Ray LaMontagne

* Page 234 *Rooms With A View If Nothing Else* the reference here is to the original late 1960's English group featuring the duo of Patrick Campbell-Lyons and Alex Spyropoulos and calling themselves Nirvana. Not the later Kurt Cobain fronted Nirvana, who went on to achieve far greater success.

77

THE MAN WITH THE CUBAN CIGAR

She's Got A New Spell (7) 1988 Billy Bragg

The tall, thin man puffing on the oversized Cuban cigar lived alone in a ramshackle house that had no curtains on the windows and a large hole in the slate roof which let the rain fall through. It had been that way for as long as we had known him.

Each winter without fail, the tall, thin man said, this time he would get the materials and fix the hole. He never did.

In all of the rooms we had seen, there was just one picture on his wall. It was very old and in places the paint was badly worn and peeling from the cracked canvas. Bound within a huge gold leafed frame it looked very much out of place.

An arched stone bridge spanned a narrow river. Large trees along an avenue either side, tumbled off into a muted haze. In the distance, dark clouds partially obscured a pale water sun. In the foreground a man wearing a top hat and holding a cane, walked hand in hand with a young girl. A tan and white fox hound trailed closely at their heels.

The shadowless thin man, smiled as he reflected. The years had flown so fast he did not know where they had gone. He shuffled awkwardly, as if paralysed by the moment. Almost resigned to his loneliness. As he went, a band of smoke drifted above his head and curled about his bony shoulders like a lock of frightened hair.

The moonlight streaking through the open window, threw strange patterns on the ceiling and the marble floor. They disappeared when the man passed by.

His right hand trembled slightly as he waved a finger. From the corner of one eye a tear ran down his cheek. He drifted back to long ago.

The girl in the painting was his mother.

78

GEORGE CALEY'S REPULSE 1804

The expedition had grown weary from all the hard work, so they paused for a brief while at the foot of the precipitous mountains. The flat marshland plain they had crossed the day before, now transformed, giving way to a totally different kind of landscape. Here at the junction of the rivers, the dense undergrowth, interspersed with towering eucalyptus and prickly shrubs that scratched and pierced the skin, made fast travel near impossible. It was decided therefore, that they would leave behind their broken horses and the heavy saddle packs and continue as best they could on foot.

Little by little they climbed until just before sunset. Hoping for a change of fortune, they turned direction under the cloak of a thick choking haze, only to be tumbled headlong into the giant arms of another unknown valley. A strong easterly punched down hard upon the saddleback, then strengthened behind them in a fit of rage. Ahead lay a hundred miles of impenetrable scrub that dropped away precariously through coal dark ravines fed by countless unnamed streams.

From this vantage point they could hear the devil's roar rasping over sharp rock and splintered timber. They could see his curling tongue spit its venom in shallow drifts that hung like clouds above the bloodwood on the ridge.

The sense of awe struck deep and chilled them to their bones.

79

HARRY'S HOUDINI ACT OR MY FIRST
ADVENTURES WITH A PIKE

_Barges* (7) 1972 Ralph McTell from the album
Not Until Tomorrow_

Good old Uncle Harry was a clever one that's for sure.
Knew more about fish and what they swam in than
most people knew about the alphabet. Well that's what we
always thought. And unassuming Harry was not the type
nor had the disposition to change our opinion.

Harry was the husband of my mother's only sister,
Lily. Ever since I could recall, he had walked with a slight
limp, the result of an injury received during the war. He
was an avid greenhouse gardener who had an envious
knack for growing supersize tomatoes, perfect pumpkins
and trellises full of the sweetest peas to be found this side
of the Pennines. But more than this he also happened to
be a most expert fisherman. Throughout the villages near
and far, Harry had gained a reputation second to none. So
much so, everyone for miles around agreed, without doubt
he was Woodlands' finest angler. A no nonsense man
worthy of a medal and a knighthood at the very least.
Like a true professional of his trade, he loved to tell
swashbuckling stories, narratives of derring-do and

the one that got away. Spin a well baked yarn about his exploits with those mysterious inhabitants of the shallow and the deep, the roach, the golden eyed perch and the ever elusive giant eel. Brave encounters with that lucky fish fortunate to strike him on his rare bad day. That day when everything that could possibly do so, went wrong. When a sudden gust of wind took him by surprise, causing him to snag his line on a piece of flotsam or entangle it in the reeds and bull rushes near the river's bank. Or worse than that, spring a leak in his expensive thigh high rubber waders at the critical moment. Just one distractive element enough to break Harry's formidable powers of concentration and thereby make him lose the catch.

Mind you, we all agreed his tall tales though fanciful and well-contrived, were concocted strictly for the benefit of the kids and to Harry that was very important. But as far as Lily and anyone else was concerned never was the quarry lost that jumped onto his trusty hook.

Lily however knew Harry more so than Harry ever realised.

Come the much anticipated annual angling tournament, we set off bright and early when the sun's narrow rays first struck the frosted meadow and when the cuckoo chimed its morning wake up call. Keen as mustard and chirpy as a nightingale, we loaded up the Austin with all manner of devices, knives, nets and rods. To be safe rather than sorry, Harry threw in a few colourful thingamajigs that took his fancy, not quite sure if they would be of any use or not. Still, the more we had the better our chances of winning. Harry shot a glance my way, stuck out his chest and proudly remarked that what he hadn't put in the tackle box, he didn't need.

"Well here's something you W-I-L-L need" Lily responded in an abrasive tone that hinted of her previous adventures in *the clever wives know better than to fish with their husbands club*. It was a large flask of good, strong Yorkshire tea and a generous serving of her famous cheese, cucumber and chutney sandwiches. *"By the time old Harry's finished, you'll be craving one of these"* she said, waving a large brown bag in front of me. It looked so enticing I could have eaten the whole lot on the spot. What better way to sate a young boy's appetite.

Leaving the crowded motorway behind and on the outskirts of town we pulled in at a general supply store so Harry could replenish his favourite stock of Capstan tobacco. He wouldn't go anywhere without the stuff. He confessed no matter how bad it was for his health it more than made up for by improving his thought process and strategic planning skills.

According to the official manual of good practice, some fisherman have a preference for spinners, furry flies and hairy lures. But not Harry. The only bait he ever used was worr-ems. The home grown variety, fat juicy ones, the reddest worms imaginable, fresh out of the deepest section of the compost heap. The sort that would make a baby blackbird's eyes light up. Nothing else compared. Harry swore by them. Knew there was no need for any other sort of fancy aquatic contrivances on his part. It was almost legend that he hadn't yet met a frisky fish that refused to swallow a wriggling meal on the end of a well concealed hook. Or as he liked to spruik, *an old raincoat won't ever let you down.* Harry would know.

Digging his calloused hands into the bottom of the hessian bag and picking out the longest worm I'd ever seen, I could see why he was so confident. *"Big is good"*

Harry grinned, revealing a gap between his bottom teeth so wide I am sure the wind could have blown straight through it.

In water almost waist deep and on his fourth cast, Harry struck. The slender wooden rod arched and trembled in his hand. *"Think I've got a gud un fert taking"*, he crowed. Happy as a peacock on the farm. Right at that moment I was nowhere near as confident as he was, but then again I had never before seen Harry put to task in such a hurry. Tension building, he rifled through his shirt pocket and shuffled oh so carefully to secure a foothold in the thick mud which sucked and teased at his boots, put out his Sherlock Holmes smoking pipe and threw it over his head onto the grassy embankment behind him.

From the shadows a patch of mottled silver slipped by no more than two feet below the surface. *"Yep, tis a pike am sure bat that"*. This time the words grew a little louder than before. A pair of eyebrows raised then lowered like a drawbridge on a moat. *"Bloodeee clever un at that"*. Harry stood bolt upright, his wiry frame silhouetted by the bright sunlight. His nostrils flared and his bow legs tightened. He looked a rare nautical sight indeed.

This was my first up close and personal encounter with a pike and in all the hoo haa and excitement I dropped the sandwiches into a clump of cotton sedge. *"Steadee there yung whippersnapper"* he murmured, desperate not to let the situation get out of control *"nowt but rain and lightning t' worry bout, 'tis only a slim whisper of a thing."* Now that was most reassuring I thought. Whispers often turn into a whole trouble load of shouts.

Closer and closer to the spiral reeds and muddy shallows the fish moved. Slowly but surely. Pulling hard against the straining birch. First to the left and then to the right in a gesture of defiance. Harry knew he was in for one heck of a good old fight.

Spellbound and slightly nervous I took the canvas chair and sat down, ready for the action. I didn't have to wait long for the fireworks to begin.

Harry flinched as if stung by a giant hornet. Sweat built on his furrowed forehead. There was a low, rumbling groan of discontent. He could see what the pike was up to and grabbed for his trusty keep net which hung around his broad shoulders. But this move only gave his clever adversary a little more time and breathing space. With one great, now or never lunge the streak of silver reached the tangled mass of roots of a large willow tree precariously teetering on the water's edge. The line quivered for a second, went taut, then caught fast upon the twisted fibres and jammed Harry's reel. He cursed again, this time at double speed. There was a sharp ping and a sudden snap, then silence as the thin strand of nylon failed and went fluttering into the air. Harry's beetroot red face said it all. With a short, submissive sigh he realised the cause was lost.

That cunning piscine fellow flicked his tail one final time, before disappearing into the murky depths, content in the fact that the river gods were on its side. Our prized would-be dinner had won the day.

Never one to panic, Harry always had a backup plan in case of unexpected emergencies. Even in the worst possible situation he knew what to do. Survival sense prevailed. He pushed the thread bare deerstalker cap back across his receding hairline. Puffed twice on his pipe for reassurance, then cracked those bony knuckles as if the solution to his predicament had hit him like a bolt of lightning. It was time to put our contingency plan into effect. There would be no egg on Harry's face tonight.

On the way home, somewhere near Kirk Smeaton we took an unexpected left turn instead of a right, popped into the fish shop for sore losers' that was there for just such emergencies and picked out the meanest looking, heaviest critter we could find. Six pounds four ounces worth to be precise. The large, bearded man behind the counter wearing a blue and white striped apron shook Harry's hand firmly, then turned and gave a wink. I am sure Harry had met that man before.

It was almost dark. The street lamps flickered to life as the sun set in a wash of red and dusty golds. Lily was waiting at the gate, anxious but happy to see us return in one piece and with our splendid, hard earned catch. *"That must have put up quite a fight dear."* Harry for once was lost for words. She leaned in close and pinched my shoulder. The perfume of lavender on her skin was strong. *"I bet you likely lads are hungry as wolves in a sheep paddock"* she said with that inquisitive look in her eyes.

We sure were.

Harry's good name remained intact and the legend of Captain Ahab and mighty Moby Dick was not forgotten.

80

THAT'S RIGHT, BLAME IT ON THE OYSTERS

There is something crawling on my window, there's something walking up my wall.....

Today was much different to yesterday. Yesterday was easy does it, French red wine, wet kisses and Cadbury Roses chocolate. Now, here I was as sick as an old dog looking for a place to hide. To make things worse it was also the day we had organised to go on our little cruise around the bay and on to Mutton Bird Island. So of course that put an end to that.

A mean yellow sun popped over the fields nice and early. Too early for some. Through the small hotel window it came streaming and right on cue I made it to the bathroom just in time to throw up my previous evening's expensive meal. I think it must have been those locally farmed oysters or god knows whatever else dragged up from the bottom of the sea I had eaten. Surely a mere peccadillo on my part. But Jutta couldn't for the life of her see anything trifling in the matter. She frowned and her cheeks turned a whiter shade of pale. The new look didn't quite suit her temperament. I could see what was coming next. Right before my very eyes the lines on her brow began to mutate into *a steer clear of at all costs* map not found in any atlas. "*Tut-tut. You should know better than to bite off more than you can chew, especially when it comes to crustaceans and molluscs"*, she snapped in a tone that I quickly deduced was not one to be argued with. For a moment I wondered what the hell I was doing here and what mud crabs and oysters had to do with the state of affairs, especially my health or the price of eggs in Denmark, until she chimed in once again *"those damn things just don't seem to agree with you. It must be your heritage or something more sinister"*. I blushed. She was right of course. She always was. I guess that was one of the reasons I married her. So she could tell me not to eat oysters and I of course in my own stubborn fashion would ignore her anyway.

So our much hyped Coffs Harbour getaway for newlyweds finished up being cut short. Three days and nine hours' worth to be exact. Isn't that always the way. Plan for a rollicking good time and *bingo* along comes something rotten to ruin the fun and romance. At this point you could cut the air with a knife. So to smooth the turbulent waters, I briefly made a passing comment about how all was not lost, that at least the fresh salt air driven in from the Pacific had cleared our heads and as an added bonus my sinuses were in the best shape they had been in for years. And *anyway* what was the problem, she never did fancy the awful *Big Banana* nor the real ones that grew here on the steep hillside.

Jutta fumbled in her hand bag of tricks for her lipstick roll. I was amazed at how such a small package could hide so many useless items. For a moment I thought she was going to stencil a nice red cross on my forearm and tell me I had been a naughty boy and how naughty boys do not deserve favours. She didn't. Then the school teacher inside her took control and muttered *"write fifty times on the blackboard I must not eat bad oysters"*. Like a broken down recording repeated herself over and over. Until her mascara mask began to run, until she reached the point where I truly believed her. Although come to think of it I would much rather have gone and stood in the corner for my penance.

Funny, I never did get to see a mutton bird.

81

A CHANDELIER OF STARS

Under The Milky Way * (8) 1988 The Church
from the album Starfish

Alex' face said it in spades. He looked lost. He sure as hell didn't quite know where we had ended up and the long, painful ride had stretched his patience to the very limit. To compound matters, he wasn't the only one on edge.

Fortunately, the old ice cream shop that appeared out of a cloud of bright blue jacaranda blossoms, quickly changed everyone's demeanour. The blackboard menu propped against the window offered exotic colourful gelato and dainty Danish morsels for all types and all tastes. It was an invitation too good to refuse.

"I think I'll try the triple tier double whammy lavender lady, no nuts" Alex chirped without so much as a second thought. Lauren, not to be outdone, remonstrated briefly and then went for something more suitable to her fiery temperament. Mango flavoured mousse with a huge cherry perched on top sounded nice and painless. She just couldn't resist. Neither could Alicia and Natalee.

So there we sat, under a blistering summer sun, in a seemingly endless field full of rippling yellow canola, surrounded by a thousand impatient flies. Stayed until every last drop had been extracted from those extra thick wafer cones. Then went back for seconds.

The broken sign pointed north, just forty five kilometres of winding road to go. Weighed down with our afternoon delights and even though we didn't have much further to travel, the prospect of those hills and nauseating bends did not fill us with great enthusiasm. The rusted cattle gate marked the spot at which our relatively comfortable journey to date, would now turn into a trip of attrition. Still, we were determined to reach Polblue and our camping site before sunset.

At the top of the range tall brown barrel and blackbutt gave way to scattered stands of snow gum. There almost hidden in a narrow band of mist, the sphagnum swamp and open grassy reaches greeted us. Dragonflies danced between banks of spiral reeds. Frogs frolicked in the tea tree stained shallow water. Unaware of our presence, a water hen warbled.

That night with the fire burning brightly, we slept beneath a chandelier of silver stars.

82

THE WISH

*The Grave** (8) 1971 Don McLean from American Pie*

The wise man, with a whole world of wrinkles on his face and a head full of proverbs and tales, looked at the nervous boy and said in a dull but soothing voice *"That is where I wish to be"*. His words danced lightly through the cold air, caught like the last petals on a summer breeze that would never more return. He drew a deep, slow breath, then paused for a moment. Regathering his thoughts and with a shaking hand, he pointed *"Up there on the side of the hill, not too far from here. Somewhere near the old gnarled tree that shall hang its tired branches over me, like restless fingers upon my bones. I shall watch the flowers grow"*

Alex was taken by surprise and even though he tried hard not to, he couldn't help but smile.

There was no hint of sadness behind the man's eyes nor a heaviness in his heart that dimmed the reason.

Brother Francis had seen the years come and go like waves breaking on a golden beach and was not the least bit concerned or overawed by his predicament.

Life is as it should be. No more no less. Therein lies the privilege. Therein lies the great mystery.

He turned slowly, wanting to finish what he had begun.

"Please find a simple place beneath (the tree) and there mark it with a stick. And when the wind that blows is at its kindest, bury me there in the morning time. Where I shall rest content and peaceful in that quiet, pleasant glade. Let me feel the warm sun's light dance forever on my grave".

83

MINUTIA
(DAMN LIES AND STATISTICS)

Thick As A Brick* (9) 1972 Jethro Tull from the album Thick As A Brick

The world is full of wise men who should have known better.

It often doesn't matter where you are, or where one stands, the simple fact is, the more you look and stare at things the less clear they can become. Unless of course, one has access to an electron microscope and just so happens to be a good old fashioned journalist or a particularly mad scientist working on some secret government X Files project. That would explain everything.

So it came as no great surprise that on this special day, either through sheer random chance or meticulous research on someone else's part, I discovered the hidden secrets of the universe. Or should I say they discovered me. Along with a little help from Dvorak, Gustav Holst and a sudden brief encounter with one particular daddy of them all, Kepler 69c.[1]

---

1. *For those with a slightly inquisitive bent, this happens to be a super earth size planet in the Kepler 62 system, some 2700 light years away. Information and statistics courtesy of NASA's Kepler Telescope space exploration program.*

The morning started off harmless enough. First a devil's brew of strong coffee to calm the nerves, backed up with short bread biscuits and some other item of sustenance whose chemical composition I cannot even pronounce. No other distractions except for the irritating fracas of cicadas caught in the great outdoors. Right outside my window.

Senses stretched to their limit and in need of a quick fix, I lean back, trying hard to keep balance and at the same time fumbling for the Sennheiser headphones that somehow have disappeared from their overnight resting place. Undeterred I carefully tweak the tone and balance switches on the amplifier and turn the volume control to seven. A reasonable number. Not too soft as to demonstrate any indifference I may have had and just loud enough to annoy the hell out of the kind neighbours who for weeks now, have been playing the complete unexpurgated recordings of Billy Ray Cyrus and Barry Manilow. In their entirety. On random repeat. Little wonder I am suffering from an episode of sleep deprivation.

So my smile is warranted and my revenge is sweet, if only fleeting.

The red light on the console blinks then shifts to a soothing blue and the pleasant aroma of Arabica filters through the room. Suddenly heaven is here in my own head. What more could one ask for? I ponder the very question as the Bower and Wilkins speakers crackle to life and I am transported to another place light years distant that as of yet, still doesn't have a name.

My wife being a stubborn, dyed in the wool Libran is unhappy with my selection of orchestral wizardry. She tells me in no uncertain terms she would much rather kick off her shoes, keep her feet warm and be entertained slow burn style. That is, start out in a transcendental state, sort of steady as she goes, then build up to the bombastic finale, something in the vein of *In the Hall of the Mountain King, 1812 Overture* or laid back in some French Canadian style like Celine Dion. Ambient soft and sensuous indigo. That's right. Mood is the key to her kingdom.

The news I have in front of me is the same news as yesterday and the day before. Yet still I cannot put the paper down, reinforcing the obvious fact that underneath this layer of skin I am a creature of old habits. What else is there to do to pass away the idle hours? There is nothing here that wasn't here last week and nothing to be alarmed about. The citizens of this vast metropolis are in good hands, served and informed by only the very best minds in their respective fields. This is where the Stephen Hawking syndrome kicks in and I shift my attention to other more distractive things. There is a large fly on the kitchen window sill. I know this because I can hear it buzzing around and around in the key of F. Getting annoyed because it is going nowhere. The sound gets stuck inside my brain and won't come out. No matter how hard I shake it. I think it is an ear worm.

The curtains start to flutter and something else catches my attention. A flash of instant colour that transforms into a familiar picture and a bold typeset I cannot avoid. I put my bi focals on and read. Line by line. Drinking in the moment. A few jumbled words at first. Then some more. Deciphering only the right amount until the room spins and numbers that weren't there a second ago fall into place. Like the first winter snow. They leave a big impression.

Some numbers are smaller than others and some I cannot even begin to comprehend. Taking a slow, deep breath, to brace for the consequences whatever they may be and wherever they may lie, I am prepared for the unbelievable. That irritating *beam me up Scotty* moment I never thought possible had arrived. Nothing left to surprise or shock the system. Here there is no place for the faint hearted. That is the nature of the beast and the beast tells me we live in a galaxy that contains a mere 250 billion stars give or take a few. In anyone's language, that is an absurd amount of gas, heat and light to share around the heavens between friends. So I figure, what has one small, insignificant sun got that all the others haven't? Apparently nothing whatsoever.

By clever calculation and an ounce of positive thinking, it so happens that we share our tenuous Milky Way existence with countless other planets similar in every respect to our own. Each orbiting a large or small star. Personally I am an optimist and prefer to think it is the latter, as most good things they say, revolve around small packages. There is some confusion. I am not quite sure which way is up and which is down. Though colour I am informed has something to do with it. Red giant, white dwarf or yellow dwarf. Each with its own progeny of carefully arranged satellites, forever bound on a carousel ecliptic. And if you follow the clues and join the dots, every third rock from the sun has water good enough to drink and bathe in, the right volume of nitrogen and oxygen and is not too hot and not too cold. Well if you look at it from that perspective, then everything is fine and dandy, the way Goldilocks[2] prefers. From here, it doesn't take a nuclear physicist to work

---

2. *Essential reading for those inclined to the principals of creation are the challenging theories put forward in The Goldilocks Enigma by Paul Davies*

out that we could be but one of 11 billion earth like planets. A truly staggering statistic indeed and a hard truth to swallow. Channelling more than just a touch of Pythagoras and $E = mc2$ into the thought process, I am relieved to find that there are lots and lots of other earths. I happen to like earth, for one thing the place has atmosphere, so that very snippet of information fills me with a great deal of confidence and makes me feel a whole lot better about myself and the current state of the universe. As unlike Carl Sagan, I was beginning to think we were totally alone in the infinite cosmos. It also struck home that whoever did the mathematics and the measuring could not possibly be married, probably still lived at home with their boring parents, seven brothers and sisters, two cats and four dogs and had nothing better to do with their time. Except make it difficult for the rest of us.

I have travelled a long way in five minutes. The newspaper drops to the floor, adding to the considerable debris of articles now piling up at the foot of my comfortable leather recliner. Armed with this latest revelation, I am suddenly wide awake. Though feeling distinctly odd and rather insignificant, like those annoying insects singing arias in the eucalyptus trees. Right here in my very own garden. In my own finely tuned galaxy.

They say knowledge is a wonderful thing when put to the right use. Knowledge is truth and power. Knowledge is also not much good if one doesn't know how to nurture it or what to do with it.

In my case, it is more-what cannot be seen, therefore cannot exist.

Worlds spin and die, new worlds are born to replace them and nothing is as it seems. Atoms and molecules, dust and light only serve to confuse and hinder what it is we might be searching for.

When all is said and done it is the smallest piece of the puzzle that is the hardest of them all to find.

Cocooned in a dense bubble, beneath a layer of plastic shrink wrap I reside. Protected from reality and thankfully far enough removed from where those billion or so stars I know not very much about, collide and collapse. Making a total mess of the system. Making black holes or Alice in Wonderland type holes. I do not like holes. They make me feel queasy. Especially those that have no bottom.

What the truth is I cannot really say. Except that I am real and you are real. And I am here in this private space and you are somewhere else in yours. I go about my business in the usual methodical way and apart from a few glitches and aberrations now and again, I try not to be overcome by extraordinary events.

Confused?

You bet your precious saucer full of secrets[3] I am. But isn't everyone. And deep down I have an awful gut instinct that confusion is the whole point of the exercise.

By now, it sort of makes sense that little green aliens, UFO's and time travel might be real after all and those quasars and quarks may be more important than we can possibly imagine. With that in mind, I can't wait to meet my other irritating self in a parallel universe. If he's anything like me, I would shake his hand and buy him a beer, because somehow I know we just might get along splendidly.

---

3. *Pink Floyd's second album was released in 1968. If you like progressive space rock music then this one's right up your alley. Or for something a little less confronting you might care to try just about anything from the catalogue of Japanese electronic maestro, Tomita*

Until then I shall stick to the New World Symphony or the Planets for my kicks. It's a hell of a lot easier than pondering the alternative. And anyway, I am Aquarius. I don't believe in making ripples. That is best left for stones and other heavy inanimate objects.

84

BOAT ON A RIVER

With yellow hair softly spun and silent, she came with all her clothes undone. Almost unexpected into my room.

Storm clouds gathered at the river's edge drawing with them as they grew in size, a sharp flash of movement from the dark water. A golden perch perhaps or some timid eel startled by the sudden stab of lightning overhead.

I anxiously looked over the side of the boat, but other than my own reflection there was nothing else to see. Whatever was down there had now disappeared.

A cool wind sprang up, fresh out of the south. It whipped against our backs in a pin prick frenzy. We turned hard upon the wooden oars until our arms and fingers ached. Then without so much as a word, headed safe for shelter through the heavy, thick straw reeds that now began to whisper in our wake.

Ahead, barely out of reach, the last of the wading birds (pressured home to bed too early), babbled in displeasure at our rude intrusion. As we gently eased the boat up on the wide sandy reaches, a band of drinking damsel flies took to restless flight.

85

SIMPLE FACTS SOMETIMES HIDE COMPLEX TRUTHS

"My master told me, that a thing he wondered at in the Yahoos, was their strange disposition to nastiness and dirt."

Jonathan Swift GULLIVER'S TRAVELS

Ok. Strike one. So some bright spark out there got it wrong. All men are not created equal. Not even close by any stretch. Fact. Pure unadulterated, ugly fact. Case in point, a middle aged male relative on my mother's side twice removed who shall otherwise for the purpose of this debate remain anonymous.

Let me fill in the jigsaw puzzle as best I can. Picture this. There is a Picasso arrangement of sticks in a ceramic bowl at the doorway and a large, heavy piano in the parlour. It looks out of place standing on the cold, stone floor as he doesn't much like music. Never has the time for it, he adds. That's not to say it's his fault. Who knows, perhaps he might fancy tickling the ivories now and then, it's just that no one's ever heard a single note struck or a feel good, gather round the fireplace song played in jest. Not so much as a *Happy Birthday Norma Jean* or *Good King Wenceslas*. Not even a jingle in times of warm, wet and fuzzy. Certainly no life for one so young and impressionable.

The black sheep of the family also doesn't take kindly to untidy people with bad habits, especially those who reside in close proximity. Not that they could by any stretch be described as anymore untidier a person than you or I. The Minister for Glass Houses just thinks they are. In addition he has an unhealthy attraction to that most ubiquitous earthly substance H_2O, so I presume that is the very reason why a state of the art swimming pool takes pride of place in his lush, garden oasis. One that bubbles and burbles with joy every time the giant multifunction barracuda sweeps its way to places no man has been before. Which kind of sucks the lemon juice out of all and sundry.

Of course deep down, by my very own admission, I am jealous. I would like a nice, clean maintenance free pool but they don't exist. And anyway in these tough economic times I can't afford one. Well that's my excuse. Plus the kids have left the nest, so if I did have one it would be home to the world's biggest vegetable patch by now. In the meantime at least, until the next blue moon arrives, I am more than happy to gaze in wonder across verdant suburban lawns, rub my limited edition sterling silver teapot courtesy of Harrods, cross my heart and make three wishes.

To sum up he pretty much doesn't have any close affiliation to anything other than his Dinky toy vintage car collection.

In my eyes that makes him the most unequal person I have ever met. Full stop.

Strike two. All dogs are not user friendly. Which says a great deal for those that are.

Strike three. All women are not converted blondes. Neither should they be. It is better that way.

Strike four. What you see is not necessarily what you get. Bleeding obvious.

Strike five. As much as I can tell clouds do not have cherub cupids shooting sharp arrows into people's hearts. Nor silver linings. At least the one hanging over my head right now doesn't. This one is just full of dust and water droplets and is about ready to pour on my *make a friend happy* parade.

Which brings me back full circle to the whole point of the argument. In life nothing is certain and nothing is ever as expected. Now where's my special bottle of Margaret River cabernet merlot.

Hallelujah and amen.

86

THE MEMORY DEVICE
(FOR MY FATHER)

"We travel, some of us forever, to seek other states, other lives, other souls" Anais Nin

How he was at the very end is not how I remembered him at all.

We were at his side the night he died. Caught in a frozen moment that didn't seem quite real and yet compelled to watch his very life unfold before our eyes.

A curtain of pure silence fell and trailed behind his ghost in a shower of shooting stars. The room filled and overflowed with light. Glowed and shimmered with a soft and peaceful whiteness that knew no fear. Bright as sun and like the air inside the chambers of the heart, it permeated each and every molecule within us.

Then having satisfied itself for the last time and with nothing left to give, dimmed and soon departed.

87

THE GREAT STONE VIADUCT

Old Friends/Bookends * *(10) 1968 Simon and Garfunkle from Bookends.*

Caught by surprise, you blushed and pointed skyward. Disturbed by the thought of scaling such dizzy heights in order to reach the heavens. From here it was a long way up and you were too afraid to climb. Perhaps for fear of skinning knees or ruining the yellow cotton dress your mother had made for your twelfth birthday. At that moment you looked sad. So sad, the colours of the rainbow fell out of you and where they touched the ground, the earth turned grey. But I said it was okay. Grey was fine.

In an exercise of Barnum and Bailey bravado I clambered up the strong, thick vine of an ivy ladder that had suckered against the stone and wooden beams of the old viaduct. For a long time I sat there at the top, silent, legs dangling over the edge. Oblivious to the world around. Keeping lookout for rocket ships or some other streak rushing across a tiffany blue horizon. But there were only fluffy clouds for miles around.

Bindweed and sweet honeysuckle twisted around the trunk of a dead hawthorn tree and the air was thick with bees. Larkspur grew in a ledge of splintered sleepers. Red

Admirals cavorted here and there, near the water filled troughs that ran between the low brick terraces. Each crystal pond stretched out like elongated teardrops and footprints on the ground. So clear I could see my reflection in each and every one of them.

Swallows skimmed and dived among the hay swathes far below. Light reflecting from their tapered wings.

It was then I closed my eyes and made a wish that I could somehow be like those restless birds.

Out of the shadows of the walled buttress, hedgerow and woodland tumbled into the distance, where daylight's thin fingers melted into mellow darkness. No longer able to see you from this point, I could still sense your presence all around, feel your breath as soft as a warm breeze upon my skin. Feel your cherry lips press silken on my tired shoulders.

When I returned, a smile was still with you. I remember, for you had picked delicate buttercups, cow parsley and wild briar rose for a garland. The brightest one I tied in a ribbon around your head and your hair grew into a garden full of all secret things.

I like flowers. I think I shall save some in a nice vase beside my window. Ready to drink up the remnants of the day. To remind me how pretty you looked.

It was the final breath of summer. Our madcap holidays would soon be over, brushed away into another golden memory.

Around the siding bend a goods train shuddered into view. Steam belching from its narrow funnel. The last rays of afternoon struck the fresh cut fields and overhead, lightning danced and thunder rolled.

It was late. We put what was left of the sunshine inside our pockets and slowly headed home.

88

THE LAST STRAW

A small, harmless looking white ball. A wooden stick. Plenty of patience. The smell of the great outdoors and as much fresh air as the nostrils can take. Surely nothing gets better than this.

Something had to give. I am afraid on this occasion it was me. On a good day given the right conditions and temperament I would win at squash. Bill would always win at golf. No assistance required in that department. It was as if he had a god given right to humiliate me at every opportunity. Which of course he gladly did. It was completely frustrating and as far as I could see, downright unfair. For when it came to the fine art of dabbling with irons and woods I never stood a chance. You see, even at my very best I couldn't so much distinguish a sand wedge from a driver or a putter from a pitcher. A bit like not knowing the difference between a HB and a 4H pencil. But that I could live with. No one kept a score sheet on that one.

Bill was around five feet four inches tall. I stood at a towering five feet ten and a half. The course marshal said Bill was handicapped more than me. I am not quite sure what that actually meant but I don't think height, girth or religion came into the equation. Whatever the logic, there were no objections on my part. I liked the sound of it. Perhaps he would be constricted at the knees, bound with ropes and chains or have stones placed in his nice leather golf shoes. Maybe have his Gatorade spiked. Better still be blindfolded. Now that would give me a real shot at glory.

Bill had a fetish for Payne Stewart. And his fashion sense gone amok. Fancy rolled up T. Barry Knickers. Peaked wool cap or Tam O' Shanter depending on the state of the economy or the mood he was in. And to round off the wardrobe department, fine Scottish tartan jumpers. Custom-made and only the very best of course. It was enough to make me sick at the sight. I preferred jodhpurs and Rod Stewart.

To begin, Bill had the full arsenal. Lock, stock and barrel. Fourteen clubs in total. Motorised buggy, Nike Dura Feel left hand glove, colour to match his socks. Regulation sweat towels and field umbrella just in case of rain. Already I was behind the eight ball with a measly seven clubs, three of which had different shaft lengths. I could see where my day was heading.

Off the first tee, I started 10 strokes ahead. It didn't take me long to put Bill's house in order.

Disaster struck at the very next hole. A picture postcard perfect, nice par five dog leg slightly downhill. A few dips and troughs along the way. I would be hitting into a slight breeze. Right to left I was reliably informed. My first shot landed in the thick rough. No such problems for Bill, he put his smack bang in the middle of the fairway. My second stripped out most of the vegetation that was in the way, but I missed the ball completely. The third through to sixth shot took me on an exhausting safari adventure via tea tree scrub and melaleuca thicket through steamy jungle. My seventh caught a favourable double rebound from a gum tree that wasn't there moments earlier, before finally steering a true course back to the elusive green. Now it was serious. With a wet sail, Bill came home in four with enough spare time to take a relaxing cuppa break. Biscuits and all. Meanwhile I paced up and down and around the perimeter of the putting surface surveying that which lay spread out before me: a formidable slope that dropped alarmingly towards the water at the northern edge. Bunker to the right. Bunker to the left. Bunkers everywhere. I chipped. I chopped and then chipped again. Finally at the fourth attempt I put the bloody Callaway out of its misery and breathed a huge sigh of relief.

And so it went. Hole after hole. Hack after hack. Not getting any better. And still no sign of those predicted afternoon thunderstorms coming to my aid.

Bill was in no danger. I finished 18 strokes behind.

So much for handicaps.

89

WE WERE FEELING KIND OF SEASICK !

Hey Bulldog* (9) 1968 The Beatles from Yellow Submarine

Awind struck in over the shallows, driven across a thousand miles of wildest ocean. Past the lighthouse at the point and between the houses nestled near the foam. It pushed hard, like pine needles on our faces and our hands, then turned itself in the other direction, allowing the delicate mist that had hung about the slopes for hours to momentarily clear. In that instant we caught a glimpse of tall ash forest marching upwards in a single pencilled line, drawn high against the steep incline and away into the clouds and the giant shadow of the Otway Ranges beyond.

We broke the heavy silence. Emerged dazed and breathless on the edge of the cliff, almost teetering at the brink. Ready to be sucked into oblivion. Stuck there in awe between the brown folded hills of Johanna (rising at our backs) and the hissing spray from the great sea breakers. You gripped my arm, too frightened to look down in case we stumbled.

Almost lost in the broken shafts of dying light, an endless speckled blanket spread out across the shoreline.

Bringing a thousand horses riding on the frosted foam, all vivid white and cobalt blue.

A LITTLE SOMETHING TO PASS THE TIME AWAY 10

I BET YOU WISH YOU'D NEVER HEARD THESE

Little Arrows	Leapy Lee
I've Never Been To Me	Charlene
Honey (5)*	Bobby Goldsboro
Agadoo	Black Lace
Baby	Justin Bieber
MMMBop	Hanson
(You're) Having My Baby	Paul Anka
She Bangs	Ricky Martin
Barbie Girl	Aqua
Macarena	Los Del Rio

Disclaimer: Other than *Honey* (which on a good day is passable fare and on a bad day schmalz of the highest order) the above songs have not been given a personal rating. This is strictly for my own safety. I therefore leave such dangerous assessments to the reader's common sense and discretion. Good luck.

Thankfully after this there is no more!

90

GRAVESTONE AT EBENEZER

As the sun struck the last of the three peaks, she turned and shook her head and whispered once again: picture yourself in a river running home.

The rough, grey gravel road rose up to meet us, then swept gently past the ruins of the old sandstone church. Its great arched windows cracked and broken. Its once neat grounds partially hidden now by the tall, speckled sheaths of wild grass twisting in the breeze. High overhead in a burnt summer sky, an orb sun dances. Weaving golden strands at the muddy river's edge.

Close by, in a dense column of reeds and flowering sedge a water hen warbles, its timid voice almost drowned by a relentless roar of sonnet crickets.

A sudden urge beckons. You turn, tugging hard at my sleeve to show me something that has struck the interest of your eye. We feel the same. United in our quest. Hands pointing in the one direction. Something there near the leaning stone cross.

The car shudders and stops with a sudden lurch. Quickly we run, as if our lives depend on it. Brushing past the creeping blackberry that sticks and tears against our skin and clothes. Clamber through the loose cables of the rusted star wire fence and catch our breath for a moment at the broken headstone.

Then like blind men reading braille, carefully glide our fingers across the cold surface of damp granite, searching for an epitaph and a name now long forgotten.

91

DIMMING OF THE DAY

The last of summer's breath passed taking with it the frenzied purple wild plain geese and the azure cloudless skies.

Giant butterflies danced in the narrow shafts of light. If she could, she would have counted each and every one of them. Frozen in the moment, she sat nestled in the cosy leather chair, her yellow skirt pulled taut across the knees. Her delicate brow, beaded in sweat and faintly patterned with the curling wisps of hair that hung about her forehead like gentle summer clouds. Trembling, ever so slightly. She smiled. It was easier to think of the past than dwell upon the road that lie ahead. Waiting here she could picture him a thousand times over and how he always said how much he liked her hands. But that was on another stage in a different play. Now he was just the remnant of a dark shadow pressed into the corner of the room. Out of reach and almost insignificant. As if his bones had long since turned to ashes.

It seemed an eternity she had been here. Stuck between worlds with nowhere else to go and nothing more to see. Yet how could she wish for anything more?

A salt breeze blows through an open window. Shutters creak. The lace curtains rise and flutter. She thinks his very breath has teased them into shape. The branches of the trees tap in gentle rhythm on the walls. Beyond the wooden framed gazebo and the broken fence line, an untamed vista of button grass and flowered meadows beckon. In the distance the great blue sea moans.

Beneath the loose hounds tooth blouse, her breasts rise as fragile moons resting on the tide. She takes one last deep breath, sucks in the fragrance of his body and in that instant lets her mind once more take flight to fancy. In a soft whisper calls his name and dreams of a great exploration beginning all over again. Heart in a flutter and lips pressed tight, she crosses her pale slender legs. In anticipation, watches for his return. Then remembers something her mother had warned her about. Snippets of life and brief pieces torn from a cold fog haze swept in from the bay.

There would be days and nights like this.

Outside the last petals of late afternoon folded into a blaze of patterns and colours she could not hope to save. The dimming of another day without him.

92

BROTHER CAN YOU SPARE THE TIME

The term writer's block is not worth the paper it is written on….

At the rate I am going I'll never get this bloody book written. Plain and simple. Some things are just never meant to be. I have been sitting here now for three weeks solid and can't seem to think of anything worthwhile to put on paper. At least nothing anyone would be remotely interested in. Nothing that would start a fire or send the earth spinning out of its delicate alignment. Where in Killarney were those precious words of wisdom when I needed them the most? Then it occurred to me the sticky situation could have been a whole lot worse.

By my count that was six weeks ago.

One morning out of a jelly brown haze that had secretly crept in under the door, she spoke to me, her sweet mouth overflowing with a thousand cotton candy words. The kind that in my world spellt a whole bucket load of trouble. *"It's just a silly book my dear"*, the voice spluttered, almost struck down by tonsillitis at the worst possible moment. *"Plenty of good people who know absolutely nothing whatsoever about anything, write books."*

The blood rushed to her face. "*What's so difficult about that. If Mort Buckmeister can make it work out then you sure as hell can*". Picking myself up off the floor, I was impressed with her straight forward tactfulness, but in short, I had not the faintest idea where she was coming from or where I was going and anyway, that didn't seem to dilute the urge that was brewing deep inside: I wanted to strangle her right there on the spot. I was however somewhat comforted in the fact that she of all persons would understand how the pieces fit and how the wheels on the bus go round and round, for she had never written so much as a sonnet in her entire life. Not even haiku.

That was two weeks ago.

Now it sure is peculiar how things turn out. How the black snake road twists its way to who knows where and then back again. Just to be annoying. And how events conspire. For right at the lowest point imaginable, the pea soup weather that had hung about my head for months suddenly cleared and the sunlight that had persisted in striking upon the right half of my brain, now struck the left side instead and those sweet sermons I so desperately craved, fell out of the sky like overgrown raindrops in a summer storm. A veritable lexicon of tedious information to save the day. A chance to boot up the word processor and activate the espresso machine once more. No point in painful hesitation. There would be no stopping me now. That's what all those who knew best told me. That's what I thought. A gut instinct also told me my nights would be better spent stargazing or philatelising, if there is such a thing.

Come to think of it, I should be doing lots in my spare time. Help an infirm lady find her way back to the nursing home, give a generous donation to the St. Vincent De Paul Society or set up an aid work program in some far distant, war torn land. Play tournament tiddlywinks for the sheer excitement of it. Mix it with society's big wigs. Maybe even join the Church of Scientology. If only they would have me. The mind boggles.

These gestures would be noble and nice. It's just that for some unfathomable reason, I never seem to get around to such things. My excuses I am afraid are feeble and boundless beyond belief.

That was last week.

This week was different. I did get around to climbing the Sydney Harbour Bridge. A bold decision on my part, but something I had been planning to do for years. To keep up with the Joneses, to make sure my dear wife didn't retain sole bragging rights in the daring adventures department. According to Jutta, I was the only person on the planet other than Alex who had not yet scaled those giddy, girdered heights. Naturally we were both embarrassed by what we had missed out on. So to put an end to the ridicule and to secure lifetime membership in the exclusive *been there done that club,* we cautiously hopped into our one size fits all, baggy pair of blue grey overalls, before tethering each other to a very thin hand rail with an even thinner chain. The man next to me with the glowing hardhat, sadistic smile and streak of humour that left a lot to be desired, explained it was for our own benefit and that nothing untoward had ever happened on his watch. And in any case we should be thankful we weren't affluent Japanese tourists.

So it was with God's blessing, we were sent along our merry way with a number of others in the fool hardy brigade who had no interest whatsoever in self-protection, but every intention of standing at the highest point of the curved steel arch and yelling out at the top of their lungs *"Look what I've done to my hair Ma"*. And of course keeping up appearances no matter the cost, for the funny girl with the braces and expensive camera. *"Stop and smile"* she said *"we have whimsical paths and endless portraits without borders"*. Click, click. That will be twenty three dollars and fifty cents if you want a nice one to put in your portfolio. Thank you very much. I thought she made a lot of sense but Alex flat out declined, his business sense refused to buckle to her feminine charms.

There was also the time I reluctantly partook in the beginner's photographic course for self-confessed dummies. Gift voucher compliments of Natalee. She must have seen something latent in me nobody else could. Something she thought was an acorn worthwhile nurturing. Even if it meant being painfully blunt and brutal. The truth however, was it sounded perfect, almost too perfect. Especially as the promotion blurb said for all types and all ages. No matter the status quo or the IQ. No discrimination there. That was fine by me.

I had a great field day, snapping away with my sleek, newly purchased Canon EOS system complete with nine point AFP, supersonic sensors, triple warp speed drive and flashy USB space port I couldn't seem to locate. Pretending to be someone I wasn't when anyone cared to ask what I was doing. Still, at that moment I had grand visions of *The Bridges Of Madison County* running through my mind, so I said I was a mature aged photo journalist on special assignment for some glossy world travel magazine they had hopefully never heard of. The ploy worked. Some even wanted to pay me to take a panorama of them alongside the international terminal at Circular Quay with *that* building with the huge white sails in the background. Imagine that. Yep, certainly enjoyed the adventure. Too bad the pictures didn't live up to others' great expectations. For that reason, I might try again if I can only find the time.

That was last year. Now I am a little older and apart from a few additional wrinkles not much has changed since then.

Yesterday I know was Monday. It said so on my calendar. It came down cats and dogs and the stock market plummeted one hundred and thirty two points. Today is not so bad. My joints do not ache and there are clouds in a deep blue sky. Four in total. One is shaped uncannily like Marilyn Monroe. Complete in every detail, right down to the breasts. The other three look just like I expect clouds should look. A cool wind is blowing through the trees outside my window and winter is just around the next corner. I can see a small spotted dog chasing the postman down the street and at such times as these I wonder what Einstein got up to when he had nothing important to do?

Maybe he took long walks in the Black forest or went fishing to calm the nerves. Perhaps he played scrabble. Perhaps he took happy family snaps. Perhaps he had his dear wife whispering in his ear to write a book about nothing in particular.

93

ALL THE LINES ARE DOWN

*My eyes were sore. My body ached. Then in a
vision bright she came, ghostlike and spectral upon
an endless sea.*

Through the long night the snow kept falling without a
break. Filling every cleft and hollow. Drifting over the
fields of stone and broken voices. So much snow, even the
smallest of hummocks looked like fairy floss mountains
rising from the plain.

Fifteen miles still to go. It may as well have been five
hundred. So much for the element of surprise. By the time
I'd reach my destination the festivities would be over. No
more sad songs to sing and the cheap red wine would be
gone. So I pondered how much I missed McCabe and
his silly Irish jokes that only he thought funny. Long tall
Sally and her one eyed rocking horse that refused to die.
Grandma Beatrice and those wonderful rum filled pies
no one could ever get enough of. And most of all how I
missed the smell of crushed pine leaves and chestnuts
roasting on the open fire.

Unable to stop shivering and shaking even in his thick
winter uniform, the policeman blew large smoke rings
from his mouth and tried to think of a better place to be.

Despite the fact he was wearing Dr Marten grip souled boots, he struggled to keep upright on the slippery surface. Taking a slow, deep breath, the words tumbled awkwardly into the darkness. "*The road up ahead is blocked and silent now, the cars are going nowhere and the singing wires are down*" he drawled, mercifully extracting nothing more than a blank expression from my numb face. I had never looked at wires quite that way before. I wondered did he know something I didn't. "*Make a wish, you might get lucky. Conditions might just take a turn. Then again...*" He was about to clarify the situation but something distracted him. The sound of children's voices in his head perhaps or the smell of fresh grilled bacon wafting through an open window. He grimaced, rubbing his large hands together in an attempt to generate some kind of instant body warmth. "*Maybe not*" he added as an afterthought. "*It looks to me you could use a nice bath and some serious shut eye, for sure and certain. But it won't be in that miserable town*". A finger stabbed through the frozen air pointing toward some vague object shimmering in the distance. "*No siree, not this god awful night*".

The faint blue beacon mounted on the dashboard threw out a howl of discontent, flashed once, twice then three times before the sedan lurched into gear and as quickly as it had appeared, returned once more into the black void from which it came. Soon there was nothing left behind to follow but old photographs and worn out memories.

The dervish wind whipped a frenzy and cut deep holes beneath the barren hedgerow. Crept its way across the empty meadow like a common hunting fox, leaving marks upon the cart tracks where the rabbits no longer run.

I had a strong urge to call Rupert and tell him what I thought about his directions. But if he had any sense Rupert was probably sound asleep by now all wrapped up in his cosy little bed. A lifetime away from here, somewhere in the arms of a pretty woman who knew better than to venture out in such foul weather.

The ice river rests silent in its course. The snow has fallen on the lilac. Over the woodland and the brae. Between the salt marsh and the red cliffs that sweep along the coast, I can see the last of the embers burning in the hearth.

It's Christmas and all the lines are down.

94

OPUS

There are lyrics hidden in the music, at rest between the lines and gentle strokes that bind. Carefully placed among the clefs and quavers to change my way of thinking.

Afloat in some hypnotic trance we chance our luck and find, as we rapidly approach the autumn of this symphony, that we are left alone to dance on catastrophic chords.

A whole new world awaits for those who listen.

Dare I strike one note allegro, another perhaps andante? Then strip back the pages that now unfold and in a moment of weakness, behold the obvious truth of clear deception.

Once summoned at the crashing end, I shall declare my hand and reveal this conundrum to be the opus of my life.

Now all that is left to finish, is with something said at the very beginning of this story:

If I could start all over again, you know, I wouldn't change a thing.

95

SOMETIMES I KNOW EXACTLY HOW THOM YORKE FEELS.

The Queen had only one way of settling all difficulties, great or small. "Off with his head" she said without looking round.

Lewis Carroll
ALICE'S ADVENTURES IN WONDERLAND

This morning arrived with nowhere else to go and plenty of time to get there. The only things I could think about were google maps, driverless cars and paranoid androids. Which one could say was rather unusual on my part as everyone knows I have a serious aversion to progress. However, first things first. I have to admit that this was no weet bix and prunes in a bowl breakfast start for the squeamish. Not today at least. Today had dilemma written all over it. I felt the twinges of last night's full moon get the better of me. Charged with electricity and ready to take responsibility for any actions I would hereby take, I knew an ill wind would blow nobody any good. So something more palatable to the taste buds would not be out of the question. I decided a half a dozen middle bacon rashers and a healthy dose of eggs benedict would do the trick. Complimented by the usual number 9 strength coffee fresh out of the flashy chrome machine that looked any minute now as if it would sprout wings and take to flight. There was nothing quite as effective at clearing the cobwebs, as the smell of frying ham and crushed robusta beans. Except perhaps, lunch with Heidi Klum somewhere in Marrakesh sharing Bob Hope travel stories. My better half was none the wiser and had no idea what was going on in my sheltered little head, which was just as well. Otherwise I would have some serious explaining to do.

I opened the curtains wide. Disappointed that no sunlight struck my eyes. Instead the only colour that greeted me was a solid grey from an overcast sky that stretched from the coast to the mountains and all the way down to Melbourne. Which was fine if you happened to live in that most frustrating city. At least where the weather is concerned. However this was not Melbourne and I was in no mood for meteorological banter of any sort.

Outside, a bunch of noisy magpies made clear their opinion on politics and world affairs. Roger the overweight engineer from four doors down finally got his mower working and with the precision of a surgeon proceeded to dismantle Mrs Cuthbert's freshly planted bed of yellow gladioli. Thankfully he steered well clear of the roses. In the nick of time the rain set in and put an end to the bloodshed and chaos.

And still I couldn't see the forest for those fake plastic trees.

96

THE ROAD TO LOST MEMORIES

This story actually happened in another lifetime I suppose. Inspired in part by the disturbing novel The Reincarnation of Peter Proud written by Max Ehrlich. By the way, Jeremy was a family friend and he did indeed own a Dodge. Chiffon Sandy was someone I once met long ago…

Sirens rang out. One after the other in some narcoleptic rhythm. Blasting through the dismal winter's night. Sending shock waves through those who were asleep. Even waking those who thought they couldn't get more wide awake. First the police, then the ambulance. Followed soon after by the fire engine scuttling its way through the empty streets. One minute they were there, the next they were dissolved into another dimension.

Jeremy looked over his right shoulder and shifted awkwardly behind the steering wheel. The noise and confusion took him by surprise. He tilted the rear view mirror ever so slightly to better see what all the fuss was about. In the clear, he nudged the duco faded Dodge with the striped decals into the inside lane until it gently came to rest at the side of the road. The engine sputtered and a ribbon of steam curled from beneath the bonnet.

It was not unexpected. He had been meaning to fix that troublesome radiator for weeks.

The long, slow drive down the PCH had numbed the senses and stretched Jeremy to his limits. He was tired and irritable and the Burger King on Brooks was closed. He rubbed his eyes then fumbled for the packet of cigarettes tucked away deep inside the pocket of his Schott fleece lined jacket. He had promised to break the habit once and for all, but right now it was the last thing on his mind. What he needed most was a quick fire nicotine fix to snap him out of his lethargy. Something to draw his thoughts away from the past and the reason he was alone out here in the first place.

Minutes scampered by in an incessant stream of numbers that engulfed him. The traffic lights at the intersection of Constitution and Main were stuck on red. So he wasn't going anywhere in a hurry. He figured nothing else in this dead end town worked and at this hour no one could probably give an uncles. He puffed long and hard on his last Lucky Strike as if his very life depended on it, then drifted once more into the clouds and the warm summer days in the cabin by the lake.

Pictures and sounds overflowed from every corner of his memory and he could still smell the scent of flowering honeysuckle and jasmine on the vine as if it were only yesterday they had bloomed. He reached to touch their delicate petals. Grey, familiar images danced on the weathered boards of the old veranda. Out of the darkness Sandy materialised like she had done a thousand times before. Extricated from the worn suitcase of their lives. She took his hand and at that very instant the moonlight caught her face. The smooth contours of her pale skin triggered inside him a rush of adrenalin and the silken locks of hair cascading across her broad shoulders jumped to life. An electric river coursed through his veins. He didn't know which way the fragrance of her perfume would take him.

For a brief moment Jeremy wanted to press her into his arms and hold her there forever. He wasn't ready yet to give her ghost away. Sandy shivered and went inside. The door creaked and clicked shut behind her. Through the half illuminated window he could see the pretty chiffon dress slip down around her milk white thighs and on to the floor. Her firm breasts glistened in the after glow of the kerosene lamp. If only she could read his mind.

A breeze came out of the hills and across the narrow stone strewn, point strengthening as it reached the shallows. A small boat anchored at the pier bobbed and shifted when it passed. High up in the branches of a pin cherry an eight hooter[1] called.

Jeremy squinted in an effort to refocus on the green arrow that hung from the cable overhead. Beyond the boulevard of concrete silos the freeway stretched away into the distance. Glass buildings beckoned like diamond stars in a seamless shroud of black. The radiator had now cooled down enough so he could pour in some water and quench the beast's thirst.

It was 12:35:40 precisely. Not too late to turn back. He got into the car, flicked the ignition switch, adjusted the FM band to 107.3 MHz then pulled away from the kerb and headed towards the sweet spruce pines where Sandy waited in the shadows.

---

1. *More commonly known as the Barred Owl or Hoot Owl.*

97

BIRDS OF NO ORDINARY FEATHER
(SQUID PRO QUO)

Without music there is no beginning and no end. Life is just an empty page waiting to be transcribed.

Summer hissed and moaned like summers do. But this one saved its best for last. The grumpy hotel manager with the perfect set of false teeth and a chip on his shoulder the size of Japan, snapped *We had no cause for complaint. We should be thankful the weather in this neck of the woods was kind, not cruel. We should be thankful he didn't have a twin brother.* So without further ado we crossed our fingers and hoped it would stay that way until we were sick of seeing his face and back once more in the city of smoke and endless smog.

I must have caught you by surprise when I said you looked cute and nigh on irresistible in your skimpy one piece polyester swim suit that was built more for Capri chic than Bondi babe. For a dangerous second or two there was that distinct *get out of jail free* twinkle in your eye and a tremble in your hand. Of course the last thing you wanted to do was bottle up the champagne froth and bubbles you had made the night before, especially since the kids had decided post haste to do the honourable thing and take themselves out of the equation, electing to make quartz castles and mud cakes instead of trouble. So in an amorous gesture, you let your hair down and I threw away my baggy board shorts and went for something more comfortable. Apple red speedos with a flash motif looked mighty impressive.

Thinking it couldn't get much better than this, we gladly savoured our short break in the pleasant port town of Huskisson. Tossed away what wasn't holiday essential and stuck with Barbara Cartland romance books, SP 15 plus sun lotion massages and doing our darndest to barbecue our sensitive bodies on a piece of sand some say is the whitest to be found on any beach in the world.

Keeping true with the traits of your average tourist, we took in the sights and sounds and a whole lot more and then at the end of a long, productive day, we trudged off in desperate search of supper.

In the late afternoon glow of peace and serenity we parked ourselves on the only vacant bench for miles around. Sat there counting dolphins and watching the fishing boats glide through the breakwater with their catch. Minding our own business until in a dark cloud of wings *they* cackled and cursed then descended to earth to spoil the party. In a matter of minutes and by sheer weight of numbers they dispossessed us of our hard earned fried chips and salty calamari. Exhausted, we tossed away our spasms of hunger and surrendered without so much as a whimper.

Alfred Hitchcock couldn't have planned it any better.

98

THE PECULIAR WORLDS OF KURASAWA CATCHPOLE

These are dark times indeed. Brain waves and infra-red images sent from somewhere on the edge. NGC 1365 comes into view and stutters to a blur. There is nothing to be done here. Until we reach the point of no return. No worries. They tell us home is where the heart is.

Scary to think about isn't it? Frozen old men in worn out cryogenic suits, not in control of their destiny. Unable to terminate the process that keeps those vital chemicals pumping. Over and over. Around a closed circuit board of arteries and veins. Pills and sleep do nothing to ease the pain or erase the memory. Sleep is a state of mind. Just separates the soul from the body or what is left of it from the stark reality.

Through the tiny porthole we call a window we can see the end even before it begins. It is beautiful and at the same time it is ugly. It is hard to resist. The ripple effect gathers like a band of light stretched above the event horizon. Shifts and twists, contorting and changing shape, devouring energy before our eyes. The beast that kills us is our food source.

Housed in a receptacle of giant clouds we carry a cargo of plants and trees. There are lots of them. Too many to number and more than enough for those who remember what a real garden was. But no one will ever see flowers blossom or leaves fall. We fly hopeless on the wings of shadows. Filled with fear. Longing for the warm touch of another sun upon our dying skin.

Do they know what they have done? This metal sarcophagus shall be our tomb. Our last resting place. It hums and whirrs. Electronic language never stops. Delicate wires on fire. Microchips strain to process the unthinkable. And still the engines run at full throttle. Cruising between galaxies at hyper speed.

By now we should have crossed the God divide. A line that isn't a line. The threshold of our dreams. Where there is only blackness and the great chasm left to chase. Where we are dust stuck in an endless vacuum.

Can anyone out there hear us call ? Star sailors on a cosmic sea, we have lost count of the years.

Cradled in the safe arms of our metal mother these voices drift and fade.

Message complete. End of transmission.

99

THE GREATEST JOURNEY IS THE ONE LEAST EXPECTED

For the last time we shall stroll along the Strand. You and I together hand in hand. Where our memories quietly run. We shall gather daisies in the morning sun and glide past dappled houses that once stood so tall and proud. Hide our faces in the broken clouds at the end of day, fumble in our frayed pockets and walk away down platforms worn and faded. We shall stumble for that evening train. One last time. You and I.

Our family is a close and happy little bunch of vegemites. That much is certain. Though the journey travelled together has not been easy nor without some hiccups along the way. We have learned from each other. We have built upon each other's dreams. Most of all, we have shared a unique bond that has strengthened over the years and we have come to realise the real meaning of love. In our time we have seen the seasons come and go. Seen the wild flowers adrift in spring's green fields. Chased the winds and storms. Braved flooding rains. Yet still we stand in awe at the beauty of a simple sunset. Been brought to tears and wondered how it can be so.

My family has now grown and transformed. It is not the same family we started out with. But in its own remarkable way it is far stronger and more resilient.

Leo is a not too small white and tan beagle. He was named in honour of my daughter's teenage preoccupation with all things Mr De Caprio. Leo has a nice warm bed and a roof over his head. He runs the house with an iron fist and we obey his every whim and command. As all good dog owners do. We also have a little bird in a rather large cage. Romeo[1] is a brightly coloured African love bird. Though I am at a loss to understand why *love* should ever factor into the equation. For long ago he got rid of Juliet. Annoyed her to a premature death. She is buried under the crepe myrtle tree in our back garden. Each summer without fail, it puts on a wondrous display of fluffy blossoms that hang like a mauve mist upon the twisted branches. Just for Juliet.

My daughter Natalee is happily settled in her new life in Melbourne with her wonderful husband and partner Anthony. They have put down roots of their own just as we did so many years ago.

My son still lives at home and thinks he is in a luxury hotel for the disadvantaged. He is a marketing executive with a high profile international company. Alex likes fast cars and keeps his own car squeaky clean. It is an obsession of youth and enthusiasm.

Whenever he gets the chance he plays guitar, Tommy Emmanuel style, listens to i tunes on his headphones and to keep fit he rides a bike.

---

1. *Since these lines were put to paper, sadly Romeo has now crossed over to the other side. Aged 14 and one half years. He is buried alongside Juliet under that same old crepe myrtle.*

Jutta now enjoys her well-earned retirement years and is as steadfast, strong and beautiful as the day I first met her. I could not in my wildest dreams have wished for a better wife, son and daughter than I have been blessed with.

With such a precious gift begins the greatest journey of them all. And unlike the character at the beginning of this story, I am far from lonely.

TAKE ME BACK THROUGH THE YEARS 1955 – 1970

The following compilation of songs provides what I hope is a reasonable and fairly accurate representation from the artists' musical canon.
Some of the recordings listed here can only be sourced on album. A large majority of the single releases noted did not achieve number 1 status.

Further reading: Virgin Encyclopedia of Rock 1993 Edition
The Great Rock Discography. 7th Edition 2004 Martin C. Strong

1955	ROCK AROUND THE CLOCK* (9)	BILL HALEY AND HIS COMETS
	SIXTEEN TONS* (7)	TENNESSEE ERNIE FORD
1956	HEARTBREAK HOTEL* (9)	ELVIS PRESLEY
	BLUE SUEDE SHOES* (8)	CARL PERKINS
	THE ROCK ISLAND LINE* (9)	LONNIE DONEGAN
	I'VE GOT YOU UNDER MY SKIN* (7)	FRANK SINATRA
	TUTTI FRUTTI* (7)	LITTLE RICHARD
	GREAT PRETENDER* (7)	THE PLATTERS
1957	GREAT BALLS OF FIRE* (8)	JERRY LEE LEWIS
	YOU SEND ME* (8)	SAM COOKE
	DIANA* (8)	PAUL ANKA
	THAT'LL BE THE DAY* (8)	BUDDY HOLLY AND THE CRICKETS
	BLUEBERRY HILL* (7)	FATS DOMINO
	ALL SHOOK UP* (8)	ELVIS PRESLEY

1958	*IT'S ONLY MAKE BELIEVE* (9)	*CONWAY TWITTY*
	FEVER (9)	*PEGGY LEE*
	ALL I HAVE TO DO IS DREAM (8)	*THE EVERLY BROTHERS*
	SUMMERTIME BLUES (7)	*EDDIE COCHRAN*
	TEQUILA (7)	*THE CHAMPS*
	CHANTILLY LACE (8)	*BIG BOPPER*
1959	*MACK THE KNIFE* (7)	*BOBBY DARIN*
	KANSAS CITY (6)	*WILBERT HARRISON*
	LONELY BOY (7)	*PAUL ANKA*
	EL PASO (5)	*MARTY ROBBINS*
	YOU GOT WHAT IT TAKES (7)	*MARV JOHNSON*
	MR BLUE (7)	*THE FLEETWOODS*
1960	*ALL MY TRIALS* (6)	*JOAN BAEZ*
	APACHE (8)	*THE SHADOWS*
	TAKE FIVE (9)	*DAVE BRUBECK QUARTET*
	WONDERFUL WORLD (7)	*SAM COOKE*
	CATHY'S CLOWN (7)	*EVERLY BROTHERS*
	MONEY (8)	*BARRETT STRONG*
1961	*RUNAWAY* (8)	*DEL SHANNON*
	RUNAROUND SUE (8)	*DION*
	I FALL TO PIECES (7)	*PATSY CLINE*
	TOWER OF STRENGTH (8)	*GENE McDANIELS*
	CRYING (8)	*ROY ORBISON*
	THE LION SLEEPS TONIGHT (8)	*THE TOKENS*

	PLEASE MR POSTMAN (8)*	*THE MARVELLETES*
	HIT THE ROAD JACK (7)*	*RAY CHARLES*
1962	*TELSTAR* (8)*	*TORNADOES*
	LOVE ME DO (7)*	*THE BEATLES*
	THE RED ROOSTER (6)*	*HOWLIN' WOLF*
	THE PEPPERMINT TWIST (5)*	*JOEY DEE AND THE STARLIGHTERS*
	SHEILA (8)*	*TOMMY ROE*
	HE'S A REBEL (7)*	*THE CRYSTALS*
	SHERRY (8)*	*FOUR SEASONS*
1963	*SHE LOVES YOU* (8)*	*THE BEATLES*
	A HARD RAIN'S A GONNA FALL (7)*	*BOB DYLAN*
	BRING IT ON HOME TO ME (7)*	*SAM COOKE*
	HIPPY HIPPY SHAKE (7)*	*THE SWINGING BLUE JEANS*
	LITTLE DEUCE COUPE (6)*	*THE BEACH BOYS*
	WALK LIKE A MAN (7)*	*THE FOUR SEASONS*
	HE'S SO FINE (7)*	*THE CHIFFONS*
1964	*SHE'S NOT THERE* (9)*	*THE ZOMBIES*
	HOUSE OF THE RISING SUN (10)*	*THE ANIMALS*
	CAN'T BUY ME LOVE (9*	*THE BEATLES*
	MY COLOURING BOOK (5)*	*DUSTY SPRINGFIELD*
	ROUTE 66 (7)*	*THE ROLLING STONES*
	MY BACK PAGES (10)*	*BOB DYLAN*
	YOU REALLY GOT ME (9)*	*THE KINKS*

1965 *NORWEGIAN WOOD* (10)* THE BEATLES
   MR TAMBOURINE MAN* (9) THE BYRDS
   LIKE A ROLLING STONE* (9) BOB DYLAN
   NEEDLE OF DEATH* (6) BERT JANSCH
   MY GENERATION* (8) THE WHO
   SATISFACTION* (8) THE ROLLING STONES

1966 *GOOD VIBRATIONS* (10)* THE BEACH BOYS
   TOMORROW NEVER THE BEATLES
   KNOWS* (10)
   JUST LIKE A WOMAN* (10) BOB DYLAN
   EIGHT MILES HIGH* (9) THE BYRDS
   HAPPENINGS TEN YEARS THE YARDBIRDS
   TIME AGO* (8)
   SUNNY AFTERNOON* (8) THE KINKS
   HELP, I'M A ROCK* (6) THE MOTHERS OF
            INVENTION
   HOMEWARD BOUND* (8) SIMON AND GARFUNKLE
   FIRE ENGINE* (6) 13ᵀᴴ FLOOR ELEVATORS
   HIDEAWAY* (7) JOHN MAYALL'S BLUES
            BREAKERS
   PAINT IT BLACK* (9) ROLLING STONES
   MELLOW YELLOW*(8) DONOVAN
   GOOD LOVIN'* (8) THE YOUNG RASCALS

1967 *STRAWBERRY FIELDS* THE BEATLES
   FOREVER* (10)
   WHITE RABBIT* (8) JEFFERSON AIRPLANE
   NIGHTS IN WHITE SATIN* THE MOODY BLUES
   (10)
   ELECTRICITY* (7) CAPTAIN BEEFHEART AND
            HIS MAGIC BAND

	_PURPLE HAZE_* (8)	JIMI HENDRIX EXPERIENCE
	_A WHITER SHADE OF PALE_* (10)	PROCUL HARUM
	_BLUEBIRD_* (8)	BUFFALO SPRINGFIELD
	_MORNING GLORY_* (7)	TIM BUCKLEY
	_YOU SET THE SCENE_* (6)	LOVE
	_SEE EMILY PLAY_*(8)	PINK FLOYD
	_LIGHT MY FIRE_* (7)	THE DOORS
	_SUNSHINE SUPERMAN_* (7)	DONOVAN
	_SHE'S A RAINBOW_* (8)	ROLLING STONES
	_WHEN I WAS YOUNG_* (8)	ERIC BURDON AND THE ANIMALS
	_GIMME LITTLE SIGN_* (7)	BRENTON WOOD
	_TIN SOLDIER_* (9)	SMALL FACES
	_HIGHER AND HIGHER_* (8)	JACKIE WILSON
1968	_WHILE MY GUITAR GENTLY WEEPS_* (9)	THE BEATLES
	_WHITE ROOM_* (9)	CREAM
	_ALL ALONG THE WATCHTOWER_* (9)	JIMI HENDRIX EXPERIENCE
	_SUZANNE_* (9)	LEONARD COHEN
	_I WALK ON GILDED SPLINTERS_* (7)	DR. JOHN
	_LAZY SUNDAY_* (8)	THE SMALL FACES
	_TEARS OF RAGE_* (7)	THE BAND
	_TIME OF THE SEASON_* (8)	THE ZOMBIES
	_SOME VELVET MORNING_* (6)	NANCY SINATRA AND LEE HAZLEWOOD
	_HURDY GURDY MAN_* (8)	DONOVAN

1969	*WHOLE LOTTA LOVE* (8)	*LED ZEPPELIN*
	HERE COMES THE SUN (10)	*THE BEATLES*
	COURT OF THE CRIMSON KING (8)	*KING CRIMSON*
	OH WELL PTS 1 & 2 (7)	*FLEETWOOD MAC*
	BORN ON THE BAYOU (8)	*CREEDENCE CLEARWATER REVIVAL*
	RIVER MAN (8)	*NICK DRAKE*
	A SAILOR'S LIFE (9)	*FAIRPORT CONVENTION*
	INDIAN GIVER (5)	*1910 FRUITGUM COMPANY*
	HE AIN'T HEAVY HE'S MY BROTHER (10)	*THE HOLLIES*
	CRIMSON AND CLOVER (9)	*TOMMY JAMES AND THE SHONDELLS*
	GET TOGETHER (8)	*THE YOUNGBLOODS*
1970	*LET IT BE* (10)	*THE BEATLES*
	LAYLA (8)	*DEREK AND THE DOMINOS*
	RUN THROUGH THE JUNGLE (8)	*CREEDENCE CLEARWATER REVIVAL*
	WAR PIGS (7)	*BLACK SABBATH*
	CHILD IN TIME (8)	*DEEP PURPLE*
	FATHER AND SON (9)	*CAT STEVENS*
	THE BOXER (10)	*SIMON AND GARFUNKLE*
	OYE COMO VA (7)	*SANTANA*
	DARK GLOBE (6)	*SYD BARRETT*
	SPIRIT IN THE SKY (8)	*NORMAN GREENBAUM*
	ALL RIGHT NOW (9)	*FREE*
	RIDE CAPTAIN RIDE (7)	*BLUES IMAGE*

TEN OF THE VERY BEST:

	SONG	ARTIST	ALBUM
1.	LET IT BE	THE BEATLES	LET IT BE
2.	PENNY LANE	THE BEATLES	1 (Original Single Release)
3.	BOHEMIAN RHAPSODY	QUEEN	A NIGHT AT THE OPERA
4.	STRAWBERRY FIELDS FOREVER	THE BEATLES	1 (Original Single Release)
5.	THE BOXER	SIMON AND GARFUNKLE	BRIDGE OVER TROUBLED WATER
6.	ELEANOR RIGBY	THE BEATLES	REVOLVER
7.	POSITIVELY 4TH STREET	BOB DYLAN	Single Release
8.	STAIRWAY TO HEAVEN	LED ZEPPELIN	LED ZEPPELIN 4
9.	HALLELUJAH	LEONARD COHEN	VARIOUS POSITIONS
		JEFF BUCKLEY	GRACE
10.	WHILE MY GUITAR GENTLY WEEPS	THE BEATLES	THE BEATLES (WHITE ALBUM)

IT WAS A VERY GOOD YEAR: 1967

Albums Listed In No Particular Order. My Rating In Brackets.

SURREALISTIC PILLOW* (8)	JEFFERSON AIRPLANE
SGT.PEPPER'S LONELY HEARTS CLUB BAND* (10)	THE BEATLES
JOHN WESLEY HARDING* (9)	BOB DYLAN
SOMETHING ELSE* (9)	THE KINKS
THE WHO SELL OUT* (8)	THE WHO
DISRAELI GEARS* (7)	CREAM
BETWEEN THE BUTTONS* (9)	THE ROLLING STONES
ARE YOU EXPERIENCED* (10)	THE JIMI HENDRIX EXPERIENCE
PIPER AT THE GATES OF DAWN* (9)	PINK FLOYD
FOREVER CHANGES* (9)	LOVE
SONGS OF LEONARD COHEN* (8)	LEONARD COHEN
DAYS OF FUTURE PASSED* (8)	THE MOODY BLUES
THE INFLATED TEAR* (5)	ROLAND KIRK
SAFE AS MILK* (8)	CAPTAIN BEEFHEART AND HIS MAGIC BAND
WINDS OF CHANGE* (6)	ERIC BURDON AND THE ANIMALS
MR FANTASY* (8)	TRAFFIC
MOBY GRAPE* (7)	MOBY GRAPE
GOODBYE AND HELLO* (7)	TIM BUCKLEY
THE DOORS* (9)	THE DOORS

ICONIC ALBUM COVER ARTWORK:

Reference Material: The Album Cover Album Edited by Storm Thorgerson and Roger Dean

1000 Record Covers   Michael Ochs

IN THE COURT OF THE CRIMSON KING	KING CRIMSON
SGT.PEPPERS LONELY HEARTS CLUB BAND	THE BEATLES
BITCHES BREW	MILES DAVIS
DISRAELI GEARS	CREAM
STICKY FINGERS	ROLLING STONES
BRAIN SALAD SURGERY	EMERSON, LAKE AND PALMER
SILK DEGREES	BOZ SCAGGS
HOUSES OF THE HOLY	LED ZEPPELIN
DARK SIDE OF THE MOON	PINK FLOYD
MIND GAMES	JOHN LENNON
TALES FROM TOPOGRAPHIC OCEANS	YES
OSIBISA	OSIBISA
VELVET UNDERGROUND AND NICO	VELVET UNDERGROUND AND NICO
OGDEN'S NUT GONE FLAKE	THE SMALL FACES
ROXY MUSIC	ROXY MUSIC
THE ROARING SILENCE	MANFRED MANN'S EARTH BAND
LED ZEPPELIN	LED ZEPPELIN
GOODBYE YELLOW BRICK ROAD	ELTON JOHN
TROUT MASK REPLICA	CAPTAIN BEEFHEART

ALADDIN SANE	*DAVID BOWIE*
VERY 'EAVY, VERY 'UMBLE	*URIAH HEEP*
TEA FOR THE TILLERMAN	*CAT STEVENS*
ELECTRIC LADYLAND	*JIMI HENDRIX EXPERIENCE*
IN SEARCH OF THE LOST CHORD	*MOODY BLUES*
ABBEY ROAD	*THE BEATLES*
OGDEN'S NUT GONE FLAKE	*SMALL FACES*
BLIND FAITH	*BLIND FAITH*
SHOOTOUT AT THE FANTASY FACTORY	*TRAFFIC*
CRIME OF THE CENTURY	*SUPERTRAMP*

ALBUMS TO APPRECIATE WITH A FINE WINE AND A GOOD WOMAN

It is to be hoped that the cross section of recording artists and musical genres outlined below, makes possible a rewarding and exhilarating introduction to some of the finest albums released. Unfortunately I must plead guilty to a bias that clearly favours those recordings of the sixties and seventies.

Placed in no particular chronological or preferential order this listing will no doubt be the subject of great debate and consternation to others who disagree with my views. Many fine albums have been omitted but based on a strict compliance criteria: choosing to limit the number of selections to just thirty albums together with the influence each has had in terms of historical importance, recording quality and technique, emotive content, musical presentation and progression this list is the best I could come up with. A brief personal synopsis for each album is also provided. Sincere apologies to all those out there who may be offended by this inventory.

Here goes anyway:

BLOOD ON THE TRACKS 1975   *BOB DYLAN*

A bleak and powerful collection of raw, emotive songs, highlighted by sparse and simple musical arrangements. In his usual eclectic, word whining way Dylan's songs touch upon the blues and folk music style he had now become a master of. From the acerbic refrains of Idiot Wind to the beautiful, understated Simple Twist Of Fate it is a collection of stories dealing with love lost, told with unexpected clarity and vivid frankness. If you had to choose just one Dylan album from his entire catalogue, perhaps this would be it. From start to finish it does not disappoint.

<u>BLONDE ON BLONDE</u> *1966*   *BOB DYLAN*

Considered by critics and public alike to be Dylan's supreme achievement. Rock's first true double album (though some scholars and analysts still debate this fact) and incorporating a gate fold cover, it is a masterpiece of musical progression, experimentation and sheer excitement that is accessible to all. Dylan meticulously explores, transforms and expands upon the country roots of rock that made him famous. There is a deep touching sadness attached to the heartfelt strains of <u>Just Like A Woman</u>. This album provided a wealth of material for others to admire and imitate. Bob did here what only Bob could do and then some. Sample with a nice dry red. One to be listened to over and over again.

<u>HIGHWAY 61 REVISITED</u> *1965*   *BOB DYLAN*

The process had well and truly begun. Not without criticism, Dylan had transformed in a few short years, from beloved acoustic folk sage to full blown electrified performer. The songs presented here are artistic, cohesive and literate and none adhere to the standard pop convention in terms of expected running time. The shortest is an airplay friendly 3.00 minutes and the powerful narrative of <u>Desolation Row</u> runs in at a staggering 11.00+. The new rambling Dylan, now an assured, complete wordsmith, master of mood and melody, rises to the occasion on this astonishing work. Aided by the accomplished pairing of Mike Bloomfield on guitar and Al Kooper on organ, Highway 61 Revisited raised the bar and set the *standard for countless other artists to follow. Just let yourself go and blow with the wind.*

REVOLVER *1966*   *THE BEATLES*

When released, it was certainly cutting edge and a substantial leap forward from the reflective, yet fairly restrained material found on 1965's Rubber Soul*(9). Sadly, Revolver was largely under appreciated by the public of the time, perhaps in part due to its alternative, unexpected subject matter and atypical Beatles style delivery. This indeed was a Beatles album unlike any previous Beatles album. Here the foursome shifted into top gear and headed off in a radical new and breathtaking direction. Fortunately the ensuing years have been kind and its true greatness is now fully recognised. In fourteen short, yet unforgettable songs, it transcends time and connects seamlessly across entire generations. Full of sounds and musical craftsmanship not heard before on a pop record. The Beatles having lost the desire and perhaps the energy to perform in live concerts and with more time on their hands than ever before, had now discovered that the very studio they were utilising was an instrument in itself. Much more than just a confined room in which the recording process actually took place. It was to prove, a cornucopia of creativity and synergy on which the Beatles would now ultimately thrive. Revolver was not just the precursor to Sgt. Pepper's, it was also the spark and the catalyst. Throw away the flimsy, child friendly (but strangely likeable and very catchy), stoned out sing-a-long ditty of* Yellow Submarine *and it is the perfect recording that sounds nothing whatsoever like pop music.* Eleanor Rigby *and* Tomorrow Never knows *being the classic cases in point. So say we all.*

<u>*ABBEY ROAD*</u> *1969*   *THE BEATLES*

Without doubt Abbey Road stands as the Beatles most technically accomplished recording. George Martin's deft precision and polished production is second to none. Spawned out of the decaying remains of a once unified entity[1] this became the Beatles swan song (although <u>Let It Be</u> was released later). Who would have thought it possible, given the acrid circumstances and media frenzy surrounding the band. Managing to cast internal bickerings aside, albeit only for a brief period, they proved their harshest critics wrong and showed that even at this terminal point of their careers no one could hold a flame to them. As progressive and invigorating as anything the quartet ever put down. Even with only a virtual hotch potch of fragmented and unfinished song material (some critics for want of a better description, suggested throwaway was more appropriate) at their disposal they somehow blended it all together in a remarkable cohesive mass. Harrison's bitter sweet statement of hope <u>Here Comes The Sun</u> sparkles like a diamond through troubled times and could there have possibly been any better way to say goodbye than with the all too short and plaintive epilogue of <u>The End?</u> With tears in my eyes and a lump in my throat I very much doubt it. Long live the Beatles. Enough said.

<u>*SGT.PEPPER'S LONELY HEARTS CLUB BAND*</u> *1967*   *THE BEATLES*

Unable to get enough of what was on offer in this tasty, seamless melange, the critics and buying public of the time raved. Delivering a complexity never before realised in modern music

---

1. *Though the painful process of disintegration had begun at least a year earlier with the White Album, it came into full effect during the often spiteful and disharmonious Let It Be recording sessions. Somehow managing to join forces once more, the Beatles cast aside their differences, acrimony and egos just long enough to put together their musical opus.*

that required an astonishing 700 hours of studio time to make, it was a giant step forward in production and sound techniques and a major departure from conventional rock recording. It set the path for popular music and musicians alike to follow. Here was indeed proof that all music styles, various effects, electronics and multi layered instrumentation could be mixed and blended into a palatable and acceptable format. From the backward loops and spliced tape jumble of the closing stanzas of (Being) For The Benefit Of Mr Kite to the unnerving final chaotic flourish and orchestral crescendo of <u>*A Day In The Life*</u> *the album remains a relevant tome for all ages. But the question begs to be asked: is there more fluff here than substance? Is this album overrated? I don't think so. In so many ways and on so many different levels it remains an outstanding musical milestone. Imagine how great this album would have truly been if the* <u>*Penny Lane*</u> *and* <u>*Strawberry Fields*</u> *recordings had been included in the final product as was originally intended. Arguably it remains the Beatles magnum opus. A statement not only for misguided youth, but for entire generations.*

<u>*THE BEATLES (aka THE WHITE ALBUM)*</u> *1968   THE BEATLES*

With its plain white album cover displaying only the group name and a simple embossed record pressing number, The Beatles could not have been any further removed from the gloss, glamour and ostentatious artwork of its landmark predecessor. On the surface at least The Beatles hinted at a welcome return to a more raw and stripped back style. A return to the good old fashioned days before they had become famous. When music was fun to make. It certainly delivered on all counts. George Martin did not disguise the fact that he believed this sprawling beast should have been prudently truncated from its large double album format into a much more user friendly single disc. The group resisted any temptation to cut back or delete any of the material. Careful scrutiny reveals the album's greatest attribute and strength lies in the sheer breadth, fragmentation and scope of material across all genres. From rockabilly, simple acoustic ballads, orchestral meanderings, ragtime, music hall, electronic collage, down-and-dirty blues to good old rock and roll. Sheer brilliance side by side with sheer self indulgence, this package has the lot. Long, Long, Long stands as one of George Harrison's most poignant, understated love songs. In a whispered, haunting voice that is about God and not a girl (as mentioned in his book I, Me, Mine) George pours out his innermost emotions. It begins with a gentle guitar statement and ends with a hair raising banshee moan, a rattling good moment[2] and a subtle brush of the drums. The White Album is an artistic multi layered cake of incredible depth and dimension, yet a flawed masterpiece.

DARK SIDE OF THE MOON *1973*   PINK FLOYD

Anxious to be rich and famous from the very early days (Roger Waters had stated in an interview in 2003) this album gave them all that and more. Meticulously engineered by Alan Parsons, whose credits included The Beatles Abbey Road, Floyd's eighth studio album is embellished with shimmering guitars, studio wizardry, spoken voice samples and pulsing, off beat electronics. From the infectious, clunky drive of Money, the subtle complexities of Brain Damage and Eclipse, through

---

2. *During the recording sessions a bottle of Blue Nun wine was inadvertently placed on one of the Leslie speakers. When Paul hit a particular organ note, the speaker began vibrating causing the bottle to rattle. Impressed with the accidental outcome, George Martin and the sound engineers decided to leave the resultant effects in the final take. (Reference: The Beatles Complete Recording Sessions. Lewisohn)*

to the soaring gospel vocals that dominate <u>The Great Gig In</u> <u>The Sky</u>, Dark Side Of The Moon proved to be the perfect example of the progressive rock concept album at the highest level. Spending an unprecedented term on the American Billboard Charts (some fourteen years in total) and selling in excess of 45 million copies to date, Pink Floyd had raised the bar. Where would the road take them from here?

<u>WISH YOU WERE HERE</u> 1975   PINK FLOYD

'Madcap' Syd Barrett was unfortunately not around Pink Floyd for long, but his spectre left an almost indelible mark upon the group he had helped establish. Recognising Barrett's frailties and indiscretions Roger Waters and David Gilmour dedicated an entire song suite to his influence, raw talent and considerable erratic genius. <u>Shine On You Crazy Diamond</u> is the astonishing product. Wish You Were Here is in many ways superior to its much hyped predecessor <u>Dark Side Of</u> <u>The Moon.</u> For how much longer could Pink Floyd keep their differences of opinion in check and hold it all together? After the quaint but soft at heart <u>Animals</u> and the erratic double set of <u>The Wall</u>* (8) sadly it was all downhill.

<u>STICKY FINGERS</u> 1971   ROLLING STONES

With its controversial for the time, cover image (courtesy of visual art movement pioneer Andy Warhol) the Rolling Stones managed to whip up a world-wide media frenzy. Would the contents prove to be as subtle as the denim jeans and zipper front piece. The album surprises on many levels. Overall it has a relaxed, laid back quality and delivers a fine mixture of raw, edgy blues, country blend (think Gram Parsons and the Flying Burrito Brothers) and infectious southern style soul. The *songs contained herein highlight the Stones ability to paint different moodscapes and yet still deliver with deft lyrical style and nuance. The ballad <u>Wild Horses</u>[3] remains one of the finest songs in their catalogue. Overall a slow burning blues and drug infused collection of dark and malevolent songs.*

<u>EVERY PICTURE TELLS A STORY</u> 1971   *ROD STEWART*

Not exactly a giant leap forward from his previous two offerings <u>An Old Raincoat Won't Ever Let You Down</u> and <u>Gasoline Alley</u>. However on this broad introspective sweep of songs, Rod Stewart came close to perfection in every sense of the word. His rootsy, folk and ambling blues style delivery combined with a newer hard edged rock and roll approach proved a virtual masterstroke. The ex Faces front man stands and lets loose with all guns blazing. Every song, be it an original composition or a carefully crafted cover, is an absolute gem, delivering an overall picture of a sometimes frail, naïve young man celebrating his life and coming to terms with the world around him. There are struggles here as well as triumphs and jubilation, side by side with melancholy and wavering sadness. <u>Maggie May</u> might be the album's towering centrepiece but the poignant, <u>Mandolin Wind</u> is its crowning glory. A timeless album that amalgamates the very best parts of folk, blues and rock. Be converted and throw away all doubts.

<u>OK COMPUTER</u> 1997   *RADIOHEAD*

Of this compilation of albums to appreciate, OK Computer is by far the latest listed by year of release. Which perhaps says a

---

3. *This has been covered by an array of artists including Gram Parsons and Molly Hatchet*

great deal about the music that falls into the period between. At once difficult to categorise and certainly an uneasy and at times frustrating armchair ride, but surely a must have for all true music lovers. Even the Beatles would have been proud to put together such a pastiche of sounds and electronic amblings. <u>Paranoid Android</u> is an epic slow ride that unfolds in layers of sonic turmoil. Odd time signatures and complex syncopations embellish these eerie masterpieces. Repeat listens and dogged persistence, enhance the overall experience. Ambitious and alluring with just the right amount of melancholia. Thom Yorke doesn't appear to know the meaning of happy and uplifting. His thin, reedy voice delivers with the perfect sprinkling of light and shade and emotional emptiness in a sad undertone that few could hope to match. Not to everyone's taste, but if you shut the curtains and turn down the lights there is a lot to be discovered in this slow unfolding tapestry. Open your mind, you will be rewarded.

<u>PET SOUNDS</u> *1966*   THE BEACH BOYS

Competing in earnest with the Beatles for creativity and song writing dominance, Brian Wilson unashamedly inspired by the Beatles <u>Rubber Soul</u>* (9), came up with an artistically stimulating piece of musical one upmanship. Pet Sounds was the result and proved to be a most radical departure from the typical Beach Boys fare that had hitherto made them famous. Here, there are no surfing, cars or happy California girl songs. The new themes contained within, reflect upon isolation, introspection and the seeming loss of innocence. Pet Sounds is an intricately woven production sound piece. A fully realised amalgam of joy and heartfelt emotion as well as deeper, sad yearnings. <u>God Only Knows</u> must surely rate as one of the greatest love songs of all time. Pet Sounds is invariably *nominated by music lovers and critics alike as the greatest album ever made. It remains a grand musical canvas of Da Vincian proportions.*

TROUT MASK REPLICA *1969*   *CAPTAIN BEEFHEART*

With the aid of old school friend and esoteric colleague Frank Zappa, who shared the Captain's much maligned musical taste and screwball oddness, Beefheart (born Don Van Vliet 1941) reached his creative zenith with this his third studio recording following the underrated 1967 underground classic Sour as Milk* (9). Evolving out of the Captain's deep fascination for Delta-derived Chicago Blues, this double album is full of strange, bizarre and seemingly fragmented song pieces that appear (on the surface at least) to lack any sort of logical direction and cohesiveness. Defying categorization of any kind, the chaotic structure of the album however is to be either cherished for its psychedelic rambling brilliance or despised for its aimless lyrical nonsense. Is it a case of pure experimentation gone mad or avant-garde noodling in its highest possible form? You be the judge, but don't say you haven't been warned!

COUNTDOWN TO ECSTASY *1973*   *STEELY DAN*

What's this you might say: You have got to be kidding. Right? No. Actually one of the finest and most refreshing albums ever recorded. Steely Dan's second studio excursion is chock full of consummate musicianship, neatly produced / arranged songs complete with exquisite jazz influences, obscure lyrics (take Bodhisattva) and great guitar hooks. Highlighting Becker and Fagan's seamless songcraft abilities, Steely Dan deliver the goods, lock, stock and barrel. My Old School is a straight out, shoot 'em down, old fashioned *style rock number that zips along at a wonderful pace. Jeff "Skunk" Baxter (later to join The Doobie Brothers) and Denny Dias provide some sparkling off the cuff guitar moments, especially on the funky, driving beats of Razor Boy, The Boston Rag and Your Gold Teeth. The much anticipated follow up Pretzel Logic, with its more muted and far less consistent fare, may have set the cash registers ringing and given the band a wider commercial audience (thanks mainly to the universal success of Rikki Don't Lose That Number), however Countdown To Ecstasy remains the best Steely Dan album bar none (although their debut effort Can't Buy A Thrill* (10) runs a close second). A compelling marriage of pop suavity, jazz elegance, rock attitude and studio finesse, which became the strength and hallmark of their music. What more could one ask for? Put this one in your pipe and smoke it.*

ARE YOU EXPERIENCED ? 1967   THE JIMI HENDRIX EXPERIENCE

In the all consuming summer of love Sgt Pepper's received the bulk of the attention and most of the accolades but the Hendrix spiked electric chords, mayhem and mischief of exuberance and youth have never been more apparent than at this particular place in time. The album was a veritable kaleidoscope of innovation and virtuoso guitar technique. From backwards taped effects, sonic feedback and howling electronic noise Jimi Hendrix proved to be the breath of fresh air that few of his peers could ignore. Like a whirlwind dervish rising out of a hot desert, Hendrix raised the bar to a whole new level and set the standard for guitar playing that every subsequent band tried to follow. The legend remains intact and undimmed. Quite simply an astounding tour de force.

CROSBY,STILLS AND NASH 1969   _CROSBY,STILLS AND NASH_

Their debut album still stands as a landmark achievement. Perhaps the world's first genuine supergroup conglomerate (predating the Eric Clapton/ Steve Winwood all too brief collaboration of Blind Faith by some three months) did not disappoint with this classic textured production piece incorporating songs from an entire world of influences. Take Guinevere and the uplifting Marrakesh Express for example. While the lengthy Suite: Judy Blue Eyes unfolds like the flavours of a fine red wine. A sparkling numbers set highlighting the groups close knit vocal harmonies. The album somehow perfectly captured the last thrilling moments of the American '60s dream. What more can be said.

THE RISE AND FALL OF ZIGGY STARDUST
AND THE SPIDERS FROM MARS 1972   _DAVID BOWIE_

Following on from the broad array of pop styles that typified the previous year's Hunky Dory*(10), Ziggy Stardust went back to where it all began – the full blown futuristic tales and twisted guitar rock anthems of the Man Who Sold The World (1970). Reinventing himself by pushing the concept of glam – rock and androgynous role playing to its absolute limits, Bowie created an entirely new standard of over the top theatricality, brashness and ambiguous sexual magnetism within the realm of mainstream pop. Fixed in a pseudo space age setting, Bowie's adopted persona is that of a prophetic rock star whose growth and ultimate decline counter play with the cataclysmic end of the world. The reflective state of this epic story's hero is no better demonstrated than in the paranoid opener Five

*Years and the moody, slow burning excitement of Starman.
Guest performer Mick Ronson delivers to perfection great
crunching guitar work, especially on Moonage Daydream
and Suffragette City. An often much underappreciated gem,
it is perhaps the only glam rock album to date, that sounds
just as fresh and vibrant now as it did when first released.
Repeated listening to Ziggy Stardust and his strange,
neurotic antics will have its sweet rewards. Take the plunge,
immerse yourself in the electric moment and you will never
be quite the same again. That's a promise.*

RADIO CITY *1974*   BIG STAR

*Disillusioned and frustrated with his first venture, the Box
Tops lead singer Alex Chilton (who was only sixteen when
they recorded the soul classic The Letter) subsequently quit
the group in search of new adventures and greener pastures.
Memphis quartet Big Star, which had been convened by
Chilton's former high school colleague Chris Bell, together
with Andy Hummell and drummer Jody Stephens, seemed
the logical alternative. For a short while at least, it proved
the perfect vehicle for their combined talents, although in
general it failed to ignite lasting public interest and create
the widespread recognition they deserved. This their second
album after the promising debut No.1 Record* (8) (ironically
anything but), is everything good about catchy and tight knit
music. Seamlessly wrapped up together in a batch of songs
that slowly smoulder and hint at something far more than
the usual standard throw away pop fare, Way Out West could
have been lifted from a classic Byrds session, while September
Gurls is nouveau classic art.*

*When this was released, Chris Bell had already left the
band in an attempt to revive his flagging fortunes. On a*

downward spiral, affected by bouts of depression, he tried without success to fulfil his lofty ambitions. Apart from the remarkable and poignant I Am The Cosmos**(8) his efforts garnered only moderate mainstream attention and his songs made little impact. Chris Bell died in December 1978 when the car he was driving struck a tree.*

If you have not heard this…do yourself a favour. Listen to the pristine pop, effortless melodies and fine harmonies. No excuses.

<u>HONKY CHATEAU</u> *1972*   *ELTON JOHN*

Will the real Elton John please step forward. Following on from the positive signs shown on the much to be admired <u>Madman Across The Water</u>** (9) with Honky Chateau he did so with confident strides, pure aplomb and sheer delight. The masterful collaboration between Bernie Taupin and Elton John has never been stronger nor more evocative than that demonstrated on this recording. A rip roaring amalgamation of material that hooks the listener from beginning to end. Drifting seamlessly between ballads, rockers, blues, countrified rock and smooth soul, it plays out as (arguably) the most focused, melodic and accomplished set of songs they ever wrote. Backed with the talents of crack producer Gus Dudgeon (Audience) and a superb team of session musicians who don't miss a beat, the finished product is a somewhat unexpected but worthwhile journey. This selection in my top thirty albums may well surprise a lot of people. But who really cares. This is a record deserving of a place in any true music collection. A real bolt out of the blue. Those not familiar with Mr Dwight might also like to try the super follow up* <u>Don't Shoot Me I'm Only The Piano Player</u>** (9) released in January 1973.*

WILLY AND THE POOR BOYS 1969   CREEDENCE CLEARWATER REVIVAL

By any measure this is one hell of an album. A finely crafted, lighter and breezier offering than its excellent and often overlooked predecessor Green River* (10) There is not a lot here to remind us of the doom, gloom and sense of foreboding that ran central and foremost through that great album. John Fogerty's high quality, gritty, nasal vocals continue to blossom and develop. The creative sound in general finds its roots in a very different sphere of Americana far removed from the streets of San Francisco and the sunshine and flower landscapes of California and the West Coast. These picture songs are drawn meticulously from the realm of mist filled backwoods highlighted by the chuggling single release Proud Mary. Heck, the band didn't even originate from the deep south, but listening to this effort you would be forgiven for thinking they did. Tight guitar playing and catchy riffs are a standout feature and form a common thread to all the tracks. Surely one of the best, purest, good fun records ever made. Swamp music or bayou music (whichever takes your fancy), rockabilly and slow smouldering blues, never sounded so damn good. Invigorating to say the very least. Please sir I want some more.

SOMETHING ELSE BY THE KINKS. 1967   THE KINKS

No one, not even the Beatles at their best, could adequately describe and narrate the wonderful peculiarities and structure of English society quite like the Kinks. Utilising a unique, evocative talent for portraying ordinary people and common situations, Ray Davies mastered in word and music form the art that painted vignettes and colourful pastiches, lucid sketches and palatable parodies. Revolving around every day

English life, they meticulously highlighted its eccentricities, normalities and maudlin awkwardness. Full of descriptive imagery, <u>Waterloo Sunset</u> is a charming, understated homage to a vibrant, 1960's bustling London, 'where the people swarm like flies'. So good you can even close your eyes and smell the river Thames. Self-conscious Englishness with all its faults, flaws and remarkable strengths never sounded so whimsical and yet oddly grandiose. It may not be everyone's slice of apple pie but this is a memorable and defining moment in the Kinks illustrious career. Brave and thoroughly engaging. We wouldn't want it any other way. Now would anyone like a cup of tea?

<u>*TOMMY*</u> *1969*   *THE WHO*

The weakest album listed in my "to appreciate selection". Not without its flaws and harsh critics, this sometimes overblown conceptual rock opera (perhaps operetta is a better description) struggles to narrate in some type of sequential format the story of a deaf, dumb and blind child born into a wholly dysfunctional family with its accompanying bizarre lifestyle. The Who's dextrous and ambitious rock infused dramatics and signature song piece moments are best highlighted in the resonating power chords of <u>Pinball Wizard</u>, <u>See Me, Feel Me</u> and <u>We're Not Gonna Take It</u>. Perhaps some prudent editing would have improved the overall sonic experience. Twenty four tracks presented over four sides of a double album might just have been too much to digest at a single sitting. Catch the movie featuring Tina Turner as the Acid Queen.

Fussy listeners may prefer the much earlier and more cohesive effort of The Pretty Things' <u>S.F. Sorrow</u>* (8) 1968, which is credited by Pete Townsend as being the major influence behind Tommy.

THE DOORS 1967   *THE DOORS*

The Doors took their name from Aldous Huxley's 'The Doors of Perception'. The train of thought contained in that work: an insight into the substance and nature of reality is widely encapsulated within their music. Described by many analysts as the best debut album ever made. Imposing comments indeed. Carried along by its clever fusion of rock, blues, jazz, classical, poetical wanderings and drug induced lyrics the album is both fresh and startling. The pathos captured in closing track The End, an 11 minute epic of Oedipal undertones and brooding darkness, says it all. A disturbing, acid trip delivered by a tortured soul with an inflated ego and devilish good looks. Striking, yet also sublime. The door has been opened wide enough, just walk on through to the far side and take a drink from the magic cup.

BRIDGE OVER TROUBLED WATER 1970   *SIMON AND GARFUNKLE*

A truly grand and dignified exit for the great sixties duo. Paul Simon's song writing skills are equal to anything that Dylan, Lennon / McCartney and even Leonard Cohen put out there into the music ether. Here he can be found at his most artistic and eloquent (perhaps not his most philosophical: that remains the privilege of the stunning Parsley, Sage, Rosemary and Thyme)* (10) and combined with the ethereal harmonies of Art Garfunkle, the pair absolutely sizzle. Style, grace and literary perfection is layered on for all to admire. From the soaring majestic vocal range of the epic title track to the delicately deceptive El Condor Pasa and the sad undertones of The Only Living Boy In New York. However it is the beautiful, melancholic, driving narrative of The Boxer that *shimmers like a piece of gold in a story spun with so much zest and clarity, Bob Dylan would even struggle to match its engaging power. Thank goodness they ditched the Tom and Jerry tag. Paul Simon pursued a highly successful solo path, culminating in his grand opus* Graceland* *(10)*

ASTRAL WEEKS *1968*   VAN MORRISON

Van Morrison (just twenty three years of age when this was recorded) had always held a strong jazz disposition. Following major hits with Gloria, Here Comes The Night (both with Them) and Brown Eyed Girl, Astral weeks saw Van Morrison excel in this new jazz instilled direction he had now taken. Madame George *is a heartfelt flight of fantasy set in his home town of Belfast. The imagery of the seasoned drag artist is sketched in the muted colours of a dream recollected. The song structures and their origins are firmly entrenched in folk, mainstream blues, jazz and classical music.*

Created without the normal constraints associated with studio pop production, Astral Weeks remains a predominantly all acoustic, non rock and roll work of the highest calibre.

EXILE ON MAIN STREET *1972*   THE ROLLING STONES

Recorded in the South of France under the most haphazard of conditions utilising their very own 16-track mobile unit. A gripping and intense experience from start to finish. Like the Beatles double white album before them, this sees the group confidently return to a more basic, raw and stripped back style. A sprawling, double album effort which on the surface at least, doesn't appear to deliver anything new or fresh in terms of creativity and musical progression. However, each subsequent listen reveals subtle nuances within a rich, textural tapestry of raunchy, down and dirty rock and roll (Rip This Joint), faithful blues (Tumbling Dice), soul, gospel and straight out country (Sweet Virginia) as only the Rolling Stones at the peak of their powers could deliver. With more swagger and sway than any of their previous albums, it was recorded with a crack line-up of session musicians including Bobby Keys on saxophone, Nicky Hopkins on piano and Al Perkins on slide guitar. Wonderful and invigorating and so damn good. Most critics agree, this was the Stone's finest hour. Put yourself in the mood. Sit back and enjoy the show.

FIVE LEAVES LEFT 1969   NICK DRAKE

Nick Drake has achieved far more in musical fame and status in the subsequent years following his death, than he ever did during his brief and tormented lifetime. Virtually ignored by the music public of the day, unable to overcome his lack of success as a live performer and fearing constant failure, Drake died in 1974 from an overdose of antidepressants.

Five Leaves Left is his debut album. Produced by Joe Boyd (whose work credits included Soft Machine, Pink Floyd and Incredible String Band) and featuring grand folk influenced guitarist Richard Thompson (of then Fairport Convention fame), it is crammed with complex, highly introspective musical meanderings of incredible emotion, warmth and equal parts sadness. Shades of light and dark, juxtaposed and melded together and delicately brushed with arrangements and production befitting a genuine pop icon. Drake had a fascination bordering on obsessive, with time and its inevitable exhausting, finality. This powerful collection of baroque styled pop songs, reflect his thoughts and feelings through the use of elegiac lyrics, expansive strings and folk –jazz infused acoustic guitar. Way To Blue, Man In A Shed and Fruit Tree are especially poignant. Listening to Drake's distinct, fragile voice almost at the point of breaking down is a chilling experience.

The tragedy remains that such prodigious talent was unashamedly shunned by his peers and the record totally failed to make any immediate impact. The passage of time, which Drake so much feared in his short life, has now subsequently brought about a deserved appreciation of this rare, musical talent. His cult status continues to gather momentum. Listen, admire and weep.

<u>ODESSEY AND ORACLE</u> *1968*   *THE ZOMBIES*

Released in the UK in the early spring of 1968 (the record failed to make any impact on the charts) this album was no doubt influenced in no small part by the previous year's ubiquitous Summer of Love. Spawned out of the acid visions and excess of glossy hippy culture and musical experimentation it delivers in subtle shades of pyschedelia. The fine edged lyrics and great harmonies echo the Kinks and Beach Boys at their very best. Think <u>Something Else</u>* (10) and <u>Pet Sounds</u>* (10) respectively, whilst the music itself draws strong comparison to Procul Harum. Recorded in the famous Abbey Road Studios the album is swathed with lush and baroque influenced pop melodies of breathtaking sweep that heavily feature the use of mellotron, flute, harpsichord as well as rich organ loops and swirls. Keyboardist Rod Argent's great love of jazz lies comfortably at the heart of each song contained on this 12 track offering. From the opening strains of the oddly derived Care of Cell 44, to Butcher's Tale (Western Front 1914) and the unforgettable closer Time of the Season (which would later become an anti-Vietnam War anthem of sorts), Odessey and Oracle does not disappoint. The CD format contains some wonderful bonus tracks such as Imagine the Swan, I Want You Back Again and the bouncy instrumental layering of Conversation Off Floral Street.

Listening to this, it is difficult to understand why the Zombies never achieved the success they surely deserved.

CLOSE TO THE EDGE 1972   YES

Owing a great deal to the pioneering antics and extensive embellishments of King Crimson, Yes refused to shirk the task at hand and overcooked everything in fine rambling style. In so doing they took the idea of ostentatious song art and the the progressive rock concept yet one step further. Featuring only three tracks, the pinnacle of Yes' work, sees them adopting an even more expansive, collaborative approach to music than on their previous breakout album Fragile*(8). With the band members shifting from jazz to hard sweeping rock almost seamlessly, Jon Anderson's loopy, obtuse lyrics and high vocal exercises (though at times sounding weak and strained) never seem out of place in the great scheme of things. Avoiding the very real temptation to showcase their own talents and drift off on an out of control tangent, they somehow defy all odds to combine forces brilliantly. The organ arpeggios, searing synthesiser swirls and delicate slices of mellotron created by wunderkind Rick Wakeman (ex The Strawbs and who had previously filled in as a solid session man for all occasions to Al Stewart and David Bowie) merely add icing to the birthday cake. Many critics at the time said the full on, in your face sounds were strictly over the top and far too contrived and self indulgent to be of any worthwhile lasting value. However, Close To The Edge a UK Number 4 hit, proved to be a cohesive, dynamic statement of voices and instruments more enigmatic than conservative. Puzzling though it may be, it stands as a true moment of greatness. Yes never really bettered this finely balanced effort.

THAT'S ALL FOLKS............. NOW TAKE A MOMENT TO SIT BACK IN THAT COMFORTABLE RECLINING CHAIR, REFLECT, RELAX AND ENJOY THE MELLOW SUNSHINE.

ALPHABET NOODLINGS: MUSIC ARTISTS FAMOUS AND NOT SO FAMOUS

A   Abba, ABC, Arcade Fire, America, Allman Brothers Band, Aerosmith, Animals, Aphrodite's Child, Average White Band, Audience, Anno Domini, Archies

B   Beau Brummels, Beatles, Beach Boys, Badfinger, Beck, Beautiful South, Big Star, Bonzo Dog Doo Dah Band, Black Sabbath, Beirut, Jackson Browne, Bad Company, David Blue, Boston

C   Calexico, Captain Beefheart, Cold Chisel, Cream, Cars, Cure, Ry Cooder, Creedence Clearwater Revival, JJ Cale, Coldplay, Can, Cheap Trick, Clash, Cosmic Rough Riders, Cross Record

D   Doors, Def Leppard, Doves, Bob Dylan, Donovan, Dire Straits, Deep Purple, Decemberists, Nick Drake, Daddy Longlegs, Del Amitri, Depeche Mode

E   Elephants Memory, Eagles, Electric Prunes, Every Mother's Son, Emerson, Lake and Palmer, Electric Light Orchestra, Eels, Euphoria, Echo and the Bunnymen

F   Foghat, Fotheringay, Foreigner, Five Man Electric Band, Flying Burrito Brothers

G   Golden Earring, Genesis, Grateful Dead, Grand Funk Railroad, Gandalf, Greenhornes

H   Jimi Hendrix, Human League, Hawkwind, Hothouse Flowers, Robyn Hitchcock, Humble Pie

I	Indigo Girls, Iron Butterfly, Iron and Wine, Incredible String Band, INXS, Ill Wind, Iron Maiden
J	Japan, Jethro Tull, Joy Division, Jefferson Airplane, John's Children, The Jam, Journey
K	Korn, Klaatu, King Crimson, Keane, Kings of Leon, Kinks, Kraftwerk, Killers,
L	Lindisfarne, Love, Little Feat, Lynyrd Skynyrd, Lightning Seeds, Led Zeppelin, Live, Lulu
M	Moody Blues, Madonna, Van Morrison, Moby Grape, Massive Attack, Bob Marley, Move, John Mellencamp, Mike + The Mechanics, Mandrake Memorial, Manassas, Mellow Candle, Molly Hatchet, Mountain, May Blitz, Midlake, Modest Mouse
N	Paolo Nutini, Neutral Milk Hotel, Nazareth, New Riders of the Purple Sage, Nice, Nirvana
O	Osibisa, Oasis, Ozark Mountain Daredevils, OMD, Ohio Express
P	John Prine, Prince, Pink Floyd, Posies, Procul Harum, Pixies, Pogues, Plastic Ono Band, Pearl Jam, Posies, Portishead, Psychedelic Furs, Power Station, Pere Ubu, Police, Pentangle, Patto
Q	Queen, Quicksilver Messenger Service, ? and the Mysterians, Suzi Quatro
R	REO Speedwagon, REM, Rolling Stones, Roxy Music, Rupert's People, Radiohead, Ramones
S	Styx, Smog, Stackridge, Splinter, Sutherland Brothers, Shins, Sly and the Family Stone, Sparklehorse, Bruce Springsteen, Strawberry Alarm Clock, Sugar, Stereolab, Stooges, Stealers Wheel, Steely Dan, Steppenwolf, Simple Minds, Smoke, Silver Apples, Soft Machine, Spirit, Specials, Soft Boys, Spooky Tooth, Suede

T	Traffic, Talking Heads, Ten Years After, 10CC, Toto, Taj Mahal, Tangerine Dream, Television
U	UB40, U2, UFO, Uriah Heep, Ultravox, Underworld
V	Verve, Velvet Underground, Vanilla Fudge, Van Der Graaf Generator
W	Who, Wimple Winch, Tony Joe White, Wishbone Ash, Wizzard, Edgar Winter Band, Wilco
X	XTC, X Ray Specs
Y	Yothu Yindi, Youngbloods, Yardbirds, Neil Young, Yazoo, Yes
Z	Frank Zappa, ZZ Top, Warren Zevon, Zombies, Zoot

FURTHER READING

Aldridge, Alan (Editor)	*The Beatles Illustrated Lyrics*	Macdonald Futura 1980
Brackett, Nathan (Editor)	*The New Rolling Stone Album Guide*	Simon and Schuster 2004
Buckley, Peter	*Rough Guide to Rock*	Rough Guides 1999
Burrows, Terry	*The Beatles*	Carlton Books 2014
Byrne, David	*How Music Works*	Canongate Books 2012
Cresswell, Toby	*Rockwiz: 1001 Songs. The Great Songs Of All Time*	Hardie Grant Books 2007
Davies, Hunter	*The Beatles Lyrics*	Orion Books Weidenfeld and Nicolson 2014
Davies, Hunter	*The Beatles: The Authorized Biography*	Norton 1996
Davies, Paul	*The Goldilocks Dilemma*	Allen Lane (Penguin Books) 2006
Emerick, Geoff and	*Here, There and Everywhere: My Life*	Gotham 2007
Massey, Howard	*Recording the Music of the Beatles*	
Friedlander, Paul	*Rock And Roll: A Social History*	Westview 1996
Giuliano, Geoffrey	*Tomorrow Never Knows: Thirty Years Of Beatles Music And Memorabilia*	Dragon's World 1991
Gold, Jeff	*101 Essential Rock Records*	Gingko Press 2013
Harrison, George	*I, Me, Mine*	Chronicle Books 2002

Heatley, Michael (Editor)	*The Virgin Encyclopedia Of Rock*	Carlton Books 1993
Heatley, Michael	*Where Were You When The Music Played? 120 Unforgettable Moments In Music.*	Readers Digest 2008
Julien, Oliver (Editor)	*Sgt.Pepper and the Beatles: It Was Forty Years Ago Today*	Ashgate 2008
Katz, Mark	*Capturing Sound: How Technology Has Changed Music*	University of California Press 2010
Larkin, Colin (Editor)	*The Virgin Encyclopedia Of Popular Music*	Virgin Books 2002
Levitin, Dan	*This Is Your Brain On Music: The Science Of A Human Obsession*	Plume/Penguin 2007
Lewisohn, Mark	*The Complete Beatles Recording Sessions*	Sterling 1988
Lewisohn, Mark	*The Complete Beatles Chronicle*	Pyramid Books 1995
Macan, Edward	*Rocking The Classics: English Progressive Rock And The Counterculture*	Oxford University Press 1997
Macdonald, Ian	*Revolution In The Head*	Chicago Review Press 2007
Miles, Barry	*The British Invasion*	Sterling 2009
Ochs, Michael	*1000 Record Covers*	Taschen Books 2005
Rees, Dafydd and Crampton, Luke	*Q Rock Stars Encyclopedia*	Dorling Kindersley 1999

Reising, Russell (Editor)	*Every Sound There Is: The Beatles Revolver And The Transformation Of Rock and Roll*	Ashgate 2002
Sarig, Ron	*The Secret History Of Rock: The Most Influential Bands You've Never Heard*	Billboard Books 1998
Sinclair, David	*Rock On CD The Essential Guide*	Kyle Cathie Ltd 1992
Smith, Chris	*101 Albums That Changed Popular Music*	Oxford University Press 2009
Spignesi, Stephen J. and Lewis, Michael	*Here, There and Everywhere: The 100 Best Beatles Songs.*	Black Dog and Leventhal 2004
Strong, Martin	*The Great Rock Discography 7th Edition*	Canongate Books 2004
Thompson, Dave	*Bayou Underground: Tracing the Mythical Roots of American Popular Music*	ECW Press 2010
Thorgerson, Storm and Dean, Roger (Editors)	*Album Cover Album*	Harper Collins 2008
Turner, Steve	*The Beatles: The Stories Behind The Songs 1967-1970*	Five Mile Press 2009
Whitburn, Joel (Editor)	*The Billboard Book of Top 40 Albums*	Billboard 1987
Williamson, Nigel	*The Best Music You've Never Heard*	Rough Guides 2008

Womack, Kenneth	*The Cambridge Companion to the Beatles*	Cambridge University Press 2011
Womack, Kenneth	*Long and Winding Roads: The Evolving Artistry of the Beatles*	Continuum 2010
Womack, Kenneth and Davis, Todd F (Editors)	*Reading The Beatles: Cultural Studies, Literary Criticism And The Fab Four*	State University of New York 2006
Yenne, Bill	*The Beatles*	Bison Books 1989
Albums: The Stories Behind 50 Years Of Great Recordings		Thunder Bay Press 2005
1000 Songs To Change Your Life		TimeOut Guides 2008
The Mojo Collection: The Ultimate Music Companion 4th *Edition*		Canongate Books 2007

Rolling Stone Collectors Issue 637 March 2005: The 500 Greatest Songs Of All Time

Uncut Magazine Issue 225 February 2016: 200 Greatest Albums Of All Time

www.Allmusic.com

A smorgasbord music site and reference source covering all genres and artists. An added feature is the Editor's review for new monthly music releases. Also incorporates a comprehensive artist overview, biography and discography.

From novices to nerds and everyone in between. Highly recommended.

www.ingramcontent.com/pod-product-compliance
Lightning Source LLC
Chambersburg PA
CBHW070016100426
42740CB00013B/2511